GET CARMAN

IN COURT WITH GEORGE CARMAN QC, BRITAIN'S MOST FEARED LAWYER – THE MAN BEHIND THE ADVOCATE

KAREN PHILLIPPS

First published in Great Britain in 2024 by
Biteback Publishing Ltd, London

ISBN 978-1-78590-898-9

10 9 8 7 6 5 4 3 2 1

A CIP catalogue record for this book is available from the British Library.

Set in Adobe Caslon Pro

Printed and bound in Great Britain by
CPI Group (UK) Ltd, Croydon CR0 4YY

For George

'George Carman QC, the most feared and admired barrister of the age, surprised legal colleagues by announcing that he had made his last appearance in court.'

THE TIMES, 30 AUGUST 2000

'George Carman was both the best-liked and most feared advocate at the English Bar. He was also the best known. In any looming libel battle, the side that was first to pay George a comfortable retainer had an incalculable advantage … His retirement means that the age of the great advocate is over. Many barristers are clever, some are skilful and a few are good-looking. But there are now none left who can fill the public gallery on star quality alone.'

JOSHUA ROZENBERG, *DAILY TELEGRAPH*, 30 AUGUST 2000

'I, George Alfred Carman QC, want you, the reader of this book, to know that putting pen to paper for myself has been cathartic. Along with the account of my life's journey up till now, I have written this chapter in the knowledge that my life expectancy has been shortened due to cancer.'

GEORGE CARMAN QC, SUMMER 2000

CONTENTS

INTRODUCTION

George Carman QC was, and perhaps still is, the most famous British lawyer within living memory. Equally feared and respected, he made his name as an erudite and incisive advocate largely in the field of libel. In the 1980s and 1990s, no high-profile libel case was complete without the diminutive QC whose ability to wipe the courtroom floor with the high and mighty, often with a smart turn of phrase that guaranteed headlines in the following day's newspapers, was unmatched.

Following a spell working in the north-west, Carman moved to London, coming to prominence with his superb defence of disgraced former Liberal Party leader Jeremy Thorpe on a charge of conspiracy to murder. The odds seemed stacked against Thorpe, but he was acquitted – and George Carman was on his way.

In subsequent years, he rubbed shoulders with many well-known faces from the worlds of entertainment, sport, politics and business, among others. Many of these were the beneficiaries of his superb advocacy; others, however, would never forget the bruising they received under his forensic cross-examination. Those who won the day include Ken Dodd, Richard Branson and Elton John.

But the likes of Jonathan Aitken, Neil Hamilton, Ian Botham and Gillian Taylforth were among those who succumbed to 'Killer Carman'.

George was commissioned to write his memoirs from the time he was forced to retire in August 2000 due to his advancing prostate cancer. He was offered a publishing contract for the manuscript and, knowing he was unwell, began to put his cases into categories, along with a personal chapter of reminiscences from his early years. However, he became too ill to complete the book and died on 2 January 2001.

Although George fully intended to complete his autobiography, I do wonder whether, had he lived, he would actually have managed to finish it. This isn't because he was indolent or easily bored – in fact, quite the opposite. George was a workaholic who tied himself up for weeks and months on end with court cases, and while his intentions towards the writing of his autobiography were good, my opinion is that he simply wouldn't have had the time.

I became George's confidante and he talked to me many times about the way he would like his memoir to flow and what he intended to include. And he certainly didn't plan that I – or anyone else – should write it for him. That said, he did leave me his papers in his will, so perhaps he was dropping a posthumous hint. We will never know.

Either way, George was a driven man who was dedicated almost wholly to his work. He wasn't much interested in having hobbies, and unlike a lot of lawyers, he didn't play competitive sports. If I invited him to the theatre or an exhibition, he'd happily come along, yet he was equally happy not to bother if he needed to work. He wasn't an unsociable person by any means; he enjoyed meeting people and chatting, though the conversation was almost invariably about the law. George had a few good friends, but on the whole, they tended to be lawyers he was working with.

So work was intrinsic to him. He didn't know what to do when he wasn't working. If he hadn't had the health issue which finally killed him, he'd have worked until his life ended. He wouldn't have retired; he couldn't have occupied his time in a meaningful way. When he was in the middle of a case, he would talk of nothing else, always pondering and picking his various arguments while trying to think what his opponents might say or do next. And every time a case ended – even if it was a high-profile one that had gone in his favour – he would experience a real dip in confidence, thinking that he might never work again. In a way, he was more like an actor than a lawyer, terrified of the dreaded 'resting' period that sometimes comes even after a successful show. As soon as he was hired for another case, he was back on cloud nine.

This is why I've decided to write a book predominantly about George's work – because his work *was* his life. We could spend time dipping into the whys and wherefores of George's day-to-day personal life, but inevitably, this would still bring us back to the subject of his work. Had he managed to finish his autobiography, there's no doubt that it would have contained a certain amount of personal reflection and, in fact, those chapters written by George shortly before he died do exactly that. He delves into his past with surprising candour, insight and a great deal of brutal honesty about himself:

> I am a complex person, a driven person and at times an arrogant person. I totally lived for my career and was in control, which I needed. At times, it was a very lonely place, unless you had people of similar thought processes around you. I now realise it

> was hard for others to understand me regarding my professionalism. I realised I was living my mother's wishes as 'the prodigal son'. My mother always sought to do her best. She was at times very judgemental of people who were not of the same thought process. Her drive and standards helped me on my journey. I realised I had her traits not my own. I have been guilty of being in judgement of those around me and again that core footprint of my mother was repeated on those occasions.

It is sad that George didn't live to write any more of his story, as it would have been fascinating to have read his thoughts about the cases he worked on and the ways in which he conducted those cases. However, we at least get a tantalising glimpse of the man beneath the barrister's gown in these brief reflections, a sketch of a person with outward charm, confidence, wit and intellect, as well as a soul that, while not quite 'tortured', comes some way to meeting that description. As he said, it's all rather complex.

Because of the Jeremy Thorpe case and various other high-profile trials, George's reputation preceded him, so, like most lawyers working in London in the mid-'80s, I had heard about him a while before I met him. Having qualified as a barrister, I was offered a pupillage in 13 Old Square, Lincoln's Inn, the chambers of Charles Sparrow QC, a bencher of Gray's Inn, my chosen inn of court. It was a fascinating time, and I would often walk back from court at lunchtime to chambers with my pupil master, Patrick Talbot QC. These Chancery chambers were unusual in that many of the tenants were in the High Court or Privy Council regularly, often making new law with intricate cases. Elizabeth Appleby QC was the only female QC and there was one other female tenant, Beverley Briggs, now Lady Briggs KC. I was one of only two female pupils, the other being a woman called Belinda. My pupil master had never worked with a female pupil before and joked he would never have a male pupil again!

I left these Chancery chambers to seek experience in common law. I was now receiving my own criminal work and had not ventured into a criminal court before. I undertook six months' pupillage in the chambers of Margaret Puxon QC, an eminent doctor. I was then invited to spend a few months at 4 King's Bench Walk with Michael Latham. He was amused that I never did spend time with him, as I was either doing my own work or acting as pupil to another tenant. I then applied for a tenancy in 2 King's Bench Walk, the chambers of Lord Campbell of Alloway.

One of my fellow tenants, George Papageorgis, was friends with George Carman. Papageorgis said he had told him about me and that Carman would love to meet me. The two Georges hatched a plan and eventually I met them both in Daly's Wine Bar in 1986. I thought I was going for a drink with my colleague, but George Carman was already there with him. I grinned at seeing the 'Silver Fox', as the press dubbed him, in the days before he was renamed 'Gorgeous George'.

I was aware that Papageorgis was trying to set me up romantically with Carman, but at that time, I had a boyfriend. Nevertheless, we hit it off, and when Papageorgis got up to leave, Carman persuaded me to stay and continue the conversation. So I did, later accepting an invitation to lunch. I can't say I approved of George's chain-smoking, especially in the confines of his car, but I liked his warmth and found him entertaining. He wasn't remotely pompous, but he was immensely clever, amusing and genuinely interested in people. In that sense, he wasn't a typical barrister! And he communicated extremely well. That, I think, was his greatest asset: he was able to mesmerise anyone he was talking to and had a wonderful command of the English language. He focused on you as a person, as he did with juries, and from that moment, you were under his spell.

During the lunch, he asked about my relationship, and I said I hoped to be married to my then boyfriend 'one day'. At the time, he was separated from his wife. George assured me he would never fully leave her. Despite the charm, however, I wasn't romantically interested in George.

'I love my boyfriend and I'm prepared to wait and see,' I said.

'You're wrong,' George insisted. 'You should marry me.'

I was taken aback by the immediacy of his proposal and turned it down, in the kindest way I could. Outlining this to him cleared the air. We were then able to have a carefree lunch discussing books, music and places we liked to visit. We appeared to have quite a lot in common.

And so began a deep and enduring platonic friendship which continued right up to George's death. If I wasn't his partner, I was certainly his companion and confidante. He would frequently test out on me his intended speech or arguments for the case he was handling, and I was in court for many of the cases I will be discussing in this book. Almost immediately, I could see why George's three previous marriages had failed: quite simply, he was married to the law and perfectionism came at a price. When he was involved in a case, he was like a dog with a bone and could not be moved from that subject for hours at a time. He was obsessed and absorbed in each case completely, and in that sense, he reminded me of some of the great actors, like Sir Laurence Olivier, Peter O'Toole or Richard Burton. He never took his focus off the job in hand and would be utterly, completely obsessed with it.

Life fell into a pattern. I would live in central London during the week and then spend some of the weekend in Wimbledon, where George lived. We didn't have a particularly hectic social life, occasionally having dinner with friends and relatives. Our favourite pastime was to watch foreign films at the Chelsea Cinema or the Curzon Mayfair. Our taste in movies was surprisingly similar – we both loved *Il Postino* and *Life Is Beautiful*.

This is a picture of George on the rare occasions he was able to relax and enjoy himself, reading books and relished interesting company from people in other professions and in other fields of work. It is at odds with the image of the fierce workaholic who laboured intensively for his clients.

George Alfred Carman was born in Blackpool, Lancashire, on 6 October 1929. His father, also Alfred, was a furniture retailer and his Irish-born mother, Evelyn, was a seamstress who owned a gown shop called Madame Louise.

She was a perfectionist with a strong personality and very close to George. She had a great impact on him and encouraged his close attention to detail. His father was a simple man who had no ambition. Evelyn was quite the opposite, even taking regular trips in the evening to check the shop window looked perfect.

George boarded at the age of seven at St Joseph's Roman Catholic school in Blackpool. This was a tough, archaic institution run by the Irish Christian Brothers, an order of priests with a fearsome reputation for discipline, corporal punishment and, as was subsequently revealed, the sexual abuse of many of their charges. George was the subject of regular beatings with a leather strap. Father Tom Walsh wrote a letter to me after George's death, saying that St Joseph's was a 'hard school of life'. He talked about the problems of adolescent faith … It seems as a matter of laws, regulations, prohibitions, loyalties. It takes you all of your life to realise what it means, a childlike trust that God's purposes for you are loving and good. If not severely crushed, this conviction can last from your Catholic childhood – from your mother's 'faith-trust' often.

George, as a clever boy, would have rationalised his worries more and the burden would have been too much. He came to the hurly-burly of St Joseph's and luckily found a brilliant teacher.

Father Tom Walsh met George at pre-rugby match sports meetings. 'George was a demon scrum-half, brave, never drew back, a terrier around the scrum,' he wrote. Although in later life George never had time for hobbies, it appears all these qualities were exhibited in his courtroom skills.

At the age of fourteen, George attended the Up Holland Roman Catholic seminary, near Wigan. He felt he had a vocation to the priesthood and this austere college would be the place it was tested.

It instilled in him a very strict, regimented way of life. George always commented on the early rising at 6 a.m. and regular prayer. He was impressed by and benefited from the extraordinary discipline. However, after two years there, he realised that the life of a Roman Catholic priest would not be for him and he left, citing 'the discovery of girls' as his reason, saying that the strict rules against priests marrying were untenable.

Yet Catholicism would never quite leave George. He had a reputation for enjoying a drink, having the gift of the gab and he felt drawn to the outcasts of the world. In a letter to a good friend, Judge Michael Sachs, I noted that there was something of George's priestly vocation that lasted through to the end.

When George returned to St Joseph's in 1945, he told me he was taken under the wing of Brother Woodhouse, particularly in the subjects of Latin and history. Woodhouse also encouraged George to broaden his reading material by delving into the classics. George took an interest in debating and decided that his goal would be to attain a place at Balliol, Oxford. But his dream nearly failed. With his usual tenacity, George sat every day at 7.30 a.m. at the top of his staircase, waiting for the mail to arrive with his post-interview letter. During the second week of patiently observing, he saw something drop through the letterbox and disappear.

He pounced down the stairs to look and could not believe there was nothing on the ground.

He was convinced a letter had dropped through a minute crack in the floorboards.

Immediately, he summoned his father to remove the floorboards – a request a furniture dealer was most unhappy to comply with…

However, the letter from Balliol College, offering him a scholarship place, had indeed slipped between the boards. If the letter had not been answered, there would have been no further correspondence.

After National Service with the Royal Army Educational Corps, George went up to Oxford, where he became a noted debater and started a Catholic journal that attracted great contributors. Fellow undergraduates included luminaries such as William Rees-Mogg, Dick Taverne, Patrick Mayhew, George Steiner and Robin Day.

After a failed attempt to be elected as a Conservative candidate in a hopeless constituency, George turned his back on politics, having received advice from an experienced QC that the Bar was too demanding to combine with a career at Westminster. However, with no family connections and no contacts among solicitors, George faced a great battle to find a chambers that would take him. He carried out mundane jobs at Lyons's Corner House to help financially until he obtained a pupillage with Neil Lawson in London. Following this, George moved to Manchester, where he received plenty of work in the fields of crime and personal injury. In 1971, he was appointed Queen's Counsel (QC) and finally moved to London to take a place with Byrom Street Chambers. What was to follow was arguably one of the most remarkable careers in British legal history.

All that said, I would be doing George a grave disservice if I were to concentrate solely on his personal life. He wanted the cases he was involved with to speak for themselves. With the help of court transcripts, press reports and George's own documents, plus eyewitness accounts (including my own) of the various trials and other reflections, I have pieced together a collection of George's most memorable cases. I have also included as the first chapter of this book his brief but illuminating account of his early life, which he managed to write before his death. My aim is to shine a light on George Carman's world; a world that has certainly changed since he was practising in it. Lawyers today are far less strident than they were and do not like to be seen to be pulling people to pieces. That, I suppose, is reflective of the times we live in now, but it certainly would've baffled George had he been around today. As he said, 'If you bring a case, you deserve everything you get.' This book looks at such cases, the times and the context in which they emerged and – fair or otherwise – the impact they had on those involved.

CHAPTER ONE

IN HIS OWN WORDS: THE FIRST THREE CHAPTERS OF GEORGE CARMAN'S UNFINISHED AUTOBIOGRAPHY

CHAPTER ONE

GEORGE ALBERT CARMAN QC SPEAKS HIS TRUTH

I, George Alfred Carman QC, want you, the reader of this book, to know that putting pen to paper for myself has been cathartic. Along with the account of my life's journey up till now, I have written this chapter in the knowledge that my life expectancy has been shortened due to cancer.

There comes a time in one's own life when one reflects on how far one has come, and my time of reflection was when I was diagnosed with cancer.

'Time stands still for no man' – I once read those words, but only when one looks at what little time one has left, do those words become very real!

I had a day of reflection, remembering myself as a boy wanting to be a man and in later years finding the true person within and becoming content within myself. Unfortunately, the time with this inner peace came later in my life and I was sad to gain this knowledge that 'it's OK to be oneself and to have one's own ideas' so late in life.

On this day of reflection, however, the moulding by loved ones and one's own ideals and values becomes clear. Many people lose themselves in the illusion of life to please others and are not of truth to themselves. This, I realised, was of paramount importance in one's life.

My regret is that I never found the 'true me' much earlier in life, as maybe I would have found that inner peace. The shortness of height and the lesser good looks would be there but would not have mattered, as I would have been happy and content within myself. Who knows, my life may have had balance, which it did not. If I could say anything, I would say hold dear and reflect on who you are and who you wish to have in your life, but most of all, be true to one's own self.

I am a complex person, a driven person and at times an arrogant person. I totally lived for my career and was in control, which I needed. At times, it was a very lonely place, unless you had people of similar thought processes around you. I now realise it was hard for others to understand me regarding my professionalism. I realised I was living my mother's wishes as 'the prodigal son'. My mother would always want to do her best. She was at times very judgemental of people who were not of the same thought process. Her drive and standards helped me on my journey. I realised I had her traits not my own. I have been guilty of being in judgement of those around me and again that core footprint of my mother was repeated on those occasions.

My father's views were of little use to anyone and very bigoted. However, I found myself also bigoted at times. Never until my reflection did I know who George Carman was! He was a product of a controlling home and school and only after I left home did I find my own thoughts. I also realised that at their core, they were still my mother's thoughts and the journey that she was never able to take. Due to the control by others, I became guarded even with my own self, but it shaped me into the person I became in my career. I am truly proud of that.

I have become a well-known name, which in a small way will always be part of history spoken and written by others who follow on. I hope if anything, I have set a solid benchmark of achievement for the people who wish to aspire to my level of commitment in their work ethic.

I would love to have had my own 'learning hall' for young members of the Bar to educate them, not with the law itself but how to perform in their career in a professional manner. I felt the code of conduct and principles were starting to lack, due to the pressure put on the younger generation. I could see they were all in the same mould, with few if any personalities given the chance to shine. I would have loved to help them on their way and give guidance to be 'themselves when working and to aspire to be great'. It is what truly inspires that makes you grow and increases one's desire to learn from what one sees and hears.

We are all of service in many ways. I remember watching a man called Fred Housego on TV and was astounded by his knowledge and photographic memory. Yet he was a taxi driver.

I thought to myself, 'Well, look at how we judge others on what they do for a living and their intellect.' I thought that I may have been one of his passengers, and would I have taken any notice of this man? The answer would be NO! Yet there he was, not only of service like oneself to others but a man trying to improve his life.

As I sat watching this man, it changed my thought processes regarding how I behaved in front of even the cleaners. In fact, this man pulled me up sharp and inspired me. I have personally grown in life more by being inspired than by doing what was expected of me by others.

I have been able to look at my life and in seeing I was harsh towards any form of health or social weakness, both in myself and others, I realise this had a very great effect on my son and probably harmed him rather than helped him.

If I could say anything constructive, it would be to embrace all the senses and let them surface. One could accommodate other feelings and still show oneself to be strong. Letting one's own emotions to the surface can heal and help one move forward. I could have been kinder to myself. As a young child, my parents were very rigid in thoughts regarding any illness, and one was told to grin and bear it. I held the same thought process in my life! I wish I had done more crying in the psychological sense. I felt inner pain caused by my struggle to get somewhere in life, and this also caused imbalance in my life. I took the wrong choices to please others and all took their toll.

I would sit in judgement of people in my early and later years, until the time of my contentment, when I saw the bigger picture in life. We are all the same but given different abilities to express this. I very often found the ordinary person would be of great help on many occasions. Their logic is straightforward and often takes a simpler view of the problem and its solution. So I stopped looking to judge and found that I was the one being educated.

I have looked at myself as an elder and now realise that I did not let people in! Including people who enhanced my life in many ways and became friends, yet still I kept my guard up and I did not let them in. I regret this and realise that my whole life has been guarded against any form of true feelings towards others. I now see I could and should have been just George Carman, instead of being afraid of letting my mask down. I prevailed along the professional routes, when in fact I could and should have had harmony to enjoy both. I have learned this now, that it is too late! If you want people around you that you like and love, then it's OK to have them in your company and not just when time allows you to do so. I now realise I'm not of this earth for much longer and I say to you all, do not leave it until time is coming to a closure for you to express your own feelings. I unfortunately am totally guilty of the very thing I have written about and that is because it's my own lesson too late. If I had been of truth to myself, perhaps the people I hurt along the way would not have suffered from my single-mindedness. I can't change the past; it's too late! But with these words, perhaps I may be able to help others like myself to re-evaluate their life now.

The biggest challenge and fight of my life was when I was diagnosed with prostate cancer. My thoughts were firstly to see it off, and secondly to also grin and bear whatever lay ahead regarding treatments – there was a very long haul after I was diagnosed! I also thought, 'I must get on with it and fight to destroy it.'

I can truly say that I dealt with it by not giving it my attention. I thought that if I was going to get cancer anywhere, it would have been my lungs due to the smoking, however that was not so. Sometimes I would cry inside but tell myself, 'Don't be so weak,' knowing my mother regarded illness in any shape or form as a weakness.

The processes of the treatment and the doctors' statements of

'You are doing well' was encouragement but after a while started to sound like a recording to encourage one, but they did not state one way or the other the likely outcome. In the latter part of my disease, I have had to face the fact that no matter what was tried to stop it, one couldn't halt it and there will be a day when I will have to be very brave and accept it is going to beat me! One can't give it any more in the psychological sense, so you're left to accept 'that will be that'.

I am quite brave in the way I have dealt with the disease, but one's inner self gets to a point where one knows the truth and has to look it in the eye and face it. That takes courage. Whatever takes you, one has to accept it's the way it's going to be.

After the news of my cancer, I enjoyed what was around me much more. I enjoyed the company of the people close to me and the lesson I learned 'to be true to myself'. That may shock you, as I seem very much in control of who I am and what I do. However, take away the title and all you have is a man. I have feared death, but once I knew it was coming, I have chosen to look it in the eye and accepted it. I would not express my fear, as that would show weakness.

I did see a 'white mist' in the hall. It did not faze me in anyway, but I knew I had witnessed something which was not of human form. It moved quite slowly and then disappeared. It did not feel like a bad energy and gave me a form of comfort and confirmation that an afterlife exists.

I am sad that there will be a day when I will not see the people that I love around me any more, nor tell those who truly matter to me how I felt regarding them. I am sad that I have to give up my career and because of the thought of not seeing the sunshine, the rain and the flowers. Of course, I believe in 'God's energy'. I believe at the end of my life, there will be a place that I will go to be received. I fear retribution for the weak side of myself, my indulgences. I thought I was one of the most positive people on the planet, but when death is looking at you and has boxed you into a corner with nowhere to go, a little self-pity is helpful. Holding back one's emotions for the benefit of others causes the emotion to go within and can cause more harm. Crying, laughter, sadness and joy have been given to human beings as a release mechanism for healing. We all arrived with a cry!

CHAPTER TWO

THE MAKING OF THE ADVOCATE

My life in law I embraced wholly. My mask was my career and I was able to hide behind it and shine, but for who, I ask? I see it was for others' approval; I copied my mother, who also sought others' approval.

I was devoted and dedicated to my career and being the best at what I did to assist others is paramount to me. I would show my true colours on the closure of cases at their final execution.

I helped many, many people in my time and joy was experienced as a result on many occasions. My work opened many interesting doors to interesting people.

Ironically, in my early years in law, I feared failure, until I saw fear in another and quickly dismissed it as a weakness! A weakness that predators can feast upon, for gain and for victory.

One could say that when I took on a case, I used sports tactics. If a boxer enters the ring with his guard down, he will be the victim of the opponent. The very best boxers watch their opponent's moves and look for their weak spots to make the kill.

I would go over and over all the evidence with a fine toothcomb. I am quite charming and witty and that was for two reasons. I used it when I was at college to throw off guard the bullies, and also when in court to make the juries feel at ease. It was also my mask, as I used to worry, but I am human after all!

Once you're at the top of any profession, there are those who wish you to fall. Jealousy can be quite evil. My profession gave me the opportunity to shine. I could wear a mask of an actor to cover the nerves. The court was my platform. I have become the very best I could be and am proud of myself for my career. I knew I wanted to be someone who set precedence for others, someone they could admire and try to become or even better! This is the way to lead people forward in the law.

All the pioneers, philosophers and explorers have the same thing in common: they are total individuals. I was unique, I made sure of that! I wanted to be remembered for what you can achieve when the chance comes along. I say chance, because of the way life can lead people to be in the right place at the right time. Some people can have all they need to take them forward but somehow it doesn't happen. Maybe that's because there are leaders and followers in life and that balance is always there, whether human or animal. One must not judge the followers; their journey is just as important. We are cogs in a wheel of life. There is balance in life – the leaders and the led.

My father once said, 'Why do you bother? You won't succeed to do anything special in life.' Those words haunted me, and from then onwards, I was going to prove him wrong. I learned to only rely on myself, even though I had people around me. I was very singular in thought. One would call it selfish, but I would call it singular. How very wrong my father was, as I was par excellence at my work. My career was my whole being and meant everything to me. I had become a great person, just like my parents' comments in my childhood regarding the 'great people' who built the railways. Those words were set in my mind from childhood and I had wanted to be great also, and there I was at the top of my career.

I worked hard. I would go over and over everything with a fine toothcomb and then again, keeping ahead of the game. I made sure I read and looked at every piece of evidence sometimes three or four times over.

I was always a people watcher. This gave me a great advantage over whom I was to take on. I learned that if their shoulders moved on the left side when I was cross-examining, that I had them on the run! Although I had what I needed in written form, the body language was also important and I was usually correct. Some, however, were clever, believing that if they said nothing, they were possibly going to get away with it. In those I watched their eyebrows: if they lifted them on cross-examination, I knew I had them and went in on the visual cues for the kill to execute the case with excellence.

I was at times tired, but then I would look at the sky and say, 'Come on, old chap. How lucky you are to be able to do what you are doing' serving others.

I also watched and listened to my work colleagues and peers. I found that people who talk about themselves gave away their weaknesses and fears, again wonderful! As in court, one knew how to rattle them before and during a case.

I always looked the judges in the eye and held their gaze, as this showed confidence. I realised early on that if one shows any sign of weakness, one is looked upon as weak or not as good at what one does. So I always made sure to give the appearance that I am totally confident in what I was doing, which I can say truly unnerved some.

Once in for the kill, I am ruthless, as I had so much retained knowledge and information of the case, I would home in on it, like a boxer punching his opponent when off guard. I love it! I was wanted, I am needed and I am talked about.

I am the best at what I do, but it could be a very lonely journey for people not of the same thoughts. You see, the main difference between myself and my colleagues was that to me, the law is my whole being, everything! To others, but not all, it is more of a job. In being so committed, I will always make sure I give over 110 per cent. Others, however, stick to the textbook guideline on deliverance and on summing up during court cases. I will always be one step ahead, as I look outside the box, shall we say.

There were one or two who were committed in a similar fashion to myself. We, however (and to mention no names), did not see eye to eye, as our egos, including mine, get in the way.

At work, I like to be in my own company, but one has to share chambers! I can be awkward company, as I like to rehearse questions and answers myself before a case came to court. I will rehearse over and over to get things perfect in my mind, in case my client could be asked an awkward question. I would be at the ready to have the knowledge at hand, verbal or written. So I would practise being my client and putting questions that I thought may come their way and how I would answer them. You see, I was clever, and the truth and only the truth mattered. So, I liked my own space to practise this.

I am a very heavy smoker and others (not to name them) were not pleased with the smoke or smell the cigarettes give off.

I often look out the window from my chambers and think to myself, 'Well, Mother, if you could see me now, I've done you proud.' We can all have bad days at work. I am no exception, but I can tell you when I put my work clothes on, I automatically change.

I become completely in control of my thoughts and completely driven.

I have a little superstition and will say to myself just before going into the courtrooms, 'Carman, you have a job to do and do it you will.'

And on leaving a completed case, I would say, 'Job well done!'

I am small in stature, but in court, I am a giant of a man. I also have to wear the same colour socks when in court! Silly to look at it now, but at the time, it was the normal way of thinking and would assist me in winning and helping things going well. My shoes also have to shine. I am not alone in these little 'safety nets'; quite a few of us in the law have them.

I will bring everyone into the courtroom proceedings. I will look each jury member in the eye during my cross-examination. I will hold the person's gaze and watch their expressions. I am quite sarcastic and very dry in court, which will make people laugh and unbeknown to them, makes them feel at ease and more relaxed. That gives me an edge on the person I am questioning. I will try to make them feel belittled to rattle them, and when people are rattled, they become angry and start to forget where they are, even for just a moment; they can then drop themselves in it by failing in their own defence. I know that my complete dedication gives me advantage over my colleagues. Hard work pays off; practice makes perfect.

I knew that my life is anything but the norm and due to this sacrifice, others suffered. I must say that with my career, luck also played its part. I was in the right place at the right time. The court is my platform, as I said before, and I have become the very best I can be. I have absolutely no regrets regarding my career. I do my best to assist the common man and those up-and-coming men of the law to be the best they can possibly be in their career. I would change my personal life to have more balance.

One morning at fifty-five years old, I looked in the mirror and saw an older version of myself staring back at me and for the first time in my life, I acknowledged I had aged. At that moment, my whole being seemed to change, including my outlook and perspective on things in many ways. I also asked myself where have all the years gone? I look much older in the flesh but not in the mind. The ageing thoughts only stayed a few moments. I had never observed myself as a person in the flesh before and it gave a sense of meaning. On that day when I recognised I was on the other side of fifty-five years, it was a trigger point for me to not stand still with time but to embrace myself much more and to do so much more career-wise. I did consider that same year to move abroad to America, but I soon dismissed it, as I knew what I have achieved here in England and I am respected. That means a lot to me.

I was greatly inspired by Winston Churchill. As I saw it, he was a genius who would ask people around him their opinions and views and take what he considered to be the positives and consolidate this with his own thoughts.

I also adopted this method in my career with my juniors, asking, 'What do you think?' This, I found, gave me respect and them a sense of confidence. However, I always maintained their respect and did not let anyone cross the line with me.

I also had respect for Douglas Bader – there was a man of great courage and determination, true grit and his dedication to the last was unconditional. How wonderful. What he did, allowed our people and others to be free, including myself.

I also had respect for Reginald Mitchell, the man who created the Spitfire. He was a genius, who also looked outside the boundaries of the normal and believed in himself.

I am a complex person and like to be in control, as losing control of oneself could show weakness. I knew when working that my life was anything but that considered to be the norm.

As a young man, I would get a great adrenaline rush after each court case and would have suffered a 'great come down' that could be avoided by alcoholic drinks after the cases. Drink would loosen my tongue and allow my voice to state how I felt. Again shyness disappeared. I have an addictive personality.

Company sometimes came at a price to one's own self. I could be in the company of what one would call 'hardened drinkers' and at times one would more often find oneself nursing a hangover. After long hours of work and after putting 'my all' into my work for that day, I would not want to just go home. Normal life in that respect was something that was dull. When I won cases, one would go out and people wanted you in their company, not for oneself but for the 'man with the title'. I knew that, but it suited me. I met many people from many walks of life, including villains and more. At the Garrick Club, I would listen to those around me and their opinions on everything. Their views on political issues and who they voted for gave me the measure of the company I had. I had many acquaintances but very few true friends of my choosing.

In my latter years, of course, one knew how to channel this energy after a court case, but as a young man, I did not. Later in my life, I preferred a social drink of quality rather than quantity.

On reflection, my smoking was a crutch or safety net, along with my addictive personality. I smoked as I thought it seemed to bring me luck. If I had a cigarette, I would have a good outcome on any case that I worked on and that escalated into my personal life. I found comfort in smoking, which switched to having to smoke, which was a silly thought process.

On reflection, I know I was a 'hail-fellow-well-met'. I loved to indulge others in my ability to pay and treat them. It gave me great pleasure. I was no fool, though; some took my kindness as a weakness. I soon saw through them, even if I was a little worse for wear at times. I was always on my guard and made sure that any form of snipe coming my way, I very quickly stopped.

I am a man who runs deep. People I met who thought they knew me did not. They would only see what was on the surface. In an odd way, I dealt with my shyness via my professionalism. I only became at ease with myself later in life, when I was at the top and had more time to engage with and choose who I wanted to be around me.

Karen Phillipps was a lady whom I let into my life. A lady of great complexity! An enigma in a way. We have common ground in our work area. She is kind and I see her as a person who needed nurturing even though one would try to guide her, but she has her own plans. I respected that in her, but it can also frustrate me. I am very pleased that she is a part of my life's journey. I never felt that either of us as individuals wanted or required more than what we have together.

CHAPTER THREE

GEORGE CARMAN'S PRIVATE LIFE AND UPBRINGING

My 'out-of-balance life' affected my home life. I want to tell my son Dominic that I love him and that I'm sorry. He has inherited my stubborn streak! I expected my son to complete a similar journey and for much I have regrets and want to apologise for myself.

I am proud of my son but expected too much from him, including him to climb to great heights. Although I was around, I never gave him balance. My career took my time and I did not show him nor tell him how much I loved him. In having given what he required 'provision and moneywise', I feel to blame for his lack of responsibility in that area 'mea culpa' (my fault). During my reflection, I realised that I too had some of my father's traits and could have been a better father to my son. I did not break the circle that was created by my father. We can all say that's a 'cop-out' to blame one's own failings on the parent or parents. Well, parents have a duty to encourage their children to go forward.

Dominic and I had a somewhat complex relationship, which is not at all unique in families with professional parents, as it can become difficult to give time to family life. At times, career and family both had to suffer, but this did not mean that I did not love my son – I do!

I wanted him to become a man who wore his own suit and reached his goals in life. I found my son to be an 'optimistic opportunist' who thought he could see the bigger picture in life without analysing where it could take him.

I feel he will please people as a 'yes man' to gain approval from others.

In my later years, I became wiser and accepted who he is, which made me more at ease with him. I accepted his journey wouldn't be as driven as mine. He always knew I was there and that's all that mattered to me in the end. I could have been a better father! History repeated itself.

My profession took precedence like my parents. I did provide for him; I felt he had my father's traits in many ways. I want to tell my son I love him and that I'm sorry.

I look at my grandson Matthew and see a 'younger me'. I mellowed with age and that allowed me to enjoy him as he brought such joy. He was an achiever and it was such happiness to be in his presence and to know he knew his life's journey at a young age.

I can say truly, I was never wholly satisfied with a 'confined' normal married way of life. I know I let all three of my wives down. My hunger to be the best at what I did, and my choice of career, took precedence. I did not see beyond that! I did what I thought was expected; I provided but inevitably the marriages broke down.

I regret hurting all three of my wives and for not having the courage of my convictions to say no. I also feel I should have ended the courtships sooner, on reflection. You see, my controlling ways in a sense made me want them to be there, even though I was totally unhappy in a marriage situation and believed that letting go was a failure for oneself.

I should never have walked down the aisle. I conformed to what was expected to be the norm. I was selfish and because of this, the people around me suffered. I helped others in their lives, but I was to blame for failing in my own.

I guess I truly found it hard to show my feelings in the correct way, and in not doing so I had three failed marriages. I can truly say that all three were very beautiful women. Marriage was not a need or requirement that wholly fulfilled me. I married because it was considered to be the norm and expected thing to do, and again mainly to please others. I could have done a better job of being a husband and father. Take away the wig and costume and you have only the man.

How things have changed. People are free to make choices now and it is no longer frowned upon if people just live together or remain single.

My childhood also had imbalance: although my sister and I were happy and my mother showed us more affection than my father, it was only experienced when time permitted. My parents were controlling in the sense that they never made the home life a place of joy; it was always work orientated. I knew my parents were not at all happy with their marriage, but for pride's sake they stayed together.

I felt that made me grow up quickly. I can truly state that my childhood was quite lonely. My parents were business orientated. Mother was a workaholic. She was a lovely kind lady but in no way empathic regarding illness or weakness that she saw in others or herself. Mother was also a very private lady and our house had very few visitors who were allowed into the home. Our family was a tight unit in that respect; we kept ourselves to ourselves. She would say we don't want others peering in at what we have and judging us. I did have a privileged upbringing, but my journey grounded me. My parents' snobbery made me not want to be condescending to less fortunate people. My mother was always working and had little spare time to give to the family. She was a driven lady and I looked up to her.

Mother would always tell me that if anyone knocks on the door unexpectedly, do not open the front door wide, as we do not want them peering in at our belongings. For the milkman, however, mother would open the front door more than the usual crack-sized gap to allow her to pay him for the week's milk. So this was how the Carman family received people who called upon us! However, the priest was always welcome; my parents considered it as great honour to have him round. Mother would fuss over him, giving him tea and cake; they felt it was a privilege, you see. I, on the other hand, saw he was only there for the cake. My family sought approval: they were in awe of those whom they felt had respect in society and that included doctors, priests and teachers. My father was very much in awe of them and would take what they said as gospel.

My mother had great order in our house and everything was done to time. After the evening meal, the table was always set for breakfast. Our house was kept clean in case we had visitors, which makes me smile on reflection since my mother was very fussy about whom she allowed into the house.

Ironically, as my mother was very judgemental of others that she regarded to be common people, she would help others and show her kindness to those less fortunate but considered herself to be upper class when in fact we were merely middle class. She would tell me that in order to get on in life, you have to do the very best you can at whatever you do. That had a big impact upon my attitude to my career and the journey to the top of my profession.

I had a good school friend called Fred Murray. He was allowed into the house and garden as my parents liked his parents. They owned a fruit and vegetable stall and wanted to own a shop, so that impressed my mother greatly. That friendship sadly ended when they moved to Sutton-on-Sea.

I had little or no respect for my father. He was sarcastic and a formidable character. He would have a look that made you stop and listen, which even now in my life I can feel the effects of deep within. He had a single-minded attitude and everything he said would have a tinge of sarcasm to it. I felt that he and my mother had parallel lives, due to their work. My mother was the strong one of the family; she pushed us forward.

My father would be in his own world, really. I sought my father's approval and wanted him to respect me. In my eyes, my father did not love nor even like me and was jealous of the love my mother showed towards me and I towards her. He never once told me he loved me, in fact the complete opposite. I considered that he did not have any feelings towards me.

He was damning, sarcastic and brutal in his way. He would speak to me in monosyllabic words on a good day. He said I would never aspire to anything or anyone of importance in life. This made me very determined to prove him wrong. Always in my life's journey, those words and his lack of love resonated in my subconscious. I realised it made me a singular person who would only look to oneself for everything and became unable to show my true feelings.

Despite this, my father was a man I loved but had no respect for. I took my father's traits of not being able to express my thoughts and personal feelings, but only in my later years have I seen that in myself.

So I became solo in thought and action. It was my way of coping with life. My career became my life as I was in control of it and oneself within that profession.

My mother was a very clever lady. She had this special knack of getting one to do the household chores. They were considered to be a great privilege. I had the honour each week of winding up the clock, cleaning the dining room table and chairs completely, including every leg and also underneath the seats, and the top of the table was polished to make it shine! She was also fastidious with regard to keeping the house spick and span, as she would say.

I was also in charge, fortnightly, of polishing the brass candlesticks, which were placed either end of the mantelpiece. My mother also had peculiarities and many superstitions. Never would she pass a green gate or attempt to walk through one. No new shoes were allowed on the table due to them bringing 'bad luck', she would say. Also lavender was never permitted indoors, as she believed it would give bad luck outdoors. As to the green gates, one never had an explanation as to why she had this problem regarding them. One could only assume that she thought it would bring her bad luck.

I also developed superstitions as a result. I can remember as a young man my left shoe had to be put on first and my shoes always had to shine. I can only imagine that my father had an influence on this from his army background. My mother used to say that shiny shoes always pleased people, it shows others you're from good stock and people judged you on shiny shoes. I also had a thing regarding doors, which I preferred to open on the right side as I entered the room. I liked things in the house to be in place, but in my later years, I was not so fussy.

I learned to accept that I would only have my own company for the majority of my youth and teenage years. I actually liked my own company, and I would take myself off to the local area and beyond to enjoy watching and listening to people's conversations. From a very young age, I would be a great listener and would observe people's behaviour, which I felt was a great asset to have and came in useful later in my life in the courtroom and on many occasions. As I was quite shy (believe it or not), most people were not aware of this young boy near them, or if they were, I can only imagine that they were not aware that I was watching and listening. I gained great knowledge from my time with this hobby.

I also remember our family train journey with my parents saying to one another how great the people were who invented the trains and railways! On that same train journey, I can recall myself looking out of the carriage window and thinking to myself that I wanted to be great one day. That thought inspired me and remained with me for my lifetime, as I said before.

My schooling as an infant was enjoyable, but I can truly say my junior school years were hellish for the first time in my life, due to bullying from my lack of height. I told my mother how horrid the children in the class were and that they were picking on me and taunting me over my height. All Mother said, and this was her standard way of dealing with any of my issues, was 'Don't mull on it too long. The bigger the person, the harder they will fall.' She felt sure that after a week or two, the bullying would all stop and that the boys who picked on me were no doubt taller boys. My mother's words, although harsh, stood me in good stead in my teens and also in court.

Alas, the bullying continued! I called upon my father for support and guidance with tears in my eyes and his only advice was to toughen up. He gave me a smirk and a sarcastic comment that he didn't want a son of his to be a wimp and then asked, 'Do you hear me?' Those words ran deep and scared me.

I realised that he probably enjoyed the fact that I was being bullied. From that moment on, I stood alone with this problem. I soon learned that if I made people laugh by being witty, they liked it, and as time went on, it became easier to cope with bullying. However, underneath, it scared me to the core of my being. I found making people laugh by fooling around helped to distract the bullies and also to overcome my own shyness. That is why I liked my own company. I always tried to excel at school and here jealousy reared its ugly head from some classmates.

My school photographs show I was just like everyone else but shorter than some.

At St Joseph's College, there were some very cruel bullies, along with control by the Roman Catholic faith. As a boy and young man, I was always in awe of the teachers and had respect for those who were going to help mould my future. I always wanted to know things and I was like a sponge for knowledge, which never left me. When we sat our exams and were marked by our teachers, I realised that we were summed up by a piece of paper that was important to go forward with one's life and career. The education was second to none at St Joseph's.

As a young child and young man one went to church as the expected thing to do somewhat automatically. I did not need to go, but that was personal between God and oneself.

I wanted to become a priest at one time because I believed it was the path I was to follow. I also thought that it would make my family proud of me, something I had always sought. However, one changed one's mind due to the fact that not all who are of the cloth are true to themselves. As one matured, one knew that some took that path with other agendas and became trapped in a life they felt they had to continue. The control over my life from home and school had been immense and I could see this being even greater if I pursued the priesthood path.

I became personally disillusioned with my Catholic religion. I looked at what I saw of the priesthood and did not like it, so I knew this was not for me as a personal view. I did enjoy Latin and Mass and the smell of the incense. I loved the architecture of the cathedrals, the choir and being in a chapel of the inner peace that gave something to me. In fact, I loved looking out for signs on the walls of the buildings and shops and the architecture and the artwork that went into them.

My life opened up when I was at Oxford studying law. Many opportunities came that I had not experienced before, and my life changed. I had the freedom to think for myself. I had always done so from an early age, but at Oxford, there was no control. So, it opened doors for me in many ways.

It was a revelation! I drove myself to be approved of and loved, having been bullied due to my lack of height and I was truly messed up by my father's attitude.

You see, all my life until this point, I had been controlled by others' wishes, views and religion and although I had my own observations and thought processes, I was not able to use them or state them. I felt I was analytical at an early age and a people watcher. I was always open to knowledge of every kind. I was never a person who had blinkered vision, unlike my parents, and I would accept that everyone was different. My childhood was controlled by the fact that I was encouraged to live my life the way my parents wanted me to. School, again, was controlling. I had a temper, because I did not speak up for what I wanted. Until my late teens, I conformed to the wishes of others. My mother had a great influence over my thoughts and on reflection, I was sad, as I should have been permitted my own way of thinking and dealing with things. It was responsible for me 'going a little on the wild side of freedom' later, when I had no boundaries set.

University at the very beginning was such a different way of life. One was taught in a completely different way. We had tutors who guided us in the right direction, but ultimately, it was up to one's own self to learn from books and texts and to drive oneself as far as one could. It all overwhelmed me and I became depressed, even suicidal, for a short period of time. I was confused about whom I was, along with memory of my father's words saying, 'I will never become anything of importance.'

I soon pulled myself up when I realised university was what I wanted. I had wanted to get to university, and it was a great honour to be there. After that self-talk, I never looked back. I welcomed and embraced all the doors and opportunities that opened up for me with my arms open.

At university, the tutors are the ones who looked outside the box. At an early age, I used to weigh up the teachers. I had observed that there were two types: ones that gave textbook teachings and were quite happy to just read and repeat others' works; and those who would write history and expand knowledge. These, I thought, are people who wish to go beyond just 'parrot fashion' in learning and teaching and saw the bigger picture and led others onwards.

History has shown I did the best, in fact extremely well, at university. I always knew as a child that I was to be of service to others and history shows that it was to be law, but whatever I had chosen, I would still have given it my all. I realised that George Alfred Carman QC was at the core a person who had the traits of both my parents.

I have lain bare whom I am. No one truly knew this information and I hope it will open a few hearts and minds into my life's journey. People can make or break you in life. My journey made me as a professional but as a mere man it broke me, and it is in this revelation of my book that you can see a part of that.

All addictive personalities go overboard on anything they take on. We all lose and gain in life as part of its journey. I was weak; I was controlled. I had too many negative things in my own person and at times was quite difficult to be around, especially as I have never tolerated fools gladly. That was the realisation to me, to accept what I did when it was too late. I took my father's traits of not being able to express my thoughts regarding my personal feelings but only in my later years did I see that in myself!

Not many people have truly left their mark in the world, but those who do were true individuals with their own thoughts and the courage of their convictions.

CHAPTER TWO

R V. JEREMY THORPE

'And you, and you, and you, and you…'

GEORGE CARMAN

In May 1979, George Carman QC was instructed to appear for his client in what the press called 'the trial of the century'. Jeremy Thorpe, the former Liberal Party leader, was accused of no less than incitement to murder and conspiracy to murder.

The case was a major turning point in George Carman's life. He was offered a very low fee, but the publicity would be immense, thereby enhancing his reputation.

In public life, Thorpe's career had gone from strength to strength. He was elected to Parliament as Liberal MP for North Devon in October 1959 and succeeded Jo Grimond as party leader in 1967. The public loved him as a witty panellist on *Any Questions?* What they didn't know was that he had a habit of picking up young men in bars. Despite this, he married Caroline Allpass in May 1968. The Archbishop of Canterbury gave them special permission to use his private chapel at Lambeth Palace. The next month, the flamboyant Thorpe gave a reception at Burlington House for nearly a thousand people, including the Prime Minister and the Leader of the Opposition. Caroline and Jeremy had a son, Rupert, the following year. Tragically, Caroline was killed while driving alone in 1970.

Three years later, Thorpe married the divorced wife of the Earl of Harewood, Marion – a distinguished concert pianist.

Despite this, it had long been believed that Thorpe had 'homosexual tendencies', as it was so delicately put; however, no newspaper had ever stated this for fear of libel. In fact, Thorpe's solicitor, Lord Goodman, 'the portly peer', was not slow in passing on a client if there was whiff of scandal in the air. This was certainly so in the case of Thorpe. A stable groom, Norman Scott, alleged not only that he and Thorpe had had an affair starting in 1961 (even consensual homosexual acts were illegal in Britain until the Sexual Offences Act of 1967) but that Thorpe had tried to have him murdered.

The alleged facts of the Thorpe case are bizarre, almost beyond belief. However, the reason that truth is stranger than fiction is that fiction usually has to make sense.

In October 1975, Andrew 'Gino' Newton, a former airline pilot, collected Norman Scott, from where he was living in Combe Martin, North Devon, and drove him to Exmoor. When they reached Porlock Hill, Newton stopped the car and they both got out. Newton then shot Scott's dog, Rinka, a Great Dane, before turning the gun on Scott.

When the case came before Exeter Crown Court in March 1976, Scott said that the gun jammed and that Newton then drove off, leaving him alone beside the dead dog. Newton always maintained that his intention was only to frighten Scott, whom, he alleged, possessed incriminating photographs of him. The jury evidently believed Scott's version of events and Newton was convicted of possession of a firearm with intent to endanger life. He was sentenced to two years' imprisonment.

During his court appearance, Scott repeated his claims of a relationship with Jeremy Thorpe and alleged that Thorpe had threatened to kill him if he spoke about their affair. Scott also sold letters to the press which he claimed were love letters from Thorpe. One of these included the memorable line 'Bunnies can and will go to France', which supposedly showed Thorpe using his 'pet name' for Scott, in connection with a promise to find Scott a well-paid job in France.

Scott's allegations forced Thorpe to resign as Liberal Party leader on 9 May 1976. He was replaced temporarily by his predecessor Jo Grimond and then permanently by David Steel.

Andrew Newton was released from prison in April 1977 and then revived the scandal by reversing what he had previously said, by claiming that he had been hired to kill Norman Scott.

An amazing fact about the Thorpe case was that it did not come about because of police investigations but largely because of research by two BBC journalists, Barrie Penrose and Roger Courtier, and the paranoia of Harold Wilson (who stepped down as Prime Minister on 5 April 1976). Wilson had later spoken to journalists in the Commons' press gallery about the interference of South Africa and how anti-democratic agencies in that country were trying to subvert British democracy.

The following day, Wilson gave a personal interview to Penrose and Courtier and told them that, while he was in office, MI5 had tried to discredit him and his private secretary, Marcia Williams, as communists. He knew about the Thorpe–Scott rumours but was firmly on the side of Thorpe. He claimed that Scott was, in fact, an agent of South Africa and advised the journalists to investigate him and also a former MP, Peter Bessell, who was allegedly part of an international conspiracy against Thorpe.

Bessell had been the Liberal MP for Bodmin in Devon from 1964–70. He had left school at sixteen and embarked on a series of feckless ventures, managing to persuade people to invest in businesses from plastic egg boxes to a potential string of motels. All of them failed and nobody got their money back.

However, Bessell did make his mark in 1953 by putting on a successful local pageant to celebrate the Queen's Coronation and was subsequently selected by the Liberals as their parliamentary candidate for Torquay. Jeremy Thorpe came to support him in the by-election of 1955 and, although Bessell came third, the two men became friends. Bessell was not gay; he had a wife and a string of girlfriends.

Once in the House of Commons, Bessell became as close as anyone to the new Liberal leader and it was to him Jeremy turned when his mother, Ursula Thorpe, received a seventeen-page letter from Norman Scott giving details of his sexual relationship with Thorpe. Scott complained about his subsequent abandonment and retreat to Ireland and, above all, his need for money.

Bessell discussed the matter over a drink with Thorpe, thinking he would gain his confidence – and the truth – by pretending to have had his own homosexual moments. Thorpe raised his glass, saying, 'Peter, we're nothing but a couple of old queens.'

Bessell became Thorpe's liege man. He flew to Dublin, where Scott had been lodging with a priest. Bessell eventually met Scott and warned him that his letter to Ursula Thorpe was a blackmail threat. He could be extradited from Ireland and prosecuted. Scott's reply surprised him: 'Well, that's marvellous. I can come to England

and get the whole matter sorted out.' Bessell asked him about the fifty letters from Thorpe, and Scott admitted that they were in his suitcase, which had been lost by Aer Lingus, when he was in Geneva.

On his return to London, Bessell tracked down the suitcase and arranged for it to be delivered to Victoria Station. He needed to go to New York for yet another of his ambitious and abortive business ventures, so he arranged for his secretary to pick it up. She was taken aback when Thorpe, whom she hardly knew, said he would come with her and further surprised when he drove them to his flat in Marsham Court, where he forced open the locks of the case. Thorpe removed the packets of letters and any evidence that Scott had been living at Marsham Court and then calmly relabelled the case and drove with it to the Aer Lingus office for its dispatch to Dublin.

Scott eventually returned to London and it was to Bessell he turned for money. Bessell managed to obtain funds, usually by conning wealthy Liberals, most notoriously Sir Jack Hayward in the Bahamas, stating it was for party matters.

When Bessell lost his seat in 1970, he was bankrupt, and Thorpe managed to get a friend to bail him out. Bessell left for the States, ending up in Oceanside, California, to start a new career writing children's books. But his charm, once again, stood him in good stead. His American girlfriend, Diane Kelly, had a rich father who bankrolled them both and even bought some other cottages on the coast to give them an income.

Hunting for a lead, Penrose and Courtier flew to California. They knew that by this time Bessell's loyalty to Thorpe had waned, as Thorpe had unnecessarily dragged him into controversy in an article in the *Sunday Times*. Bessell told them that the idea of him or Scott being a South African agent was nonsense. It was a red herring that Thorpe himself had produced. Bessell was prepared to tell all, especially for money.

Bessell told the reporters that Jeremy allegedly said to him, 'We've got to get rid of Scott. It's the only way. If I don't, this man is going to haunt me all my life. It's no worse than shooting a sick dog.'

Thorpe's best man, David Holmes, was assistant treasurer of the Liberal Party who took over from Bessell the task of doing Thorpe's dirty work. Thorpe, said Bessell, had suggested that Holmes lure Scott to the Florida swamps, where he could shoot him and the alligators would eat the body to hide the evidence. This proved impractical. But Holmes did initiate the events that led to Andrew Newton and the shooting of Rinka.

One of Holmes's business contacts was carpet salesman John Le Mesurier (not the actor of the same name). He also gave financial advice to one of the latter's friends, George Deakin. Holmes told Deakin that a friend of his was having trouble with a blackmailer and needed someone to frighten him off.

At a charity dinner, Deakin was introduced to an airline pilot, Andrew 'Gino' Newton. Later on, Newton took Deakin aside and whispered, 'I understand you want someone bumped off. If you haven't got anybody, I am your man.'

This was to be financed by payments from Sir Jack Hayward, a benefactor who lived in the Bahamas. Hayward liked Thorpe and loaned him some money to bail out the bankrupt Liberal Party and then made further personal loans to the party and to his friend Nadir Dinshaw, who lived in Jersey and was Rupert Thorpe's godfather. Unknown to Sir Jack, £10,000 of this would make its way from David Holmes via petty criminals to Andrew Newton.

Satisfied with their discoveries, Penrose and Courtier returned to England to write their book, but none of their sensational material could be printed in the press, due to the laws of libel. This didn't prevent *Private Eye* and other papers hinting at what Thorpe and his accomplices had been up to. Matters came to a head on Wednesday 19 October 1977 when the *London Evening News* came out with the headline: 'I was hired to kill Scott. Gunman tells of incredible plot – a murder contract for £5,000.' Andrew Newton, recently released from jail, had sold them his story.

Now the matter could no longer go uninvestigated. It would be normal for the Attorney General, Sam Silkin, to ask the police to make inquiries into matters of 'public interest'. However, Silkin was in a difficult position. On the one hand, there had been press allegations of a possible political cover-up. On the other hand, the nature of the evidence gathered so far did not necessarily merit a trial. From Scott to Bessell to Holmes to Thorpe himself, there were too many slippery and barely trustworthy characters.

So Silkin relied heavily on the advice of the Director of Public Prosecutions (DPP), Sir Thomas Hetherington, who firmly felt that they had to go ahead, and thus the Avon and Somerset Police, who had hitherto been rather reluctant to pursue the matter, were ordered to investigate.

Thorpe knew he had to respond to the *Evening News* article and ten days later called a press conference, which was held in the National Liberal Club in Whitehall. He was joined on the platform by his wife Marion, Sir Clement Freud (then a Liberal MP and friend but who, posthumously in 2016, was exposed as a paedophile who sexually abused young girls) and a partner from Lord Goodman's law firm.

Thorpe rose and read from a prepared statement:

> I must stress that anyone expecting sensational revelations is likely to be disappointed. Not a scrap of evidence has been produced to implicate me in any alleged plot to murder Norman Scott … No sexual activity of any kind took place … Had I known of David Holmes's negotiations to purchase Scott's letters, I would have stopped them at once.

This completely terminated any friendship between Thorpe and Holmes. Indeed, were the case to come to trial, Holmes's lawyer John Mathew QC later told me, his client was prepared to plead guilty to 'conspiracy to frighten'. Had the Crown accepted this, it would have put Thorpe in an impossible position. But the plea was not acceptable to the prosecution.

Detective Chief Superintendent Michael Challes and a colleague from the Avon and Somerset Police now began to interview the main suspects. They didn't really know where to begin, so Challes went to see Penrose and Courtier to get their story. It is to the journalists' credit that they gave Challes all their research, since if a court case did ensue, they would be unable to publish the sensational story in their book as the matter would prohibit discussion elsewhere. They even accompanied Challes back to California, where Bessell provided him with his damning accusations.

Thorpe, meanwhile, urged those implicated to say nothing to the inspector. When his own turn came, he merely provided Challes with a written statement. He refused to say another word except 'Ditto' to every question. Amazingly, *Private Eye* got hold of a transcript of this conversation and labelled Thorpe the 'Ditto Man'.

On 4 July 1978, Challes provided the DPP with his findings to see if there was sufficient evidence for a prosecution. There wasn't.

Sir Thomas Hetherington said there were 'gaps' in the evidence that required Challes to do some more work.

There cannot have been very much missing, since by the end of the month, the Attorney General announced there would be committal proceedings against Thorpe, Holmes, Le Mesurier and Deakin.

A committal hearing was set for 20 November 1978 in the sleepy seaside town of Minehead in Somerset for three magistrates to hear the charges. Jeremy Thorpe was accused, along with David Holmes (deputy treasurer of the Liberal Party), George Deakin (a night-club owner) and businessman John Le Mesurier, with conspiracy to murder. Thorpe was also separately accused of inciting Holmes to murder Scott.

Normally, the local bench would pass the matter on to the Crown court after a relatively brief hearing, but Sir David Napley, Thorpe's solicitor, advised Thorpe to have an old-style committal under Section 6(1) of the Magistrates Courts Act, so they could hear the detailed prosecution case and take a look at Bessell and Scott in the witness box. In retrospect, this was unwise, particularly as Napley cross-examined Scott as to whether Thorpe had any unusual marks on his body. He stated that Thorpe had three nodules in his armpit.

In the eventual trial, one of the reasons George Carman did not allow Thorpe to give evidence was that Scott might have disclosed his intimate knowledge of Thorpe's body.

All counsel had agreed to have no publicity at the committal. Amazingly, Gareth Williams, the QC for Deakin, later Attorney General and a Cabinet Minister under Tony Blair, not only ratted on the agreement but asked for reporting restrictions to be lifted, as his client had 'nothing to hide'. From that moment, the town was engulfed by reporters from Britain and overseas wanting to cover the sensational saga.

The press had a field day as everything from Thorpe's alleged relationship with Scott to the botched plan to have Newton murder him made headlines for the next three weeks.

The Crown knew that allegations from the unstable Scott were unlikely to be enough to make a case. Holmes was hardly going to assist them, as he was one of the accused. Crucially, the Director of Public Prosecutions granted Bessell immunity from any sort of prosecution, so he arrived from America, his hair dyed red and wearing a selection of flamboyant suits, to tell the court and the world press what he claimed was Thorpe's insistence that Scott be killed.

That did it. The magistrates knew they had no other option than to send the accused to the Crown court for a full jury trial. This would usually have taken place in nearby Exeter, but the prosecution asked for committal to the Old Bailey, where the jury would not be selected from Thorpe's constituency.

The case was set for 30 April 1979, the day after Thorpe's fiftieth birthday, but another major event intervened. The government fell and the Prime Minister, James Callaghan, called a general election for 3 May. Thorpe, although no longer Liberal leader, was determined to stand again for the North Devon seat. Not to do so would be an admission that he had something to hide from his impending trial, the date for which was moved to 8 May. George Carman was appointed as Thorpe's lawyer.

An unexpected candidate for the North Devon constituency was Auberon Waugh, son of Evelyn, a journalist who wrote primarily for *Private Eye*. Waugh had chosen to stand against Thorpe on behalf of the Dog Lovers' Party (so called because of the death of Scott's dog, Rinka).

So George Carman's first action, on behalf of his client, was to apply to Lord Widgery, the Lord Chief Justice, for an injunction to prevent Waugh's election address being published. It was a vilification of Thorpe which Carman thought he should not have to tolerate. In Carman's opinion, the address was nothing more than a barely veiled attempt to prejudice the minds of potential jurors and thus amounted to a contempt of court.

Surprisingly, Lord Widgery dismissed the application, saying he could find no real risk in the document. Carman disagreed and took the matter before Lord Denning in the Court of Appeal. Lord Denning, after noting that 'the Dog Lovers' Party is an unusual name for a political party to choose', agreed with Carman. He declared that it was as plain as could be that there was a risk the address could prejudice a fair trial.

With or without the Dog Lovers' Party, Thorpe failed miserably in the May general election, his comfortable North Devon majority of 6,721 being overturned by the Conservatives with an overwhelming 8,473 majority. A bad omen, perhaps, for Thorpe's case to come.

So it came to be that, after twenty years, he lost his seat as MP for North Devon. Not all his constituents had lost their faith in him: he succeeded in achieving 23,338 votes, but the Conservative candidate had the majority. In the country, the Conservatives had an overall majority of forty-four and Europe had its first female Prime Minister: Margaret Thatcher.

Thorpe and the three other accused were put on trial in Court No. 1 at the Old Bailey on 8 May 1979, a week after Thorpe had lost his seat. Thorpe was charged with incitement to murder and, along with the other three defendants, conspiracy to murder.

Not only was it 'the trial of the century' – it proved to be the premier media circus trial. The number of photographers outside the court forced some to use stepladders to get their shots. Earlier, a media crowd had besieged Marion Thorpe's house in Orme Square in Bayswater. Junior counsel Graham Boal had to sneak ten-year-old Rupert Thorpe through a neighbour's garden to take him to school.

Jeremy Thorpe arrived at the Old Bailey in Sir David Napley's Rolls-Royce. He kept an expressionless face as he walked through the crowd of cameramen. In Court No. 1, he and his fellow accused – Holmes, Deakin and Le Mesurier – sat together in a glass and oak-panelled box. Thorpe's wife, Marion, and mother, Ursula, had appointed seats near them. Mr Justice Cantley, who, like George Carman, had worked primarily on the Northern Circuit, was the presiding judge, while Peter Taylor QC, later Lord Chief Justice, was leading counsel for the Crown.

Deakin was represented by Gareth Williams QC, who became Labour Attorney General and Leader of the House of Lords; Le Mesurier by Denis Cowley QC, who appeared on the Midland Circuit; and Holmes by John Mathew QC, a very able and former Senior Treasury Counsel at the Old Bailey, who now reversed his role as a defender.

Behind the scenes, Mathew indicated to Taylor that his client might plead guilty to the lesser charge of 'conspiracy to frighten/assault'. Taylor declined; the serious charge of conspiracy to murder had already been laid down and to add this alternative would weaken the more serious accusation.

After lunch on the first day, Thorpe kept on his overcoat with its velvet collar as he returned to the dock. 'I hope you don't think it disrespectful,' Carman said to the judge, 'but he tells me he is sitting in a draught.'

Taylor painstakingly set out to demonstrate the existence of a homosexual relationship between Thorpe and Scott. He outlined how Scott began to tell people about their past and pestered Thorpe for money. He was given an 'allowance' of £7 a week. The allegations continued, that ten years previously, in his room at the House of Commons, Thorpe had incited David Holmes to murder Scott. Peter Bessell had also been present. In the witness box, Bessell told Taylor that poison had been rejected as a method of killing Scott because 'it would raise too many questions if he fell dead off a bar-stool'. One alleged plan had been to shoot Scott in Cornwall and dispose of the body down a disused tin mine shaft.

Mathew, representing Holmes, opened first for the defence in cross-examination on day six. He put it to Bessell that he had told 'a considerable number of lies about this matter over a period of years'. Bessell was forced to agree but said he had only done so to protect Thorpe. Mathew got him to admit to his deal from the *Sunday Telegraph* for his story – he had already received £17,000; he would get a further £8,000 if Thorpe were found not guilty but would double his money to £50,000 if Thorpe was found guilty. Mathew asked Bessell if his departure to the States in January 1974 was 'the lamentable last act of a discredited figure' and Bessell admitted that it was.

Up next, George Carman put forward four possible reasons to Bessell for returning to England to give evidence against his former friend:

I. A sense of justice – Bessell agreed.
II. Loyalty to the Liberal Party – again, he agreed.
III. Revenge – 'No, sir, I had no occasion for it.'
IV. Money – 'No, sir.'

Carman then asked Bessell whether, as a lay preacher, it was his duty to tell the Liberal Party that 'their leader was a man intent on murder?'

Bessell replied, 'My first loyalty was to Mr Thorpe.'

Carman then picked up on his lies. 'Have you told any whoppers since 1976?'

'Not to my knowledge,' Bessell answered.

'You've told quite a few in this case, haven't you?' questioned Carman.

'No, sir,' Bessell countered.

Carman then turned to Mr Justice Cantley and suggested this might be a suitable time to adjourn, but the judge, hardly bothering to disguise his view of the witness, replied, 'Oh, I think we've got time for one more whopper, if you like.'

Previously, Bessell had also alleged that Thorpe had asked him to have another alleged blackmailer killed.

Carman took him to task. 'If the jury are to believe at all that the leader of the Liberal Party had seriously proposed to you not one, but two murders, I suggest it is a figment of your imagination. You must have thought that you had a ghastly maniac leading the Liberal Party.'

'Yes,' Bessell replied. 'At one stage, I thought Mr Thorpe had a crazy, sick imagination about murder.'

'But I thought you said he was a man of the highest political integrity?' queried Carman.

'Yes, personal and political integrity, but those were different matters.'

Carman now had Bessell where he wanted him and used ridicule to hang him out to dry in front of the jury.

'You haven't left out any other murder proposals, have you?'

Flustered, Bessell retorted, 'No, it was the first time – there were no others.'

'You're not going to tell us of a third or fourth murder proposal tomorrow, are you?'

'No, sir,' promised Bessell.

The following day, Carman attacked from a different direction to pull the rug of plausibility from under Bessell. He got him to admit that for more than five years, he had been addicted to Mandrax, a sleeping pill listed as dangerous.

'Did it not cause you to fantasise?' questioned Carman.

'It had a dulling effect and clouded my judgement,' replied Bessell.

'Did it remove your moral values or muddy your sense of values?' pressed Carman.

'I don't think it removed them, but it could have muddied them.'

On Friday 18 May, Peter Taylor called Norman Scott into the witness box. Scott described how on the fateful day in November 1961 when Thorpe took him back to his mother's house, Scott was very distressed about losing his job, so Thorpe invited him to stay the night. He later came into Scott's bedroom to comfort him and got into bed beside him. He then returned to his own room and came back with a towel and a tube of ointment. Both men stripped naked. Thorpe put some ointment on his penis, instructed Scott to turn over on the towel and they had full sex.

Scott recalled, 'I had had relationships with men and women before, but I had not had a whole physical relationship with a man. Nobody had ever come into me before.'

'After this penetration of which you have spoken, what did Mr Thorpe do?' Taylor asked.

'He just got up and wiped himself and went out,' Scott replied.

'He patted my thigh. I just lay there with my dog. She was by the bed. I picked her up, brought her into bed with me and just lay there, crying. The next morning, Mr Thorpe came back to my room at 7.30 a.m. I thought he was going to do it again. But he just asked me how I liked my eggs boiled.'

Scott told Taylor that Thorpe took him back to London, bought him shoes, shirts and silk pyjamas and found him a room in Draycott Place, Chelsea, where he would regularly come and have sex with him.

On the eleventh day of the trial, George Carman cross-examined Scott. He quickly established that he had a history of psychiatric problems and had once been compulsorily detained in hospital.

Scott had only spoken to Thorpe for less than five minutes when first they met, but the following year, he told the police he already had a sexual relationship with him before he went to see him at the House of Commons.

Carman questioned the validity of this.

'Yes,' Scott admitted. 'It wasn't true.'

'Were you saying it because you were suffering from a delusion?' Carman asked.

'Yes.'

Already, Carman had dealt a sharp blow to the credibility of Scott's evidence. He took Scott through his 1962 statement to the police.

'You told them that the sexual act did not involve penetration, but in this trial, you have said that it did.'

'I was afraid of being prosecuted,' Scott replied. 'Homosexual acts were illegal then.'

Carman appeared to acknowledge that Thorpe had gone to bed with Scott at his mother's house but wondered if Scott had consented to this. The witness began to shout.

'There was nothing I could do because I was at their house, tired and woozy. I was broken and crying! I did not know what was happening until it was too late!'

Scott became hysterical and screamed at the judge that he wouldn't answer any more questions. The judge asked him if he wanted to go home. Scott sobbed, 'I don't mind where I go. I won't have myself destroyed in this way when he knows very well his client is lying. I have had enough.'

But he did continue and when Carman suggested to him that he was flattered that Thorpe introduced him into a different social world, and that he was upset and annoyed that Thorpe did not want any longer to have a sexual relationship with him, the witness retorted, 'Of course that is ridiculous, because he did.'

Carman asked Scott if he had talked to newspapers and made money out of the matter. Scott agreed that he had. The *Daily Mirror* had paid him £4,000 for a series of interviews.

Scott had gone to Westminster to appear at the Liberal Party inquiry run by Lord Byers, David Steel and Emlyn Hooson.

'Did they listen to your story?' Carman asked.

'They patiently copied the documents I had – including the "Bunnies can and will go to France. Yours affectionately, Jeremy. I miss you" note – and read through them to see if there was anything that would help them to get rid of their leader, which is what they wanted to do. That was what David Steel told me – that Thorpe must go.'

Peter Taylor called several other witnesses before he proceeded to call Andrew 'Gino' Newton. In evidence, Newton told Taylor he had been shown photos of his intended victim and had been offered £15,000 for the job, which was later reduced to £10,000. Taylor asked him if he had asked any questions, to which Newton, who, like Bessell, had immunity from prosecution, impishly replied, 'Only the sort of questions one would expect a hit man to ask.' He had wanted to know who wanted the victim killed and why, but he was informed he had too much information already.

Questioned by Taylor, Newton said he had various meetings with Holmes but that 'it was something I knew from that day on, I could not carry out'.

In view of the money, Newton went on with the pretence and repeated the story of his drive with Scott and his Great Dane, Rinka. 'If it had been a Yorkshire terrier or something not very big, that would have been all right, but if I thought I had to frighten Scott, I was not sure whether the dog would attack me.'

So when they got out of the car in the Devon countryside, he shot Rinka. He then pointed his Mauser gun at Scott and said, 'Right, it's your turn now.' But his gun jammed.

At this stage, things looked very grim for Jeremy Thorpe and his fellow accused. Taylor had presented the case for the prosecution with a simple and persuasive logic. It was not in doubt that the twice-married Thorpe had 'homosexual tendencies', nor that he had had a dominant relationship with the fragile Norman Scott. The plan to later murder Scott had so nearly been carried out and might have occurred if Newton had not lost his nerve. Also, the money to hire the hit man, requested by Thorpe in a distinctly shady manner, might itself have led to a guilty verdict.

Prior to the commencement of the case for the defence, Taylor had telephoned George Carman to discuss something of immense sensitivity in private. They met in chambers alone. Taylor informed Carman that significant evidence had emerged to prove that Thorpe was gay. A postcard had been intercepted by the FBI showing that he had had a sexually explicit relationship with a man called Bruno, in San Francisco in the early 1960s. It was made clear that if Thorpe denied his homosexuality, the prosecution would have to refer to this relationship.

As a result of the honourable behaviour of Taylor, Carman agreed to refer to 'Thorpe's homosexual tendencies', however, he did now not have to fear that further evidence of Thorpe's homosexuality would emerge during the trial. He later told me how much he respected Peter Taylor for his behaviour in a very embarrassing situation for Carman.

At the committal, John Mathew told David Napley there was no way Thorpe or Holmes could be called at the trial. Napley's reaction was to acknowledge the problem and declare that such was Thorpe's personality, it would be impossible to keep him out of the box.

Carman remained worried as to what Thorpe might say in cross-examination, as he seemed almost arrogant in his belief that the case against him would not succeed.

Eventually, a meeting was held by all counsel because everyone wanted to know what everyone else was going to do. In the end, the only defendant to insist on giving evidence was Deakin. Thorpe and Holmes agreed to accept the advice of their counsel, not to go into the witness box, as did Le Mesurier.

By this time, Mathew QC had formed a very unfavourable opinion of Thorpe's arrogant personality and had no faith that any trust could be placed in his word. His client, Holmes, was first on the indictment and Mathew feared that if Holmes did not give evidence, when Thorpe's turn arrived, he might renege on his agreement to do the same. These concerns were met when Carman and Graham Boal, his junior, agreed that if Thorpe ratted on the agreement and insisted on giving evidence when his turn came, they would withdraw from the case. A statement was then prepared setting out this fact together with the other relevant matters.

Nevertheless, Mathew insisted that the statement be signed by Thorpe declaring he understood that both his counsel would withdraw if he gave evidence and he would be cross-examined on the contents of the statement. Thorpe subsequently signed this statement.

The court was packed and rapt with anticipation as they awaited Thorpe's side of the story. Instead, George Carman rose to his feet and quietly said, 'My Lord, on behalf of Mr Jeremy Thorpe, I call no evidence.' The courtroom gasped. George had been waiting for that moment, anticipating the feeling in the courtroom as a result.

It was a surprise to Peter Taylor that the defence had ended so promptly, having expected some time in which to prepare his closing speech to the jury. As a result, he applied for and was granted an adjournment on Thursday 7 June, until the following Monday, to prepare.

Taylor's closing speech for the prosecution took two days. He said that Thorpe's career had been 'blighted by the Scott affair', describing Thorpe's behaviour as 'a tragedy of truly Greek, or Shakespearian proportions – the slow but inevitable destruction of a man by the stamp of one defect'.

Taylor conceded that some of his witnesses had lied in the past but that was not a reason to believe that they were not now telling the truth. The fact that some of them were indeed making money out of the case did not, in itself, invalidate their evidence.

Moreover, he pointed out to the jury that there were nearly seventy facts that the defence had not disputed, and he listed them, primarily about the deceitful way the alleged conspirators had raised money to pay for their crime – especially Thorpe, who had 'lied, lied and lied again' with varying explanations of why he needed £20,000 to be paid to Holmes.

John Mathew maintained that if his client, David Homes, had been involved in a conspiracy, it was only one to frighten Norman Scott.

Gareth Williams, for Deakin, argued that his client was not a man with friends in high places and that he should never have been charged.

George Carman chose to argue less about the facts but concentrated on the personalities. Jeremy Thorpe, he said, was a man whose frailties and weaknesses had been remorselessly exposed to the public gaze, but he was not guilty of the charges laid against him, especially by what he referred to as 'the unholy trio of witnesses'. Peter Bessell, Carman warned the jury, was the Judas Iscariot of British politics. 'A man so devious, so unprincipled, so cunning, so sophisticated a liar that you could not, in all conscience, safely act on his evidence.' Norman Scott and Andrew Newton were liars, too.

Carman needed to explain to the jury why Thorpe had not gone into the box. 'It does not prove his guilt. On the contrary, it is a right, invested by law, that a defendant can remain silent. We are not here to entertain the public or provide journalists with further copy.'

He continued:

> Privately, Jeremy Thorpe is a man with a life that has had more than its fair share of grief. Nature so fashioned him that we know that, at the time he had the misfortune to meet Norman Scott, he was a man with homosexual tendencies. He's human like us all. We learn, do we not, that idols sometimes have feet of clay.

He said that Thorpe's political life and future were now irrevocably and irreversibly denied to him. 'Mr Thorpe has spent twenty years in British politics and obtained thousands and thousands of votes in his favour. Now the most precious twelve votes of all come from you.'

In a bold and dramatic gesture, George came closer to the jury and, moving his eyes and finger to each of them in turn, he said, 'Yours, and yours, and yours…' It was as if he was hypnotising them.

'The case justified that kind of drama,' George later recalled:

> I thought for a long time about doing that. I went alone to a hotel on Sundays in order to let the case run through my mind. I remember trying to think about how to make the closing speech, starting probably about four weeks in advance of it, because, of course, going back to 1979, one had to counter the danger of homophobia and prejudice in that regard, which was much more prevalent in those days.

His final words to the jury were: 'In accordance with your oath, in accordance with your conscience, I say to you on behalf of Jeremy Thorpe: this prosecution is not made out. And I end by saying of the prosecution in the words of the Bible: let this prosecution fold its tent and quietly creep away.'

On Monday 18 June, Mr Justice Cantley, described by journalist Robert Chesshyre as a 'perky man with something of the aspect of a large red bird', began his summing up. He told the jury that the fact that the accused did not go into the witness box should not mean his good character should be ignored. He castigated the parts of the press that had offered money to witnesses.

Pointing to inconsistencies in Bessell's evidence, he concluded that the man was 'a humbug'. Scott came in for much worse, with Cantley telling the jury, 'He is a spineless, neurotic character, addicted to hysteria and self-advertisement … He is a crook.' And the next day's *Daily Mail* merely listed the learned judge's opinion of the Norman Scott in bold letters covering its entire front page: 'PARASITE. WHINER. SPONGER. CROOK AND LIAR'.

Andrew Newton got off more lightly. 'What a chump the man is!' said Cantley. He noted that Newton had made nearly £11,000 in fees from newspapers and television stations since his release from prison and cruelly speculated, 'I doubt whether he has paid any income tax.'

He dealt with the accused rather more gently, pointing out that Holmes's counsel had conceded he was party to a conspiracy to frighten. Had the Crown actually accused him of that, he would have been found guilty.

In a piece of social snobbery, Cantley said that Deakin was the type of man 'whose taste probably ran to a cocktail bar in his living room'.

And the judge firmly stated that the evidence against Thorpe was 'almost entirely circumstantial'. Moreover, if the jury thought that Thorpe's request for the money to pay a hit man was obtained by telling lies, Cantley highlighted that this does not do anything for the prosecution case. 'The fact that a man obtains money by deceit does not amount to any sort of proof that the man was a member of a conspiracy to murder someone else.'

Peter Taylor was fuming by now. He might have expected to have his main witnesses discredited, but for the judge to say that this vital stepping stone in the conspiracy was irrelevant was palpably not true.

On Wednesday 20 June, Mr Justice Cantley dismissed the jury

with the words, 'Take as long as you like; there is no hurry. We shall wait for you.'

The accused were taken to Brixton Prison; Thorpe handcuffed to George Deakin. Thorpe lay on the floor of the prison van so as not to be photographed. At Brixton, the warders were obliged to strip search them before they were sent to the cells. It was to be the first taste of prison for the Right Honourable Jeremy Thorpe, but he managed to mitigate some of this indignity by claiming he had a bad stomach and was taken to the prison hospital.

The jury, meanwhile, were sequestered in the Westmoreland Hotel and ordered not to discuss the case nor listen to the radio.

They were brought back to the Old Bailey the following day, as were the accused, to await the verdict.

During the day, the four defendants spent much of their time playing Canasta, a Uruguayan card game not unlike gin rummy. It was open to a player to throw in his hand with the Spanish word '*acaba*', which meant 'the end'.

George Carman asked his junior counsel, Graham Boal, to see Thorpe to talk about mitigation in the event of a conviction. Boal admitted it was unlikely to achieve much and was very hard to frame without an admission of guilt. Jeremy agreed that George should not bother, with the surprisingly light-hearted words, 'You're the pros, I hope we're not the cons.'

We learned later that the jury immediately did a straw poll when they retired and were split 6–6. After an hour, that had moved to 10–2 in favour of acquittal because 'reasonable doubt' remained. It was to be more than a further fifty hours before they became unanimous.

On those two days spent waiting at the Old Bailey, the Liberal MP Clement Freud supplied the accused with salmon, beef and claret for lunch. Fortunately, Jeremy's stomach had recovered sufficiently for him to enjoy it.

Lunch was interrupted on Friday 22 June. The four accused were escorted back to their glass-walled box. The jury filed back into court at 2.30 p.m. The accused were asked to stand. They all looked straight ahead, betraying no emotion.

The clerk of the court asked the foreperson, Celia Kettle-Williams (a schoolteacher and, incidentally, a member of the Liberal Party), if they had reached a verdict. She said they had.

The clerk read out each name in order: 'David Holmes.'

Kettle-Williams, in a clear and confident voice, replied, 'Not guilty.'

'Michael Deakin.'

'Not guilty.'

'John Le Mesurier.'

'Not guilty.'

'Jeremy Thorpe.'

'Not guilty.'

'Jeremy Thorpe on the charge of incitement to murder.'

'Not guilty,' Kettle-Williams concluded.

Thorpe's mother, the 76-year-old Ursula, broke down in tears. The tension and the pressure had been so great that Le Mesurier, a large man, literally fell over backwards. David Holmes might have done so, had two warders not supported him as he swayed on his feet.

Jeremy Thorpe, at last, unfroze. He looked towards Marion and smiled. He scribbled a note, 'Well rowed, Balliol,' and had it passed to Carman. Then, realising it was all over at last, he threw the cushions that had been supporting his bad back out of the box. He thanked the court officials for their splendid work, then leaned forwards and embraced his wife.

Hand in hand with Marion, he stepped out into the sunshine and the huge crowd outside the Old Bailey. He raised his hands in the air as if he had just won an election, which, in a way, he had: certainly, they were the twelve most precious votes of his life.

On the steps of the Old Bailey, he delivered a short statement to the innumerable television cameras and huge crowd.

'I have always maintained that I was innocent of the charges brought against me,' he began. 'The verdict of the jury I regard as totally fair, just and a complete vindication. Quite apart from the devoted and unswerving support of my wife and family, I want to express my very deep appreciation for the countless messages of encouragement and support received from all over the world.'

Although the acquittal made front-page news, due to the libel laws, the press was now more wary than ever of any innuendoes about Thorpe. This did not inhibit the satirist and *Private Eye* owner Peter Cook, who, dressed as a judge, delivered a parody of the summing up in a West End Amnesty show less than a week after the trial ended. It was later broadcast on television.

'We have been forced to listen to the whinings of Mr Norman St John Scott,' Cook joked:

> A scrounger, a parasite, a worm, a self-confessed player of the pink oboe. A man, who by his own admission, chews pillows. On the evidence of the so-called hit man, Mr Olivia Newton John, I would prefer to draw a discreet veil. He is a piece of slimy refuse, unable to carry out the simplest murder plot … You should now retire, as indeed should I, carefully to consider your verdict of not guilty.

Two years later, David Holmes wrote in the *News of the World* that he had lied to protect Thorpe who had demanded that Scott be killed. 'The incitement charge was true, and if I had gone into the witness box, I'd have had to tell the truth.'

When asked about the case by Sue Lawley on *Desert Island Discs* some years later, George said, 'It is not the duty of a barrister to find out the truth. That is for the jury. A barrister's duty is to his client, to present his case as best he can.'

Following the brilliance of his court defence of Thorpe, especially the spine-tingling final approach to each member of the jury that may well have swayed their verdict, George Carman was about to become one of the country's most celebrated QCs.

CHAPTER THREE

R V. DR LEONARD ARTHUR

'He could, like Pontius Pilate, have washed his hands of the matter. He did not, because good doctors do not turn away.'

GEORGE CARMAN

On 28 June 1980, a baby boy was born to Molly and John Pearson in Derby City Hospital. As with every set of new parents, the Pearsons had every reason to celebrate this everyday miracle. They did so by immediately naming the child John, after his father. However, the celebrations were short-lived. Within minutes, the Pearsons were informed that their newborn had Down syndrome with complications, including severe abnormalities of the lungs, heart and brain. The chances of the child surviving were minimal, and even if he did, John would have little chance of any reasonable quality of life. After consultation with paediatrician Dr Leonard Arthur, the Pearsons decided they did not want their son to live. So began a chain of events that hinged around a question later posed in a Crown court: was this baby 'positively put to death' or allowed to die?

At the time of John Pearson's death, Dr Arthur was fifty-four years old and the married father of six children. His wife's mother was Stella Langdon Down, the granddaughter of physician John Langdon Down who, in 1867, had given the first detailed description of the genetic condition that would be named after him – Down syndrome.

Dr Arthur became a consultant paediatrician in Derby in 1965, also serving on the Council of the British Paediatric Association and chairing the Trent Regional Advisory Sub-committee in Paediatrics. According to those who knew him, he was a highly compassionate man with firm moral principles underpinned by a strong Christian faith. Not a man to take decisions – particularly morally and ethically based ones – lightly. After the consultation with the Pearsons, he made one of those difficult yet, as he saw it, necessary decisions. A note was placed on little John Pearson's cot which read: 'Parents do not wish the child to survive. Nursing care only.' In addition, Dr Arthur prescribed the drug DF118 – dihydrocodeine, a mild morphine – so the child would not be in pain. He died within three days; the cause of death being described as bronchopneumonia.

Tragic as it was, that might have been the end of that had the circumstances not been related to a member of an organisation called Life who was present in the hospital. Life, which exists to this day, was founded in 1970 and became the UK's foremost anti-abortion group, as well as campaigning to preserve the sanctity of human life from the cradle to the grave. The Life member, a nurse, reported what had happened to the police and eventually the matter was referred to Sir Thomas Hetherington, the Director of Public Prosecutions (DPP). He reviewed the paperwork from the hospital and, after what he described as 'the most difficult decision of my career', in February 1981 recommended that Dr Arthur be charged with the murder of baby John Pearson.

From the start, the case was destined to be controversial. Thousands of people signed a petition supporting Dr Arthur and, unusually for a person charged with murder, he was not remanded in custody. Instead, he was granted bail on condition that he surrendered his passport. In a case that centred on difficult decisions, one of the best and wisest ones was to retain George Carman to defend Dr Arthur.

The case began at Leicester Crown Court on 13 October 1981 and was to last for eighteen days. Douglas Draycott QC conducted the prosecution. He told the witnesses, many of them nurses and doctors who had been involved in carrying out Dr Arthur's decision, that the DPP had given them a verbal guarantee of immunity, although they were technically accomplices of the defendant.

Draycott delivered a heart-rending description of the few hours of the baby's life: that his breathing was rattling, he was sick, his feet and hands were blue and he flung his arms upwards as he tried to get air. On the second evening of John's life, the hospital vicar was called in to christen the baby and at 5.10 a.m. the next day, baby John died.

The jury heard that after the Life complaint, the police interviewed Dr Arthur. He said, 'I would like you to know that I accept full responsibility for these events and the nurses were acting on my orders.'

Kathleen Simcock had worked with Dr Arthur for eleven years. In response to a question from Draycott, she said there were two divisions in the medical profession on the question of malformed babies. 'One faction believed that nature should take its course and the other, that every effort should be made to keep them alive,' she said. She knew of no malformed babies who had survived with 'nursing care only' written on their case notes.

In answer to Carman, Simcock said that Dr Arthur would have 'strained every effort' to keep a disabled baby alive, if the parents felt they could cope. Carman pointed out that *The Sun* newspaper had suggested, on its front page, that the baby was 'starved' to death. This was totally ill-founded.

The prosecution called Margaret Slater, a state registered nurse, whose daughter had been born with brain damage. Far from making any accusation against him, she stated quite bluntly, 'But for Dr Arthur and his team, my child would have died.' This evidence was a totally unexpected gift for Carman. He was shocked that the prosecution witness gave such positive evidence in favour of Dr Arthur. He had no idea this was coming. Later, he told me, 'This was a gift from heaven'!

Slater said the drug DF118 had been given to the baby in syrup form in distilled water, purely to relieve symptoms of distress. When the child ceased to take the feed, there was no attempt to make it. 'You cannot force a baby to take a meal,' she said.

The Home Office pathologist, Professor Alan Usher, who had carried out a post-mortem on John Pearson, told the court that aside from a diagnosis of Down syndrome, the child was otherwise healthy. The greatest single factor in causing his death, the professor said, was the administration of the drug DF118. The prosecution's case rested on the belief that the child had died of bronchopneumonia due to lung stasis caused by dihydrocodeine poisoning and that he had been deliberately deprived of food and medical treatment.

At this point, Carman asked for an adjournment, during which Professor Usher was shown, for the first time, photographs that showed the baby had brain and lung damage at birth. When

Carman, on resumption, asked him if the prosecution had presented a case that the baby was healthy when born, Professor Usher acknowledged, 'Yes. I think that was because the Crown was not aware of the situation.'

A fissure had appeared in the prosecution's central argument and Carman was not slow to probe further. 'So, for the past seven days, the Crown's position was inaccurate and misleading in important respects?' he suggested. Professor Usher was forced to agree. This caused a dramatic change in the case. Had the Crown been provided with *all* the details of the baby's condition at birth? The judge, Mr Justice Farquharson (who had been at Oxford at the same time as Carman), sent the jury away and listened to two days of submissions from counsel for the defence and prosecution. As a result, the charge of murder was dramatically dropped.

However, any sense that victory had been achieved was to be premature. After listening to submissions, the judge decided that the charge of murder should be substituted for one of attempted murder. Carman was infuriated. 'It is a consummate irony that the criminal law points a finger at a man so caring, so dedicated, so devoted as this doctor,' he said. He told the jury that Dr Arthur would not be giving evidence in his own defence because of the strain that had been imposed upon him. 'You may think that his position is clear and enough is enough.'

Carman made the point that Dr Arthur had not been present at the birth of the child. It was the weekend and he was called in when the complications were diagnosed. 'He met the parents for the first time that morning,' he told the court. 'It was their time of greatest need. He could, like Pontius Pilate, have washed his hands of the matter. He did not, because good doctors do not turn away.'

Privately, George was perceiving misgivings among the jury.

There was 'a sense of disquiet', he later told me and wondered if it was merely because they would have to spend more time in court just at the point where they might have been sent home. However, he mused on a further theory: that some jurors might have felt that the prosecution was trying to hide its own mistake by coming up with a different charge against Dr Arthur. The feeling seemed to be that if there is a British sense of fair play, it was wholly absent from Leicester Crown Court that October.

George, to put it plainly, went for it: 'It has to be considered whether the law is a clear beacon, or a light, shrouded by mist and fog,' he said:

> You, the jury, face a formidable and awesome responsibility. Are you to condemn a doctor as a criminal because he cared? Are you to condemn him because he helped two people at a time of their greatest need? Does the law allow the Good Samaritan to be condemned and he who passed by to be applauded? Did the law criticise the doctor who faced the problem and applaud he who passed by? I cannot believe the law is in such a state.
>
> This prosecution was conceived in ignorance and inaccuracy. After Dr Arthur detailed the treatment for the baby, an anonymous informer emerged from an organisation called Life. That organisation no doubt has high moral ideals and they are entitled to express their views forcibly and vigorously in the proper forum.
>
> But you may think there is something slightly repugnant and distasteful about people acting as informers under the cloak of anonymity.

The drama intensified as George called his first witness, Professor Alexander Campbell, head of the department of child health at Aberdeen

University. Before the learned physician spoke, however, Mr Justice Farquharson cautioned him about possible self-incrimination. He had done his homework and knew Campbell had used the 'nursing care only' practice himself. Should Dr Arthur be convicted, this could leave Professor Campbell open to the same crime.

The professor was undaunted and, questioned by Draycott, agreed that in four or five cases of children with Down syndrome with complications, he had prescribed nursing care only with the intention that the child should not survive. The regime was similar to that prescribed by Dr Arthur with the use of a drug to alleviate distress.

Witness Dr Peter Dunn of Bristol University, who had written 200 papers on paediatric medicine, said that intensive care would be given to any child regardless of how severely disabled it was *when it was the wishes of the parents*. Dr Dunn had, before baby John was born, given evidence to a parliamentary social services committee which had subsequently recommended that sophisticated technology and surgery should not be used to save severely malformed or brain-damaged infants unless there were overwhelming reasons for doing so.

He told the court that in the USA, he had seen a child aged two with no brain, who had been kept alive by technology. The baby had died twenty times and had to be resuscitated. The paediatrician was afraid to let the child die 'because of the retribution of the law'.

Answering Carman, Dr Dunn said that had he been Dr Arthur's locum, once he had satisfied himself of the position of the parents, the nursing staff and the doctors, he would have done exactly the same.

Although the judge had not prevented Douglas Draycott QC from describing 'the dying baby thrusting his pleading blue hands into the air', he ruled that Carman could not show his prepared photographs of malformed babies. The judge told the jury that there were about forty young women outside the court carrying banners demanding better screening for foetal abnormalities, but they were to ignore them.

George could have produced any number of eminent doctors to say that Dr Arthur was a highly professional and compassionate man; in fact, even the prosecution conceded as much. However, it was considered that raising the status of his client from surgeon to saint might have an alienating effect on the jury. Instead, he invited Sir Douglas Black, the president of the Royal College of Physicians, to give evidence. This would not be about Dr Arthur; instead, it would focus on Life, which had prompted the prosecution. Sir Douglas said:

> I feel quite emotional about this and would like to express an adverse opinion from the point of view of my profession on the activities of pressure groups such as Life and Exit [a pro-euthanasia group]. I think they are trying to apply simplistic rules to situations which do not admit to the proper application of such rules.

He went on: 'Among the consequences are that doctors and parents, consulting together, might well be deprived of solutions which might be compassionate.' Sir Douglas pointed out that Life's encouragement of 'information systems' within hospitals 'cannot but be destructive to the confidence of the medical and nursing professions'.

George's final witness was Dr Norman Bluett, paediatric doctor at the North Devon District Hospital. Dr Bluett had faced such situations and when the parents agreed on non-treatment, he would let nature take its course.

'Do you think this baby was positively put to death or allowed to die?' asked Carman, getting right to the nub of the case.

'It was allowed to die,' Dr Bluett answered.

'Did Dr Arthur stray beyond his proper province and duty?' Carman questioned.

'He certainly did not,' Dr Bluett concluded.

In Douglas Draycott's final address to the jury, he told them that the baby had had at birth an 80 per cent chance of survival. No single one of Dr Arthur's actions had been responsible for the child's death, but the combination had been. Draycott stated:

> The time has not yet come in this country when a doctor can say, 'Because you are mentally handicapped and that condition is irreversible, because your mother does not wish you to survive, I'm going to take steps to see that you do not survive.' That is not permissible under English law and it is there that Dr Arthur has come into conflict with the law.

Carman, in turn, did not mince his words. 'This melancholy prosecution is now in a state of retreat and disarray.' It was a tragedy that the charge had been brought, he added, and that it had been brought in ignorance and misunderstanding of how the science and art of paediatrics were practised. He asked the jury to bring in a decision that would mean that, in the future, 'parents and doctors could make decisions, on this awful problem, without unidentified informers rushing off to the police'.

George did not even bother to mention his client. He had sensed the jury's dismay at the amended charge, which he now called 'in disarray', and the unfairness of a third party 'rushing off to the police', and it was sufficient to hit home those points in a brief speech.

In a back-handed compliment to Carman, the judge agreed, 'If this man had not been represented by those with such skill and thoroughness, it may have been there was no conceivable way to challenge Professor Usher with all the skill and dignity his position commands.'

In his summing up, the judge returned to the facts of the case. However noble Dr Arthur's motive was, it was irrelevant in law, compared to what he intended to do. As an example, the judge gave the instance of someone putting a pillow over the head of a sick and elderly relative suffering from an incurable disease. He also told the jury they had to decide whether Dr Arthur's treatment of the baby was intended to cause his death, which seemed to awaken the spectre of the original charge of murder.

Eventually, the jury retired to consider their verdict and the court adjourned. They didn't have long to wait. On the eighteenth day of the trial, the jury reached agreement in just two hours: 'Not guilty.' The relief in the courtroom was palpable.

Leonard Arthur and his wife came out onto the steps of the court and the media and public were able to hear him speak about the case for the first time. 'I would like to express my heartfelt sympathy for Mr and Mrs Pearson in their sorrow and bereavement,' he said. 'Then I would like to thank all the people who have thought about us, prayed about us, sent flowers to us and helped us in all sorts of practical ways. Things would have been hard for us without their support.' He added that he would not answer any questions.

The front pages of most newspapers on Friday 6 November 1981 proclaimed: 'WOMEN CRY "THANK GOD" AS DR ARTHUR IS CLEARED'.

The case opened up a nationwide debate in newspaper leaders and letter columns and on television and radio. Its immediate practical effect was for the DPP to announce that there were no more cases of the type involved in the trial being considered. Carman had discovered that previously, the police had asked the health authorities, in Derby alone, for the case notes of thirty-three newly born children who had died in the past five years. The health authority now declined to do so, as this would be a breach of confidentiality.

Following the trial, Dr Arthur sent George a couple of photographs of him and his legal team, which he had taken outside the court. I still have them. In a brief letter from his home, at Royal Oak Cottage in Derby, Dr Arthur simply wrote:

> Dear George,
> This comes with all my thanks,
> Signed, Leonard.

The case had put a tremendous strain on the doctor. He returned to work but was not the same man. A fellow paediatrician and close colleague of Dr Arthur, Dr Keith Dodd, said he seemed exhausted. The following year, he went abroad for three months. But on Christmas Day 1983, Leonard Arthur died of a brain tumour. He was only fifty-seven years old.

Dr Dodd said the case had put 'a tremendous strain on Dr Arthur. I think what upset him most was not the charge but that other people should be adversely affected by it.'

Dr Leonard Arthur's daughter, Linet, wrote to George when he retired in September 2000. She said:

> I have always been grateful for your brilliant defence of my father.

> You built up such a strong case that it seemed inevitable he would be acquitted.
>
> I can remember Dad saying about the trial, that he had felt like a patient: relatively helpless in the hands of experts who knew far better how to put things right.

Linet continued, 'I do know Dad would have liked to testify at the trial, but he respected your judgement, that it would be unwise, and agreed not to give evidence.'

She added:

> He had hoped that, by explaining his actions, he would be able to bring to public attention the dilemmas for doctors in treating severely handicapped newborn babies. He felt strongly that doctors should always act in the best interests of the baby, with the full support of the parents. In some cases this meant not prolonging the baby's life, in order to prevent future suffering. He hoped his case would create a precedent, ensuring that doctors were protected in these circumstances, as he felt that a doctor's clinical judgement about the baby's interests should not be influenced by fears of litigation.
>
> He also hoped that his trial would help to open the debate about this very sensitive issue. Although it apparently confirmed one important fact – that 'Nursing care only' was an acceptable form of treatment – he was disappointed that more was not achieved.

George told me that this was the most important case he had ever been instructed in. He really wanted to succeed on behalf of Dr Arthur, as he respected him immensely and thought it very wrong that he had found himself before the court on the most serious charge of murder.

Carman's junior, Graham Boal QC, concurrred:

> This was the most important case he was instructed in. Dr Leonard Arthur mattered. I won't say it was a prosecution that should never have been brought; in a way, it had to be, because of the law of compassionate medicine.
>
> In law, Dr Leonard Arthur was guilty of murder, he had no defence, but it would have been an absolute tragedy if he had been convicted.

It was Boal's idea to call the consultant Mr Bluett. He encountered him when his own son had been born prematurely, at North Devon District Hospital in Barnstaple. 'I am sure he saved my son's life,' he said:

> When this case arose, I suggested that as we had professors coming out of our ears, we needed someone who was going to appeal to the jury. I telephoned Mr Bluett and asked if he would be a supporter of Dr Arthur's behaviour. He said, 'You just tell me when the first train to London is.'
>
> I am not sure what the state of play was before, but I had no doubt, after he gave evidence, that no jury was going to convict. At the conclusion of the evidence of Mr Bluett, he asked the judge whether he could say something to the jury. The judge agreed and he said, 'If Dr Arthur is guilty of murder, then so am I, many times over.'

Boal disclosed that Carman always liked to pull a rabbit out of the hat in his cases. He advised him that he should not do so in this case. This fell upon deaf ears. George didn't exchange the evidence with the prosecution in advance and thereby caused them embarrassment when it came to light that the experts had not been privy to the full facts. The charge, consequently, was dramatically reduced from murder.

George Carman also would delegate some unpleasant tasks to his juniors. In this case, the duty of explaining the consequences in the event of a conviction for murder was left to Graham Boal. 'When I explained to Dr Arthur that the only sentence a judge could pass would be one of life imprisonment, I saw the absolute shock on Dr Arthur's wife's face,' he said.

CHAPTER FOUR

R V. GEOFFREY PRIME

'What sort of man is Geoffrey Prime? Two phrases tell it all: desperately lonely and totally inadequate.'

George Carman

On my bookshelf sits a small grey paperback that George gave to me. It's a modest-looking volume and its title, *Time of Trial*, rather underplays the sequence of events contained within. Perhaps that, and its modesty, gives a clue about the nature of its author – a deeply Christian woman who had to choose between loyalty to her husband and her conscience.

The author, Rhona Prime, was prompted to write the book after all the circumstances that had occurred. Had they not been true, they might have come straight from the pen of John le Carré. In April 1982, two police officers knocked at the door of the Primes' cottage in Cheltenham, Gloucestershire, seeking Rhona's husband, Geoffrey. He was forty-four at the time and a taxi driver; a quiet man, by all accounts, who kept himself to himself and seemingly bothered no one.

Except that he did bother certain people – specifically young girls. Unbeknown to Rhona, Geoffrey was an active paedophile and the police had come calling on this pleasant late spring day to deliver some exceptionally unpleasant news. A fourteen-year-old girl had been faced with an intruder at her parents' remote Herefordshire farmhouse who'd asked her to remove her pants. The girl screamed so loudly that the man fled in a two-tone brown S-registered Cortina Mark IV. The car's registration plate was traced to Geoffrey Prime and he was arrested. Later, following a search of his home, police discovered 2,287 index cards containing details of young girls who might be alone in the early evening. Prime confessed to his crimes almost immediately, first to his wife and, the next day, to the police.

'He told me, "I'm the man they were talking about this afternoon; I'm the man that they want,"' she subsequently told a BBC interviewer. 'And I went into complete shock and numbness. I just couldn't believe it. And he was a bit upset about that because he really wanted a reaction.'

That was bad enough, but later that night, when Prime told his wife what he'd been up to, he decided to drop another bombshell on her. 'Not only that,' he said, 'but I've also been a spy for the Soviet Union for many years.' Prime was later taken to Gloucester Prison and charged with child molestation. For nearly three weeks, Rhona agonised over whether she should tell the police about the other side of her husband's life. That is, of course, if Geoffrey Prime wasn't a complete fantasist…

Mrs Prime's mind was made up after discovering some microfilm and letters addressed to East Berlin at their home. She decided that her Christian conscience demanded that she tell the police. 'I believed before God that this was what I had to do,' she said.

Detective Chief Inspector (DCI) Smith of the Hereford Police came round to see her.

'Well, Rhona, what is it you want to tell us?' he asked.

She handed him a statement about her husband's espionage and a carrier bag with evidence in it. The DCI's eyebrows rose rapidly northwards as he read the statement and gazed at the letters. Police officers across the world hear many claims from those they have arrested that are quite literally incredible, and we can perhaps forgive DCI Smith's apparent incredulity at this stage.

'Try not to worry too much,' he reassured Mrs Prime. 'Some people do fantasise that they're James Bond or whoever. They're the ones who are more likely to leave evidence lying around because often they get a kick out of seeing it there.'

'I really hope that's all there is to it,' she replied.

Unfortunately for her, and her husband, it wasn't – not by a long stretch.

Rhona's descent into unimaginable strangeness began when she and her first husband, Peter, had fallen on hard times and decided to take in lodgers at their Cheltenham home, where they lived with their three young sons. Their marriage was also falling apart. By the time Geoffrey Prime took a room with them in 1976, they had divorced. Prime, after eight years as a Russian linguist with the government in London, had been posted to the Government Communications Headquarters (GCHQ) in Cheltenham. A year later, he and Rhona got married. Then, after only three months, he abruptly resigned from GCHQ. He took odd jobs as a taxi driver and wine salesman but became moody and retreated into himself.

Since childhood, Geoffrey considered he had been thwarted in life. When called up to do his National Service in the Royal Air Force (RAF), he worked as a store man. It transpired that he was adept at languages, so he was made a sergeant and sent to study Russian at London University. Unfortunately, he flunked that and was demoted to the stores once more. Despite this, he became a Regular. During a spell in Kenya, he listened to communist radio broadcasts and read their literature. Thereafter, the RAF gave him a second chance in language training and he was sent to Berlin, where he eavesdropped on the Russians. However, he did more than listen in; he contacted the KGB and offered his services as a spy. When returning from leave, he smuggled a note to a Soviet officer manning a checkpoint, indicating that he wanted to make contact. Later, he found a metallic cylinder attached to the door of his car. In it was a note setting up a meeting in Friedrichstrasse Station. It was there that he met two Russian agents, Igor and Valya, who provided him with a miniature camera to photograph secret documents at RAF Gatow.

Prime left the RAF on 31 July 1968, but his Russian masters told him to apply for a job at GCHQ and, almost incredibly, after positive vetting by them, he joined the British intelligence agency. Prior to commencing work there, he flew to Karlshorst in East Berlin, where he was trained in the art of spying. Prime was given the codename 'Rowlands' and a password to be used when meeting contacts. In reply to the contact saying, 'I believe we met in Pittsburgh in 1968,' Rowlands was to reply, 'No, at that time I was in Berlin.' He was given further spy apparatus: a briefcase with a false bottom, invisible writing paper, the key to send and receive secret radio transmissions, instructions on how to use microdots and £400.

Back in London, he sent a continual feed of information to the Russians, usually by radio and often telling them what KGB information GCHQ had intercepted. He was variously rewarded: in 1969, he was sent to a secret hiding place by a lake in Esher, Surrey, to find an envelope with congratulations and more money; in 1970, he took photographs of secret documents with his miniature camera and left them at a marked tree in Abbey Wood, London; in 1971, he collected more money and spying materials hidden near Banstead Station, in Surrey. His findings were often compressed into a used Coca-Cola can. The art was not to create a pattern and it succeeded.

Sometimes, he had so much material that he would fly to Vienna and give it to his handlers. He was rewarded with amounts up to £1,000 and told if he ever wished to defect, he would be given a pension and the rank of colonel. On one trip to Vienna, he gave his masters fifteen rolls of film, amounting to 500 photographs of top-secret documents. Not only did he regularly pass positive vetting by the British secret service throughout the 1970s but he was also made section head in GCHQ Cheltenham, with access to matters of the utmost secrecy and the right to take classified papers home in the evening.

By 1977, when he married Rhona, Prime found the double life was taking its strain. He toyed with the idea of defecting by flying to Helsinki, even buying tickets, but lost his nerve. So, he remained in Laburnum Cottage and cut off contact with the Russian agents.

The KGB eased off on him for a bit – and this gave him more time for his paedophile activities. Overall, though, the KGB had a hold on him from which he could never escape. In 1980, he was obliged to fly to Vienna with fifteen further rolls of film of highly top-secret documents. His reward was a three-day cruise down the Danube on a Russian ship, during which he was cross-examined about the material and given £600. The following year, he made his final trip to Berlin, where he was closely questioned about Allied activities and given a pay-off of £4,000. That, claimed Geoffrey Prime, was the end of the affair.

Two years later, Prime was in police custody, facing allegations that were tantamount to treason. Given the gravity of the situation he found himself in, it was somewhat surprising that Prime turned to a Cheltenham-based solicitor by the name of Davies, who specialised in conveyancing. A little out of his depth, one might argue, but nonetheless Mr Davies had the presence of mind to engage George Carman for the defence. On 3 November 1982, Rhona received a call from Mr Davies telling her that her husband's Old Bailey trial had been brought forward from the end of the month to the following week, due to 'certain pressures' on the Director of Public Prosecutions. As a result, they should travel from Cheltenham to London immediately to meet his QC, George Carman.

When Rhona came to London, she first went to Carman's room in the Temple. He arranged for tea to be served and Mr Davies tried to put her at ease. Carman took Rhona through the details of her marriage and then asked, 'Do you have any communist leanings?'

'None whatsoever,' she replied. 'I dislike all political extremes, right or left.'

He asked her why she had cooperated so willingly with the police about her husband's spying activities, even leading them to his radio transmitter, which he used to contact the Russians, and other incriminating materials such as a miniature camera, a method for sending photos by microdots, paper for invisible writing and instructions on how to leave dead letters for the KGB go-between.

'I'm a Christian,' said Mrs Prime. 'I had to follow my conscience. I want to stand by my husband, but I also have to tell the truth.'

'Would you be willing to stand up in court and testify publicly what you've told me about your husband?'

'Yes, I will,' she replied.

'You don't have to do this,' Carman counselled.

'I know. But I think I should and I believe it's right.'

Carman congratulated her. 'Mrs Prime, I think you're a likeable, intelligent woman and I admire you.'

At that stage, the Crown was playing its cards very close to its chest and even Carman did not yet know the extent of Prime's treachery. He was aware that the Director of Public Prosecutions had brought the case forward to avoid any leaks. The trial would largely be held in private, with the press effectively gagged. Despite all the secrecy, it was George's intention to visit Prime in Brixton Prison and so he instructed his junior, Tony Clover, to inform the governor that they would be attending.

Clover made the call, but, after a moment, his face fell. Covering the receiver, he said to Carman, 'They say it can't be arranged at such short notice.'

Carman bristled, took the phone and then let rip. 'The Director of Public Prosecutions has assured me that I can have access to my client at any time, day or night, and I fully intend to see him this afternoon.' This was of course granted.

At the prison, Carman informed Prime that despite his confession statement, the Director of Public Prosecutions intended to bring charges under Section 1 of the Official Secrets Act: in other words, for spying. Prime had hardly slept since his abrupt move from Winson Green Prison, Birmingham, and became even more distressed at this news. Carman tried to take him through his statement, but Prime was not in a fit state to concentrate, so Carman asked Clover to call in Rhona, in the hope that she might be able to calm him down sufficiently to continue.

When they returned, it was suggested to Rhona that she might like to be with her husband while they finished the statement. She held her husband's hand in silent prayer as Carman plied him with cigarettes, in an attempt to try to forge through the distressing task.

They left the prison at 8 p.m. Carman told Rhona that she would be able to see her husband again the next day and that Mr Davies would deal with any further questions Prime had. Carman took them to a West End hotel for a much-needed drink. They all knew Prime was in a very bad way.

Carman gently questioned Rhona further about her relationship with her husband. At the end, he said, 'I've dealt with a variety of cases, but never one like this. It's stranger than fiction. I find it almost unbelievable and I'm sure you must feel the same at times.'

Rhona nodded her head, 'I certainly do.'

Carman asked Mrs Prime how she and her boys had weathered these terrible days. The press, naturally enough, had been bothering her and Carman enquired how much she had been offered for her story. '£100,000,' came the reply. There was no need to ask if she had accepted this.

In the greatest secrecy, the Attorney General had allowed Carman to see every document in the case – however sensitive or secret. On his final visit, Carman learned they were going to throw the book at him – seven counts of communicating information useful to an enemy under the Official Secrets Act.

The following day, he broke the expected bad news to Rhona. 'I've just been with the Security Services people. They said the situation is very grave. May I suggest your husband co-operates fully with them after the trial. This could help when it comes to the matter of parole.'

Very serious crimes, such as espionage, are traditionally heard by the Lord Chief Justice at his court, No. 1, at the Old Bailey. It was there on Wednesday 10 November 1982 that Geoffrey Prime was to meet his fate. The sad, shattered and crumpled figure was brought to the court as if he were an international terrorist, a convoy of blaring escort vehicles and police motorcyclists accompanying his high-security van with a cordon of armed policemen surrounding the building. The press benches were packed – more than seventy journalists from all over the world – leaving only six seats for lay onlookers.

In his opening speech, Attorney General Sir Michael Havers (father of the actor Nigel and solicitor Philip) dealt with Prime's guilty plea to three charges of indecent assault under the Sexual Offences Act 1956. With the first, an eleven-year-old girl, in April 1980, he obtained entry to her home by saying he had come to inspect the plumbing. Certain that her parents were out, he put his hand over her mouth and asked her to lift her skirt up. However, he was disturbed by someone at the front door and rapidly left through the back. In May 1981, he arrived at a thirteen-year-old girl's house, claiming he had been asked to give some decorating estimates. He threw her into the bath and told her to take off her jeans and pants. He then masturbated, his semen being prima facie evidence. The third charge was the one that led to his arrest.

The court sat in camera (meaning that the press and public are excluded as matters of sensitivity are discussed). Sir Michael Havers outlined the seven treason charges, the defendant's spying equipment laid out as exhibits for those remaining to see. 'Prime came to have access to information ranging from the simply sensitive to matters of the very highest secrecy, such that their communication to an enemy would cause exceptionally grave damage to the interest and security of this country and its allies.' Possibly to reassure CIA interest in the case, he added that the evidence did not support the speculation that Prime had leaked the whereabouts of nuclear weapons or clandestine British agents.

When George Carman rose to his feet, he first thanked the Lord Chief Justice and Attorney General for letting him see every document in the case, however sensitive or secret. He continued:

> My client may now be able to see that a civilised system of justice affords him the right to be properly defended in a country whose interests he has damaged, whereas the irony of the case is that the country whose interest he sought to serve would have denied him such rights.

Carman was at pains to point out 'as a matter of the greatest public importance' that Prime's activities were conducted with the representatives of the Russian intelligence services alone. 'No other colleague at GCHQ, or indeed any other citizen of the United Kingdom or any western power, was in any way involved directly or indirectly in his wrongful activity.'

The QC told the court that, having confessed his guilt freely, Prime had expressly authorised him to say he was anxious to co-operate, after sentence, with the authorities to furnish further information that might help repair the damage he had caused.

Carman now turned to the matter of his client's sexual offences. 'So much for public matters, a matter of private concern, but no less important to your Lordship's court, is the utter shame and profound remorse that he would wish to express to the children concerned and to their parents.'

This led Carman to pose the rhetorical question, 'What sort of man is Geoffrey Prime? Two phrases tell it all: desperately lonely and totally inadequate – a sexual and social misfit,' adding that the ruthless propaganda of the Soviet system found a fertile breeding ground in the misfits of society to foster treachery under the guise of idealism.

Probably knowing it was to little avail, Carman took the court through Prime's troubled childhood, how he was a victim of sexual assault by an adult relative and his psychiatric treatment for severe depression. 'This man was not a potentially ruthless and not a totally rationally activated spy,' he concluded.

Rhona Prime, now thirty-six, was called to the witness box. To emphasise the middle-class normality of the Prime household, she was smartly dressed, in a light grey suit and wide brimmed grey hat trimmed with a blue ribbon, a bright blue jumper and even a string of pearls.

Carman began by saying to her, 'I think you are a practising Christian, are you not?'

'I am,' she replied firmly. She went on to say how Geoffrey had been a good husband and a marvellous father figure for her sons, giving them a much higher standard of living than they would otherwise have enjoyed after her divorce.

When asked why she went to the police after she discovered his spying equipment, she replied, 'I took legal advice and I had a choice. I didn't have to do it, but morally, I had to go to the authorities and tell them because I could not live as a Christian with that on my conscience.'

'What is your husband's attitude to the fact that you are the person who provided this prosecution with the ammunition it possesses?' asked Carman.

'He has taken it incredibly well,' she replied. 'He has become a changed man; the man I always thought he was underneath. He has lost his burden and is now a new man.'

Whether her testimony had much effect on the Lord Chief Justice is open to doubt. Before sentencing, Lord Lane told Prime that in his fourteen years as a Soviet spy, he had done 'incalculable harm to the interests and security of this country and our friends. It is said you are anxious to repair the damage you have done, but it is perfectly plain that a huge proportion of it is quite irreparable.'

He jailed Prime for thirty-eight years – thirty-five for spying and an additional three for his indecent assaults on young girls.

Carman took the case to the Court of Appeal, saying that Prime had been given 'a sentence without hope'. Prime's original confession to the police must have been of enormous value to the security authorities. Carman further pointed out that 'this court has to provide a positive incentive to any future traitor, or innocent relative of such a traitor, to come forward'.

Lord Justice Lawton rejected the appeal, while agreeing that the argument about an incentive was appreciated by the court, saying, 'In the end, the scales have to come down on the side of deterrence. It is much better that spying should never start than that the spies should subsequently confess.'

The case had made headlines throughout the world, causing Britain's allies to doubt how secure the secret services actually were. It gravely embarrassed the Prime Minister, Margaret Thatcher, who put Lord Bridge of Harwich in charge of a commission which, not surprisingly, recommended a more thorough vetting of those who were admitted to GCHQ.

Prime served half of his sentence and was released from Rochester Prison in March 2001. The Parole Board has the power to do this if prisoners show remorse and are judged to no longer be a risk to national security. Prime was placed on the Sex Offender Register.

Rhona had visited him for a few years but then started a new life in the West Country.

George found Prime to be a very ordinary man and was astounded that he was able to hide both his spying and his paedophilia from his family. He was a man of great complexity, a complete misfit who survived in a society that had no understanding of him. Yet he placed his trust in George and admired the extent to which he delved into the enormous details and paperwork involved in understanding the extent of the criminal activity.

Throughout this sorry tale, the person who impressed George the most was Rhona Prime. He admired her strength of character, particularly her ability to support her husband during such a distressing time while managing to shield her children from the dramatic impact of Geoffrey's behaviour.

George also admired – and even envied – Rhona's deep religious faith, understanding that her Christianity had helped and guided her through this immensely difficult time. George knew what faith was; he too had once had it, though it had lapsed.

CHAPTER FIVE

CRIMES OF PASSION

When George Carman set out the draft for his book, which sadly he didn't finish, he placed these cases together. They are all linked by one theme – love. Love that was spurned, love betrayed, love that turned sour. Here, I have fulfilled George's wishes by presenting these unusual and thought-provoking cases into one chapter.

R V. JENNIFER DAVIS

'I've shot him; Christopher is dead.'

JENNIFER DAVIS

As Christmas presents go, perhaps a twelve-bore shotgun wasn't the wisest purchase former army captain Christopher Davis ever made for his wife, Jennifer. The gift was given to her on 25 December 1980. Just over two years later, 44-year-old Mrs Davis used the gun to shoot her husband dead following a disagreement over a sherry decanter.

In truth, the row over the decanter, which Christopher Davis had sarcastically declared was 'under your nose' when Jennifer looked for it during a drinks party, was the tip of a particularly frosty iceberg. It appeared that Mr Davis had wanted to leave her and that she was determined not to let him go – a loyalty that she was to demonstrate in a most lethal fashion. Mr Davis had been a captain in the Gloucestershire Regiment when they married in 1971, later becoming an estate agent. They had two children together and two from Jennifer's first marriage.

On the evening of 11 January 1983, the couple invited over a neighbour and his wife for drinks at their home in Winsley, Wiltshire. The neighbours were keen to talk to Mr Davis about a survey of a house their daughter was keen to purchase.

During the evening, there was a disagreement between the Davises about the whereabouts of some sherry. Mr Davis told his wife that 'it is in the tantalus under your nose'. When she asked her husband why he was being so surly, he replied that he was giving her a taste of her own medicine. Then, just after their guests had left, Mr Davis informed his wife that he had a girlfriend. She was, apparently, 'beside herself' and went into his study, where he gave her a 'look of hatred'.

His callous admission was to cost him his life. Mrs Davis was, by now, a crack shot and a committee member of the local gun club. Her passion was clay pigeon shooting and, indeed, that very day she had been out shooting rabbits.

As the neighbours walked away from the house, they heard Mrs Davis shouting from a bedroom window, 'I've shot him; Christopher is dead.' They returned to the house, where an agitated Mrs Davis said her husband had another woman. She was arrested and charged with murder.

The subsequent trial, held at Bristol Crown Court in the summer of 1983, saw Mrs Davis plead not guilty to murder but guilty to manslaughter, by reason of diminished responsibility. This was accepted by the Crown, although as prosecuting counsel David Webster stated, this was not without some reservations.

George Carman was instructed for the defence by his friend and family solicitor, John Palmer, who later became president of the Law Society. Carman agreed to act for Mrs Davis on legal aid.

Carman told the court that the marriage had become unhappy and that Mr Davis had told his wife he was leaving her. Days before his death, he had spoken critically of her and she was confused.

'It spelled out for her great despair and then followed what the doctors say is an almost reflex type of reaction, a subconscious reaction due to her mental state,' he said.

Carman said the greatest punishment would be to live with the fact that she had taken the life of her children's father.

Psychiatrist Peter Trafford said she had a depressive illness caused by outside circumstances and suffered from 'hysterical dissociation' as a result, thereby reaching breaking point.

Mrs Davis was lucky to have two excellent character witnesses in Sir Ian Amory and Mr Etherington-Smith, a former British Ambassador to Vietnam.

Sir Ian Amory was a distant cousin of the accused. He described Mrs Davis as 'a highly respected person, a refined person, devoted to her family'. In his letter to me, he said he 'didn't remember hearing the evidence in mitigation … Whatever was said must have been persuasive because, considering the crime, the sentence was minimal. On release, Jenny [Davis] took Holy Orders and served as a parish priest in Devon.'

Mr Justice Stephen Brown told Mrs Davis that the court accepted she was a woman of the highest character. Her unhappy marriage had imposed strains, but in passing sentence, he said, 'The court has to bear in mind that what you did was an act of "appalling violence".'

She was sentenced to two years' imprisonment – a light sentence, given all the circumstances – and later she sent a letter of thanks to George.

R V. RHONA RITCHIE

'Let no one believe she was a spy.'

George Carman

A young British woman who passed confidential information to an Egyptian diplomat, Rifaat al Ansari, while working in Tel Aviv was 'misguided but not a spy', according to George Carman, who was tasked with defending her on serious charges under the Official Secrets Act 1911.

Rhona Ritchie had just turned thirty when she was charged with 'wrongfully communicating information contrary to Section 2(1)(a) the Official Secrets Act'. As she stood in the dock of the famous Court No. 1 at the Old Bailey on 29 November 1982, she must have wondered how she'd got herself into such a terrible mess.

The answer was love. Ms Ritchie had fallen deeply for Rifaat al Ansari, an official at the Egyptian Embassy in Tel Aviv, Israel. She had met him in London 1979, shortly after being recruited by the Foreign Office. At that time, she was working on the Hong Kong desk, and their affair began when she moved to accept her post in Tel Aviv and he followed as her Egyptian counterpart.

Rhona Ritchie was a high-flier who had been destined for great things. Born in June 1952 to parents who were both medical practitioners, she graduated with an honours degree in law from Glasgow University in 1973. She was a research assistant with the Scottish Law Commission in Edinburgh, prior to studying at the Faculty of Law at Aix-en-Provence University, before returning to Glasgow as a law lecturer. She joined the diplomatic service in September 1979, something of a late entrant into the civil service.

In late 1981 and early 1982, Ritchie, who as the Second Secretary at the British Embassy in Tel Aviv, wrongfully communicated the contents of a number of confidential telegrams to Ansari. She pleaded guilty to the charge.

Ritchie had regularly revealed to him the contents of secret official telegrams and was recalled to London, not knowing the true purpose of the recall. Upon her return, she was interviewed by the security services and admitted that she had indeed disclosed classified information to him. As a result of this, the Metropolitan Police was contacted to consider the offences and she was subsequently charged in relation to one telegram; however, five others had also been involved. The relevant telegram contained a message from Lord Carrington, the Foreign Secretary, to Alexander Haig, the United States Secretary of State. It concerned the willingness of Britain to take part in the multinational force in Sinai. Copies of the telegram were sent to a number of British Embassies, including Tel Aviv.

Prosecuting, the Attorney General Sir Michael Havers said there would be no further charges around five other telegrams, as the substance of the case was that Ritchie's conduct as a whole put the public interest at risk, rather than that the disclosure of a particular telegram was damaging to the public interest.

He said that she had been 'more foolish than wicked' and that, while having the affair, she had been 'so carried away' that she revealed to Ansari what was in the official telegrams.

Sir Michael said that there was a diplomatic service procedure which gave guidance to those employed in the embassies abroad, alerting them to the risk of being suborned by officials of friendly countries on behalf of other powers.

He said this case was very different from the case of Geoffrey Prime, who was imprisoned for thirty-five years.

Sir Michael said the damage Rhona Ritchie had done to Britain's interests was not great. Egypt was a friendly power and most of the information would have become public in due course. The mischief lay in the breach of confidentiality and the fact that her conduct caused doubts about Britain's trustworthiness in the minds of others.

George Carman said that Ms Ritchie had not believed she was breaking the law and pleaded guilty as her state of mind was not recognised legally as an issue. He said:

> Although she may on occasion have had doubts about some of the information, this young woman mistakenly made a serious error of judgment in believing that the Egyptian diplomat concerned was someone who could be trusted and that nothing she was disclosing was in any way damaging to the interests of the British government.

Addressing the judge, Mr Justice Croom-Johnson, Carman added, 'Let no one believe she was a spy. She was misguided in her judgement, and her loyalty to her country is unsullied.'

He said that since her arrest nine months earlier, she had been under sedation, had lost weight and was incredibly stressed. He added that Ritchie, aged thirty, was 'a sadder and perhaps a wiser woman. One's hope for her is that she can rebuild a career and a life that is so gravely wounded by this prosecution.'

Carman told the judge that Ms Ritchie felt she had never given any information that wouldn't be disclosed from other sources. Nonetheless, she expressed her remorse and regret that she in any way let down her own friends and colleagues in the diplomatic service and her own family.

After hearing an hour of evidence that was held in camera, Mr Justice Croom-Johnson told Ritchie, 'It is a tragedy that somebody who gave rise to the testimonials which have been put before the court, and who had that character, that promise, and that ability, should find herself in the position you are today.'

He stated that when Ritchie went to Tel Aviv, the declaration she signed relating to the Official Secrets Act and the consequences of any breach made it perfectly clear what her duty was. He pointed out that she herself had said she felt 'uncomfortable', which showed that she realised what she was doing was wrong.

However, he felt that she had suffered enough. He handed her a nine-month prison sentence that would be suspended.

George felt very sorry for Rhona Ritchie as she had been misguided, rather than dishonest. She genuinely fell for the Egyptian diplomat and discussed matters with him as a friend, with no thought that he would pass matters onto others. Sadly, she was wrong about that.

R V. KATHLEEN CALHAEM

'Riveting, bizarre and macabre.'

George Carman

This case, involving a spinster of fifty-seven who was so eaten up by jealousy that she had a love rival murdered, was both intriguing and horrific in equal respect. George Carman defended Kathleen Calhaem, and while he often found at least some redeeming features among his many and varied clients, he was only able to describe her as 'very cold, calculating, unfeeling and wicked'.

Calhaem, a retired antiques dealer living in Cheddar, Somerset, became obsessed with her solicitor, Kenneth Pigot. However, Pigot was having an affair with Shirley Rendell, a delightful lady who was married to his best friend Hugh, who was also a solicitor. Calhaem was said to have been spurned by Pigot, which led to a jealousy so deep that she was determined to have him at any cost – even murder.

Calhaem employed Pigot as her solicitor and formed an unusual affection for him, even telling him he could move in with her and blaming Mrs Rendell for keeping them apart. Calhaem pursued Pigot with intensity; she would even wait for him in the early morning when he was on his way to work.

On a few of these occasions, she had actually kissed Pigot and there had been 'heavy petting' between them. But Pigot was largely indifferent to Calhaem and often told her to leave him alone.

She was, however, undeterred. Pigot and the Rendells were all members of Somerset Cricket Club and frequently all met there. Calhaem would also attend matches, spying on the trio from the other side of the ground with binoculars, spending hours watching them.

Still not satisfied, Calhaem took matters further, employing a sometime private detective and foundry worker Julian Zajac to spy on Pigot. In January 1983, she met with Zajac at her home, telling him that she wanted Mrs Rendell killed. He was asked to select a pair of gloves from several available, as she didn't want his fingerprints anywhere. They had a drink and she gave him an envelope containing £5,000 in notes, saying she would pay another £5,000 upon completion of the deed. She handed him the notes, which had been cleaned in methylated spirits to remove any contamination.

She said, 'I want Shirley Rendell got rid of.' She asked him how she would be killed, adding, 'If she is found to be sexually assaulted before she is killed, that would be more in her way of life.'

Zajac made an appointment with Shirley Rendell's husband at his office, to make sure she would be alone at home. He then personally delivered flowers to the victim's home in nearby Yatton with a gun, hammer and knife concealed in the floral bouquet. Zajac intended initially to frighten her with an unloaded gun and to not carry out the killing, but make it look as if he had tried, in order to justify the payment. When she opened the door and screamed, he panicked and battered her with the hammer and stabbed her throat.

When her husband returned from work, he found her lying dead on the floor.

In April 1983, both Calhaem and Zajac were arrested on suspicion of murder. But at a committal hearing two months later, the court was told that there was insufficient evidence to proceed against Calhaem and – possibly to her astonishment – she walked free from the magistrates' court. Meanwhile, Zajac was sent for trial and in September 1983 pleaded guilty to murder, claiming that Calhaem had paid him £10,000 to do the job. The day after Zajac was sent to prison for life, Calhaem was arrested and charged with murder.

George Carman was instructed to defend Calhaem with his junior Michael Brompton, now KC, upon a charge of murder, by counselling and procuring Zajac (a third party employed by her) to carry out the killing of Shirley Rendell.

The case was heard at Winchester Crown Court before Mr Justice Stuart-Smith. Notably, the star witness for the prosecution was none other than Julian Zajac, the man who wielded the knife. He had decided to turn Queen's evidence, a means by which convicted criminals give evidence in court to lessen their own punishment.

Zajac said he planned a charade to kill, hoping that Calhaem would believe a serious attempt had been made to kill Shirley Rendell and he could keep the cash. He told the court that he lost his self-control, 'suddenly went berserk' and battered the woman to death. Zajac said that he was more frightened of Calhaem than he was about being found out.

The defendant did not speak during the trial, except to lodge a 'not guilty' plea. Carman divined that she was very quiet and largely kept herself to herself. He did not call her to give evidence, as he wanted the prosecution to prove their case beyond reasonable doubt without her assistance.

Instead, Carman called just one defence witness, a convicted double killer, who asked for his identity to be kept secret. He claimed that in prison conversations with Zajac, he discovered that the latter had sought to involve Calhaem, not only to mitigate his part in the crime he carried out but to minimise his involvement by saying he did not instigate the crime and to give false evidence so he would receive a lighter sentence.

He also said that Zajac had told him he had an arrangement with the police that he would get a recommended minimum prison sentence if his evidence ensured Calhaem's conviction.

Zajac was recalled as a witness and denied doing a deal with the police.

George Carman said the jury should not draw any adverse inference from the fact that Calhaem had not given evidence, as there was no duty upon her to do so. Whether that was a factor or not we shall never know; Calhaem was unanimously convicted of murder after four hours of jury deliberation.

Sentencing her to life, the judge said that her actions 'were those of a cold, calculating and evil woman'. The description was undoubtedly accurate, but it rather belied Calhaem's appearance in court. She always dressed smartly, if conservatively, and bore something of a resemblance to moral crusader Mary Whitehouse. Calhaem's crime, however, and the tale of intrigue leading up to it were enough for Carman to comment that 'the love tangle was so riveting, bizarre and macabre that it made TV's *Dallas* sound like a children's bedtime story'.

George's personal view was that Calhaem was a very odd person, a truly old-fashioned spinster, living in her own imaginary, small world. She genuinely believed that if she succeeded in disposing of Pigot's girlfriend, she would spend the rest of her life with her loved one. She had built up her relationship with Pigot in her mind to be one of great importance to both of them. In reality, she meant nothing to him. She had pursued him relentlessly to try to gain his affection and her infatuation became an obsession beyond her control.

George said Pigot was a very dull man, not good-looking or charming in any way.

There was an unsuccessful appeal by Calhaem in February 1985, on the basis that Zajac's evidence proved no causal connection to her. The Court of Appeal upheld the conviction. It was held that the offence of counselling a person to commit an offence, if proved to be committed by the person counselled and not accidentally, was a criminal act.

Michael Brompton KC, Carman's junior in the case, observed:

George's great strength as a barrister was that he combined a Balliol intellect with a street fighter's pugnacity. In preparation, he had an astonishing ability to simultaneously read, absorb and analyse complex and voluminous material, grasping the issues as quickly as I've ever seen it done. In the courtroom, the same abilities, applied to the oral evidence of witnesses, enabled him to see flaws and contradictions which in the time available would have evaded most others.

He was the master of the telling phrase and the apt metaphor, which he combined with a common touch that was pleasing to juries. He was ruthless and unrelenting, never afraid to continue to turn the knife, even after the witness had died! I have never known an advocate with such little need for notes or aides-memoire.

R V. MICHAEL TELLING

'If she pricked, did he not bleed?'
GEORGE CARMAN

In September 1983, the body of a headless woman was discovered in woods on Telegraph Hill, near Exeter in the south-west of England. The police published a photograph of her clothing in the newspapers and from that a woman came forward and told them that she might be Monika, the wife of a man named Michael Telling. Monika had been missing since March, so the police obtained a search warrant for Telling's home in Buckinghamshire and found a severed head in a plastic bag hidden in the boot of a Mini in the garage. It was indeed that of his wife, 27-year-old Monika, whom he had married in 1981.

Michael Telling was arrested and charged with murder. In custody, he admitted the killing, but, on the advice of his solicitor, he pleaded guilty to manslaughter on the grounds of diminished responsibility. The Crown did not accept this, so on 19 June 1984, he appeared at Exeter Crown Court, charged with his wife's murder.

Since 1965, the death penalty for murder had been abolished. Murder still carried a mandatory sentence of life imprisonment. But the sentence for manslaughter remained within the judge's discretion. It could be as little as community service or less, but the judge could still impose a life sentence. If the defendant were found to have diminished responsibility, they could be sent to a secure mental facility.

Telling was a very wealthy man and his solicitors instructed the person they considered the most persuasive barrister in England to defend him: George Carman QC. It was his brief to persuade the jury of seven men and five women that Telling's crime was manslaughter. Alan Rawley QC, prosecuting for the Crown, sought a verdict of murder. The case was heard before Mr Justice Sheldon.

Telling, now thirty-four, had a background which was both privileged and miserable. He had no need to work; he was a member of the Vestey family, at the time one of the richest in England, having made their money from meat. By 1925, the Vestey Brothers were the largest retailers of meat in the world, with a chain of more than 2,000 shops in Britain alone. The founder was made a peer and his grandson, Lord Vestey, Michael's second cousin, played polo with Prince Charles.

Telling's side of the family had no title but a large share of this immense wealth. However, he claimed, his parents were exceptionally uncaring and negligent. He was drinking and smoking from the age of nine. He kept carving knives in his room and once threatened his mother with one. He was cruelly bullied at school and twice expelled.

The marriage to American-born Monika was a disaster. In a police statement, Telling admitted that after seventeen months of marriage, he could no longer put up with her 'lesbianism and alcoholism'. He said, 'She often taunted me with her affairs with both men and women and constantly belittled my sexual efforts, saying I was only good for money.'

Alan Rawley told the jury that it seemed Telling's wife was a difficult young woman. It was also true that Telling had suffered mental health problems and could even have been suffering from some form of mental illness at the time of the killing. He also said there was evidence that he had displayed intelligence, cunning and an instinct for self-preservation in attempts to cover up his crime.

Telling shot her with a Marlin .303 rifle, which he had bought in Australia when contemplating a divorce. He hid her body in their partially built sauna for five months. He then disposed of the body, dressed in salmon pink shorts and a T-shirt, and chopped off her head, which he kept in the boot of his Mini for months at his home in High Wycombe.

On the morning of the shooting, Telling was due to go to hospital to see a psychiatrist. In his statement, he said:

> Monika was in a bad mood and kept telling me to hurry up and go into hospital so that she could live her life. She would not stop. She came charging towards me shouting; I thought she was going to attack me, so I picked up my rifle and shot her. I shot her three times. I shot her in the throat – a ricochet – and then twice in the top right-hand side of her chest. I was very confused in my mind at the time and have no idea why I shot her. I picked her

> up and looked at her. I knew she was dead. I was too distressed to do anything. I went into the kitchen and sat down for half an hour and then I vomited and cried for about an hour and a half.

He subsequently moved the body to his sauna. There were often visitors, including his son from an earlier marriage, Matthew. Often girlfriends came to the house, and he made love to at least two of them in the property where the body lay.

Five months later, he decided to dispose of the body in ferns and bracken in Exeter Forest. He hired a van to drive there and wrapped Monika's body in a plastic motorcycle cover. He returned home with the head chopped from the torso and wrapped it in a polythene bag.

Telling said, 'I didn't want to throw her just in a ditch or river. I knew a forest close to Exeter. It is a very attractive spot, so I decided to leave her there.' He said that if the body was not discovered, he would collect it at some time in the future.

Following the publicity surrounding the discovery of the headless body, a friend, Cheryl Richardson, said that Telling had admitted to her that he had killed his wife and her body had been in the sauna. He confessed to the police that he had disposed of the rifle in pieces in a river.

When asked why he had killed her, he replied, 'There were a hundred and one reasons. I can't really explain. She kept pushing me. I just snapped in the end; she was horrible in many ways.'

Opening for the defence, Carman asked the jury to put aside prejudice, sympathy, passion and emotion and urged them to try the case by rational processes.

It was not their job to decide if Telling was, or is, insane but to decide if, at the time of the killing, he was, more probably than not, suffering from an abnormality of mind which substantially impaired his mental responsibility.

Carman said that the defence proposed to set before the court the real picture of Telling's personality disorder, rather than the isolated selections which had been produced by the prosecution:

> We hope to lay before you a pattern from infancy to adult life. The man's conduct as an adult can be seen to mirror his conduct as a child. You will hear echoes of his infancy in his adult behaviour.
>
> He suffered from rejection as a child and suffered from rejection as a man. He was unable to cope with the stresses and strains of adult life. He was a man who never really grew up.
>
> Monika was the worst person for a man with Michael Telling's disordered personality to have married. A normal man might have been driven to near distraction. How much more would the effect be on the emotional cripple Michael Telling?
>
> If she pricked, did he not bleed?

Evidence was then given by several witnesses recounting the behaviour of Monika. Cheryl Richardson and her husband, an odd-job man, talked of their distress at seeing Monika's public humiliation of Telling.

Cross-examined by Carman, Mrs Richardson said that Monika had attended AA meetings and 'Mr Telling went to a similar organisation to help him understand and overcome her problems'.

Regarding Monika's sexual inclinations, Mrs Richardson said she once saw a vibrator in her handbag. Mrs Richardson went on, 'She did not hide the fact that she would take girlfriends home when her husband was in the house.' She even revealed that Monika had made an advance to her, which she had rejected.

Mrs Richardson said she had seen Telling extremely distressed and almost in tears. 'Michael Telling worshipped the ground Monika walked on, but she showed no affection whatsoever.'

Telling's mother, Mrs Joyce Strong, came from Australia to give evidence about his mental state. The 63-year-old granddaughter of Lord Vestey said her son had threatened to kill her with a carving knife when he was nine years old.

Telling had been on a visit to Australia just a few days before the murder. George Carman suggested to her, 'It was almost the first time in your life that you and he had communicated as mother and son?'

Mrs Strong replied, 'Yes, he felt really rejected and he prayed for affection.' She added that his father had showed him no affection and Telling proved to be a very disturbed child indeed.

She said she was so bound up in her own unhappy life with an alcoholic, violent husband that she could not cope with her son, who was impossible to control.

For years, he was kept in a separate suite in the house and looked after by nannies. At six, he started a fire at his school; he was running around with matches and chasing other children. He stole money during his time at school to go home and he kept four carving knives in his room when he was nine.

Carman asked her, 'I don't mean to say this in any way critically, but as far as that young child was concerned, you really found it hard to cope as a mother? Is it fair to say that many of his problems stemmed from a very unhappy and unloving childhood?'

'Yes,' said his mother.

Robert Bluglass, professor of forensic psychiatry at Birmingham University and a member of the Mental Health Review Tribunals, was then called by Carman.

He gave evidence that Telling had told him that his wife frolicked half-naked on the floor with another woman before they were married. She also allowed a solicitor's lesbian wife to photograph her nude in the bath and refused to make love to her husband on their wedding night. She also belittled his sexual capabilities to friends, and for the last seven months of her life, would not have sex with him at all.

Carman asked Bluglass what effect this would have had on Telling's personality.

The professor replied:

> On any normal man, it would be profoundly humiliating and hurtful and distressing and upsetting. But Telling wasn't a normal man. He was an abnormal man of considerable immaturity and lacking confidence in himself generally and sexually. Even when he finally disposed of Monika's body in Devon, he explained he could not bear to be apart from her and on impulse decapitated her with an axe.

The psychiatrist added, 'I don't consider that Michael Telling is a cool, cold-blooded, calculated individual. He is a man of mixed and barely controlled emotions, who acts on impulse – not with cold-blooded or calculated planning.'

Dr Paul Bowden, a psychiatrist at the Maudsley Hospital, was next. He said of Telling:

> To see him as cold-blooded and calculating would be to fly in the face of the evidence. He rated eight out of ten for the evil generated by his abnormality of mind at the time of the killing.

> That hypothetical scale, he said, was based on St Francis of Assisi at zero and Attila the Hun on ten.

In addressing the jury, Carman stated:

> Telling has suffered throughout his life rejection after rejection – and has been the victim of rejection. Are you going to deliver a final and ultimate rejection? I suspect not. Don't be repelled by the horror of it all and overlook the sickness of it all. The horror of the case is the product of the sickness of his mind. Built up inside him was all that sickness of mind which needed help and understanding and not taunting and humiliation.
>
> A manslaughter verdict would be a true one, not one of sympathy. Heavens above, you must have felt moments of sympathy for Michael Telling, mixed with the horror of what he did.

Alan Rawley QC made his final speech for the prosecution:

> Despite his mental abnormality, this man determined to kill his wife. He could have prevented himself from doing so if he wished. He went to gruesome lengths to cover up the killing, including using his wife's bank cashpoint card on the evening she died. He installed an electric air freshener to get rid of the smell of the body, destroyed the gun he shot her with and the axe with which he chopped off her head. The decapitation was simply to avoid identification of the corpse. Despite his mental abnormality, this man was determined to kill his wife.

Mr Justice Sheldon, in summing up to the jury, told them to put aside their emotions and dispassionately consider the evidence. 'Although it might be bizarre and unusual in some respects, you might think that, in essence, the story amounted to a variation of a not-unknown theme of an ill-matched couple, of love alternated with intense hatred, of the killing of one spouse by another.'

He referred to the evidence of three psychiatrists called by the prosecution and defence and reminded them that psychiatric medicine was not a precise science.

The burden of proof is usually on the prosecution to prove the case beyond reasonable doubt. In this instance, the burden was on Telling to establish, on the balance of probability, that he was suffering from such diminished responsibility as the law recognised. The burden shifts with this defence. All three doctors had agreed that Telling was suffering from an abnormality of the mind, arising from inherent causes. The question was whether his condition substantially impaired his mental responsibility for the act of killing.

The judge concluded, 'That is the question which is essentially one for you, the jury, an answer which is incapable of scientific proof and should be approached in a common-sense way.'

The trial had taken nine days, but the jury returned with a verdict after two and a half hours. Their verdict was that Telling was guilty of manslaughter by reason of diminished responsibility. They accepted the opinion of Professor Bluglass that Telling's disorder was 'a deeply rooted, ingrained failure to adapt to life as he matured and to people around him'.

Telling's mother and first wife, Alison, smiled and hugged each other.

However, on 29 June 1984, Mr Justice Sheldon passed a sentence of life imprisonment, saying he had no alternative. Telling showed no emotion at the verdict.

He was to serve nearly ten years of his sentence and was released from jail on 24 January 1994. Three months later he returned to Perth, Western Australia, where he had spent part of his childhood. He paid A$750,000 for an extensive house and another A$300,000 for an adjoining property. Neighbours later described him as an English gentleman but something of a recluse. For fifteen years until his death, just before Christmas 2009, Michael Telling quietly played the part of a modestly wealthy member of Perth society. He was accepted among the elite coterie of lifetime members at the WACA (the cricket club) and was a popular contributor to the Jaguar Car Club and a collector of Beatles' and sporting memorabilia. It must have come as a considerable surprise to the Australians who thought they knew him when the newspapers posthumously revealed that he had killed his wife while living in England.

This case illustrates how clearly George Carman understood the human condition and its frailty and succeeded in admirably representing Telling. He presented the facts so clearly to the jury, none of whom was necessarily experienced with or understood psychology, so that they could appreciate the dynamics operating in this case.

CHAPTER SIX

R V. KEN DODD

'Some accountants are comedians, but comedians are never accountants.'

GEORGE CARMAN

To say that the city of Liverpool was in a state of turmoil during the 1980s is something of an understatement. Deeply affected by drastic spending cuts brought in by the Thatcher government, the city's legendary strength and resilience was seemingly tested to the limit as traditional industries fell like ninepins and unemployment reached close to 20 per cent.

In response, there were protests, strikes and riots. The militant-dominated city council rebelled against the feeling that Liverpool was somehow being singled out for 'special treatment' by refusing to cut budgets. TV shows like *Boys from the Black Stuff* and *Bread* highlighted the daily deprivations endured by Liverpudlians as the city became a byword for decline, poverty and misery. The Hillsborough disaster of April 1989, in which ninety-seven Liverpool FC fans died in a crush during a cup match in Sheffield, seemed to sum up every misfortune that had befallen the city over the decade. It was all a far cry from the glory days of the Beatles and the sound of Merseybeat.

Yet even as resilience was stretched to breaking point, Liverpool's famous sense of humour seemed to be able to withstand anything. And just two months after the terrible disaster at Hillsborough, the city rediscovered its funny bone in a court case starring one of the most eccentric and original comedians this country has ever produced – Ken Dodd.

Born in the Liverpool suburb of Knotty Ash – which would remain at the centre of his world, both onstage and off – Ken Dodd was a celebrated son of the city when the Fab Four were still in short trousers. With his distinctive buck teeth (the result of a cycling accident) and array of Diddymen and 'tickling sticks', the man universally known as 'Doddy' was the instigator of a comic act that epitomised the originality and often surreal nature of the Scouse sense of fun.

He was a highly popular entertainer across the UK, playing night after night, often for hours on end, at venues from Blackpool's Central Pier to the London Palladium. The man who had made his debut as Professor Yaffle Chucklebutty, Operatic Tenor and Sausage Knotter was, by 1989, a living legend.

However, not everyone found him amusing, especially the sharp-eyed tax inspectors employed by the Inland Revenue (IR – now known as His Majesty's Revenue and Customs, HMRC). After investigations, the IR concluded that Ken Dodd had not been declaring all his substantial income for the purposes of tax. It decided to prosecute him on charges of cheating the IR from 1973 to 1986 and counts of false accounting from 1982 to 1988. The IR had already taken another celebrity scalp in the form of jockey Lester Piggott, who was jailed in 1987 after failing to declare income of £3.25 million.

The IR considered that making examples of well-known people for fraud or tax evasion had a galvanising effect on the general public, reminding them not to attempt any form of 'fiddle'. In short, the IR was out to make an example of Ken Dodd.

It was well-known in showbusiness circles that Ken kept his wallet firmly closed. He never lost an opportunity to refrain from spending money and even his close friends had little compunction in criticising him for his legendary meanness. Yet it was close friends who would come to his aid during the trial, telling the jury about Ken's unique comedic skills and – perhaps surprisingly – his contributions to charity.

Despite the parsimony, Ken was frightened enough about the prospect of going to jail to consider hiring the best defence lawyer money could buy. Several 'names' he approached saw the inevitability of a prison sentence as a fait accompli. However, one name kept cropping up – that of a fellow northerner, a native of Blackpool (that most comic of British seaside towns) and a QC who was gaining the reputation of swaying the jury, even in the most unlikely circumstances.

'I want to see George Carman,' Ken told his solicitor. 'I ought to see George Carman.'

Ken's wife told me, 'He was adamant that he would have to be represented by the best QC and that having met George Carman in the beauty parade, he was the only one!'

Ken was warned that this would be an expensive hiring, but with his liberty at stake, he was prepared to spend whatever it took to stay out of jail.

When the case began on Tuesday 6 June 1989, Carman informed the judge, Mr Justice Waterhouse, that his client was too sick to stand trial. He asked for an adjournment for further medical tests.

The judge was annoyed. Why had he only learned of this that day? The answer was obvious: Carman was beginning the uphill task of winning the jury's sympathy. He produced a consultant cardiologist, Dr Rhys Williams, to give evidence.

'The defendant,' Williams said, 'had a long history of chronic bronchitis and emphysema. He was suffering from ventricular tachycardia, brought on by a disease of the heart muscle and arteries.'

Carman wondered aloud if his client would ever work again.

Although the judge said he suspected that this might be the case with an awful lot of people in their sixties, he was nevertheless obliged to postpone the trial until Monday 19 June. And in that thirteen-day gap, it was hoped that the good people of Liverpool would find some sympathy for one of their own – not least because the trial was being held right on their doorsteps, at Liverpool Crown Court. It was a notable decision not to hold the trial in a more neutral place, especially when Doddy's popularity in the city was solid, and, it might be argued, because of the Liverpool public's natural distrust of government institutions, the Inland Revenue being a prime example.

On that day, Brian Leveson QC opened the case for the prosecution. Much later, as Lord Justice Leveson, he would lend his name to the inquiry into press standards that brought to light the notorious News International phone-hacking scandal. Incidentally, the QC was no stranger to Ken Dodd – he himself had been born in Liverpool and was educated at Liverpool College, before studying at Merton College, Oxford.

Leveson spared no punches, telling the court that for years Dodd had been 'up to his eyes' in tax evasion – not least with his overseas accounts. Since 1973, he had been receiving cash for his appearances, which he put in his pocket and failed to declare to the revenue.

Instead, he made trips to the Isle of Man and Jersey and deposited his money in banks there. By April 1987, Dodd had £777,000 in these banks and owed the IR more than £370,000 in tax.

In the 1960s, Dodd had created a limited company, Ken Dodd Enterprises, but he treated the money as his own. He had a local accountant, Reginald Hunter, who proved to be dishonest: in 1983, he was prosecuted for false accounting, and while Dodd's company was not included in that prosecution, the accounts Hunter submitted for Dodd and his company bore little resemblance to his earnings. 'Why should Mr Hunter have made this sort of mistake?' Leveson wondered. 'Mr Dodd must have known.'

In the mid-1970s, Dodd had bought a six-bedroom house in Whitchurch, Shropshire, for £26,500 for himself and his then girlfriend, Anita, who sadly died within two years. By 1989, the house was worth £250,000. When the IR began its inquiry into Dodd's tax affairs, Arthur Young Associates, a new firm of accountants, was brought in. It was discovered that Dodd had earned more than a million pounds up to 1982 but had evidently spent very little, as only £23,000 in cash was unaccounted for.

He was asked by the IR and Arthur Young whether he had any accounts outside the United Kingdom, but he insisted he did not. 'At one time,' Leveson said, 'he had twelve. He was given the chance to come clean and tell the truth, but he became devious and deceitful.' Seventeen days after his denial, Dodd went to the Isle of Man and withdrew £181,000, which he hid in wardrobes, cupboards and under the stairs of his three Liverpool houses. Nearly £336,000 was later found there. His home in Knotty Ash was as disorganised as his finances. He kept everything in boxes, piled high and everything was a muddle. Carman thought it would be worth visiting his home in order to view the disorder. As a result, he decided to have a video made recording the state of the property. He was convinced the jury would then understand more about Ken Dodd, the man.

There were other examples of allegedly fraudulent behaviour, including Dodd receiving two fees for one performance: the first was a cheque for £250, on which he would pay VAT, and the second was £750, in cash. And if the comedian really thought there was nothing wrong in having bank accounts in the Isle of Man, why did he open some in his father's first name, Artson, and another for his new girlfriend, Anne Jones?

When George Carman rose to his feet, on the third day of the trial, he was faced with a near impossible task to refute this avalanche of evidence. He began by blaming Reginald Hunter, quoting a letter from him to Dodd indicating that the accountant was the perpetrator. With regard to his share from Ken Dodd Enterprises, Hunter wrote:

> Your own bonus is fifty thousand pounds, but by the time [Denis Healey, the then Chancellor of the Exchequer] has finished with it, it will be worth a long weekend in Rochdale with a girl of your choice, two sacks of spuds, a 1934 lawnmower and a year's supply of artichokes.

Why, Carman wondered, had Dodd not been part of Hunter's eventual prosecution? Surprisingly, Hunter had not been called by the prosecution for Dodd's case, although his secretary Yvonne Rice was. She told the court that Dodd was a little 'scatterbrained' when it came to keeping records. She described how Ken would rush into their office with plastic bags full of receipts and invoices, before driving off to a show in another town. 'He would bring in his tax returns at the eleventh hour and the fifty-ninth minute, before they were due in,' Mrs Rice said. She also confirmed that he withdrew £1,000 a month for himself.

Joseph Atkinson, of the Inland Revenue, was called as a witness. When it was investigating Hunter in 1977, it found a letter from him to Dodd.

> You will notice that once again the Ken Dodd Enterprises balance sheet omits its greatest asset – i.e. the great drum better known in Stock Exchange circles as the Aladdin's Cave of Knotty Ash. Long may that priceless possession remain secluded in the Merseyside Mangrove swamps; seen but rarely, and by the very few.

The implication was that the 'great drum' referred to a hoard of cash. Carman refuted this, saying it was a reference to an Aladdin's cave of stage equipment. He pointed out that Dodd lived a frugal existence. He drove an old Ford Granada. Admittedly, on one occasion, he bought a new Jaguar, but he never bothered to pick it up and eventually the showroom sales staff drove it to his garage. Dodd never drove it.

With reference to Leveson's assertion that Dodd had earned a million pounds between 1949 and 1982, Carman pointed out that 'Mr Dodd paid more tax in a month than the average man does in a year. Yet he never put in any expenses, claims for helicopters, a chauffeur or bodyguard or entertaining people.'

The idea was to show that his client had little idea of how to manage his books. Carman then asked Joseph Atkinson, 'Do you think Mr Dodd was a fool?'

Atkinson replied, 'No – a man of above average intelligence. But he obviously had difficulty in understanding the basics of finance.'

As the case progressed, the tabloids had a field day – 'KEN'S KNOTTY ASH STASH' being just one of the many punning attempts. *The Sun* went as far as to ask its readers to send in a 'Daily Dotty Doddy Ditty'. George leapt on this, ironically regretting so distinguished a newspaper should stoop so low, and the judge agreed to report the contempt of court to the Attorney General. *The Sun* was unabashed and had a go at Carman. 'We believe Ken Dodd's brief to be beyond belief,' it crowed.

Meanwhile, back in court, the probing of Dodd's finances became even deeper. The Inland Revenue had asked – and Dodd had agreed to pay for – a report by the accounting firm of Grant Thornton into his financial affairs. It cost the comedian £54,000.

When John Collier, a partner in the firm, took the stand, Carman wanted him first to agree that Dodd's properties in Thomas Lane, Knotty Ash, were unkempt – a mess. 'Hundreds of stage props were stored in a rusty, old lorry container, nearby stables and a cottage next door. Waist-high weeds! Rather reminiscent of Steptoe's back yard. If Dodd's homes were the Aladdin's cave in Hunter's letter to him, they were certainly lacking in the treasure department,' he commented.

Then it came to the matter of Reginald Hunter's accounting. It transpired that Hunter had submitted £37,000 in Dodd's annual expenses 'out of the blue'. There had been no paperwork to back it up, just a figure plucked out of the air.

'On any view of the matter, this is *Alice in Wonderland* behaviour, by any competent firm of accountants, isn't it?' Carman questioned.

Collier agreed that it would be 'incompetent and dishonest' to work out expenses without paperwork. But he later pointed out that if he had known Dodd had deposited more than £200,000 offshore, his financial statement would have been a waste of time.

'Dodd was a little like a barrack room accountant,' Carman said. 'They are very inconvenient because you have to educate them out of their ignorance.'

Lamenting Hunter's absence, Carman said that the trial was like 'putting on *Hamlet* without the prince'. Apparently, Hunter had never been interviewed and the IR didn't even know where he was.

George seized on this:

> Mr Hunter could have said to you, 'I relied on Mr Ken Dodd and I never verified or checked what was correct.' Or he could have said that he invented the figures himself. He could have said that he invented things together with Mr Dodd. He could have said, 'I was careless, and I am sorry.' But you never even contacted him to see what the position was, did you?

'No,' came the meekest of replies, from the IR representative.

Carman addressed the jury, 'Away from the showbiz glitter, Dodd was a very ordinary man to whom accountancy was a mysterious science which passes all human understanding. It was as fanciful to him as the world of the Diddy Men and the Jam Butty mines of Knotty Ash, which he created.'

A substantial part of Dodd's 'ignorance' was fuelled by Isle of Man advertisements which said that interest was not subject to tax. They have since been outlawed in the United Kingdom. Dodd told the IR he had put his money into banks there because 'I would have been taxed at ninety-eight pence in the pound. Banks were collapsing and the pound was collapsing. I thought we were nearly caught up in civil war in this country.'

Grant Thornton eventually drew up a report on Dodd's finances, which the comedian fatefully signed. The accountants said they would not have let him do so, had they known he had £777,000 in banks in the Isle of Man and Jersey. Anthony Brown of Grant Thornton, a man whom Dodd described as a cross between Bertie Wooster and Brian Rix, had asked him to provide receipts for everything, even bus tickets. 'It was like a Chinese laundry,' Dodd said. 'No *tickee*, no laundry.'

The court laughed but not the judge, who interrupted impatiently, 'Let's get on with it. We don't want a character sketch of everything.'

Dodd countered that the firm did not understand the workings of show business. 'They even asked me how many pairs of underpants I bought a year.'

Leveson cross-examined him and when asked why he had told the IR about his £45 in the Co-op Bank but not the hundreds of thousands in the Isle of Man and Jersey, Dodd repeated his belief that the interest on them was not subject to tax.

On one occasion, he admitted bringing £180,000 home in cash from the Isle of Man. This awakened the judge's interest. 'What does it look like, all this money in a briefcase?' he asked the defendant.

'The notes are very light, my lord,' Ken replied.

The judge was further intrigued when Dodd said that by 1980, he had more than £300,000 in his attic. 'I saved it out of my own legal earnings,' Dodd maintained. 'My taxed earnings.'

'If it was in the attic, how could it be declared for tax?' the judge wondered.

Leveson seized on this, pointing out that from 1966–79, it would not have been possible for him to have built up cash savings of £300,000 out of taxed income.

'Well, I did,' the comedian stoutly replied.

Leveson said Dodd had only revealed his Isle of Man and Jersey accounts after he became aware the IR knew about them.

Ken stuck to his story. 'I earned every penny in those accounts, perfectly legitimately in my own name. I am an honest man and I realised I had made a mistake. I have done nothing dishonest – mistaken, maybe, but not dishonest.'

So there it was. Dodd had as good as admitted his guilt. Given that the most well-known legal maxim is 'Ignorance of the law is no excuse', the King of the Diddymen did not appear to have a leg to stand on.

Carman thought otherwise and with his practised sleight of hand managed to move the goal posts before the jury's very eyes. First, he was keen to point out that Dodd's deception was not to fuel an expensive lifestyle. He had never had a holiday until he was fifty-one and then he used cut-price tickets. He had not had a new suit in three years. His idea of luxury was a daily pint of lager.

He went on:

> To allegations that Mr Dodd has lived in a world of fantasy, a world on occasion of folly and a world of insecurity, we say 'Yes'. To the allegation that this man is devious, this man is deceitful, this man is dishonest, we say 'No' and we shall continue to say 'No'. His conduct, so obviously eccentric as to be explained, not by dishonesty, but by the close-knit upbringing of which he was so much a part for most of his family life. It was an upbringing which stamped on him, for the rest of his life, the values of another age: thrift, relentless hard work, family loyalty and great charity for others. Money is not the beginning and the end for Ken Dodd – far from it.

Taking the stand, Dodd told the court his grandmother was the first female magistrate in Liverpool and chairman of the Old Swan Labour Party.

Carman added, 'And she had sixteen children?'

'She knew all about labour, yes,' Dodd confirmed.

The laughter in court indicated that there was more than a modicum of sympathy for him. So, he told the jury how, from the age of fourteen to twenty, he stacked his father's lorry with coal and took it to places around Knotty Ash and West Derby with his brother, Billy. For this, he was paid £2.10s a week.

'We saved money because we didn't want to go back to the bad old days,' he added. 'It sounds old-fashioned, but my mother and father didn't trust banks and it rubbed off on us. Our money was stored in labelled envelopes at home under the care of my mother.'

Milking it further, he continued:

> I had no children, I'm sorry to say. I had no Rolls-Royce. I didn't want anything else. I wanted to live as I have always lived and be a successful comedian. But you have to have something to show that you are successful. I had a nest egg. It was my security and reassurance that I had made it. It made me proud that I had generated that kind of cash.

In his early years, he discovered he had been blessed with the magical gift of making people laugh. Aged twenty-six, he made £4,000, all stored in the attic. Aged thirty-three, it was £30,000. In 1963, his weekly earnings were about £1,500. He made it to the London Palladium on £3,000 a week. In 1966, eighteen months before his mother died, she gave him her life savings of £15,000 because his dad liked to gamble. By 1980, he had cash savings of £330,000.

Carman pointed out that he was devoted to bringing happiness to other people, but behind the scenes, he was possessed by haunting insecurity in his private life. He had made no secret of deposits in the Isle Man and the Channel Islands (he would entertain people with his tickling stick when he entered the various banks, sign autographs for the staff and they would take photographs), therefore he was far from dishonest or deceitful. The performances – and the photographs – evidently did not reach the inspectors of the Inland Revenue.

Carman highlighted:

> At the end of the day, we shall establish that deviousness is not part of his make-up. Insecurity is the theme. Caution is the theme. Reserve about private affairs and, on occasion, a little bit obstinate, a little bit of blinkered vision. Outside his own special world, where he is a master, he is really a very ordinary man from Knotty Ash.

Prompted by his QC, Dodd told the court:

> It is a strange thing that happens to you when you get paid a lot of money. Some people go crazy and go in for all sorts of things and some people don't. Most entertainers suffer from fear of not getting any more work – the basis of stage fright is when you wonder what the audience will be like and whether they will like you. But the big fear is that maybe next week, or next year, you may not get a summer season or a pantomime season. Show business is littered with people who have gone bankrupt.

The judge was getting a little fed up with these sob stories and told him to speed up.

Carman asked Dodd why he didn't use UK banks.

Dodd replied:

> After my father died in 1979, I realised our house had a serious case of dry rot and I would have to move my savings before I allowed workmen in. Then I saw advertisements that said interest earned in the Isle of Man and Jersey was tax free. I was paying 83 per cent, the top rate of tax plus 15 per cent on top of that. I would get £2 out of every £100 I earned. I was misled about tax-free interest and, on discovering my error, immediately informed the Inland Revenue about each of the Manx and Jersey bank accounts.

In the fourth week of the trial, Dodd spoke about his new girlfriend, Anne Jones. She was desperate to have a baby and had injections to help this. It was necessary for them to have intercourse within thirty-six hours of the injection and Dodd described a hectic day in 1986 when they were due to make love, but he had shows in Liverpool and Lincolnshire (both for charity), then he did one in Norfolk, before going into a long meeting with Grant Thornton. He was absolutely whacked but agreed to sign a document about their meeting with the IR without properly reading it.

Despite touring the country with his 'Happiness Show', the same could not be said of the star's private life. 'I have had five years during which I have not had one happy day,' he mumbled to the jury, his head in his hands.

Although the judge was keen to move the trial on with more dispatch, Carman had lined up a series of further witnesses. They were famous names and most likely to talk about Dodd's compassionate, charitable character, rather than produce a miracle piece of evidence that Dodd's financial dealings were completely above board. But the judge could not rule that out, nor rule them out. They were hardly going to disprove of what Dodd had done but had come to remind the jury what a wonderful man they might be sending to prison.

Comedian Eric Sykes was first up and told them he had known Doddy for thirty years. 'To me,' he said, 'he is the greatest contributor to comedy in this country. I volunteered to come here. I thought it was the least I could do to pay my homage.' Dodd wept.

Fellow comedian Roy Hudd said that many celebrities worked for high-profile charities that obtained the greatest publicity, but Ken was not like that. He preferred to work for smaller, less well-known organisations – Cinderella charities.

John Fisher, who had been a TV producer, spoke of the ten-page letter Dodd wrote to him when his wife was in hospital with cancer. 'He is the most life-enhancing personality I have ever met in show-business,' he said.

Anne Jones talked about her fertility treatment between 1982 and 1987. Carman asked her what effect its failure had on them both. 'Great stress – probably more on him,' she confessed.

Anne organised his schedule and paid the performers who worked for him. George asked her if there was any truth in the allegation that Ken was partly paid in cash for his shows and put that money in his pocket. Anne was steadfast, 'None whatsoever.'

Carman even called the veteran *Guardian* theatre critic Michael Billington, who declared that Ken was a comic genius.

It was revealed that Ken had raised millions for Clatterbridge Hospital where his partner Anita had died in 1976. The local secretary of Equity, the actors' union, said that not only was he supportive of young artists but that he would regularly perform at shows to help older artists who had fallen on hard times.

The trial wrapped up in the fourth week, a surprisingly long time for a case where the facts seemed no longer in dispute. Brian Leveson QC rose to give his concluding remarks to the jury:

> If this trial was about Mr Dodd's rating as a comedian and entertainer, it would not have lasted very long. My words about four weeks ago were that Mr Dodd is one of the great entertainers of our generation. If this trial had been about the extent of his charitable activities, it would not have lasted very long. I described them as undoubted. If it had been about his love of the theatre, the assistance he has given to younger artists or his relations with his fellow men, it would have been over very quickly. What you are concerned with are not these issues but whether Mr Dodd had a very different attitude towards a very different institution, one which affects every one of us: the Inland Revenue.

It is often said that the best means of defence is attack, and the following day, George Carman did just that, censuring the IR for failing to produce Reginald Hunter.

'One thing we have learned from this trial is that some accountants are comedians,' he said, 'but comedians are never accountants.' As ever, Carman pulled out a classic headline-grabbing phrase, and the next day's newspapers obliged him by repeating it.

Carman pointed out that since the Inland Revenue had not produced any evidence that Dodd had been paid in cash by reputable promoters, it switched the charge to 'inflated expenses'. He reminded the jury that Dodd had opened his offshore accounts in person, and this was hardly the behaviour of a criminal. He knew that Dodd could be strange and eccentric, but he had called the numerous character witnesses to reveal the true nature of the man.

Carman's concluding words to the jury were, 'We ask you to find, by a verdict of not guilty, that Ken Dodd's life reflects the life of a man who lived up to the advice to be found in Shakespeare's own words: "To thine own self be true."'

Mr Justice Waterhouse, in his summing up, said that it was for the prosecution to prove that Dodd had deliberately acted dishonestly. He too seemed to think it strange that the prosecution had not called Reginald Hunter and appeared to agree with Carman's criticism of their failure to do so. He told the jury to give 'appropriate weight' to this omission.

The judge spoke for nine hours, summarising the evidence of most of the forty-four witnesses. He thought that Dodd's good character was relevant to the case. But the crux was whether the defendant dishonestly required a payment in cash because the balance of the fee was not recorded. This deliberate dishonesty was the essence of all the charges. 'If you are left in any little doubt about an essential ingredient of the count you are considering, then it is your duty to acquit the defendant on that count.'

Unanimous verdicts were requested and, after nine hours of deliberation over two days, the jury filed back into court. They had only managed unanimity on the charge of intent to defraud and the four charges of false accounting. Not guilty.

There were still three fraud charges, about which they could not reach agreement, so Mr Justice Waterhouse said he would accept a majority verdict on them. There can only have been one or possibly two jurors dissenting from the rest, as they were back in court within two hours. Again – not guilty.

Cheers rang out from the public gallery. Ken Dodd was in tears as he embraced George Carman, who had achieved the seemingly unachievable. Ken had escaped jail, and he thanked the jury for that.

Later, on the courtroom steps, he was besieged by the media and by his supporters. The police had to hold them back. 'Thank you, thank you all,' Ken told them. 'Thank God it's all over. Thanks to the thousands of people in Liverpool and Merseyside who have said prayers for me. God bless you all.'

Clutching a mug of champagne and followed by his supporters, he and Anne retired to the nearby St George's Hotel. Once more Ken addressed his supporters. 'Normally, I'm a very private man, but this trial has stripped me bare. But I shall say "Thank God" for every day from now on.'

He went on to thank Carman and said he was 'the general of the campaign. He presented all the facts and said: "This is what happened. This is the real Ken Dodd."'

The Reverend Michael Rooke of St John's Church, Knotty Ash, where Dodd had been a choirboy as a child, had held a two-day prayer vigil while the jury was considering its verdict. He announced to those assembled, 'This has literally been an answer to our prayers.'

After the verdict, George spoke to me about the case. It was his opinion that behind the clown's mask lived a man in a world of insecurity. George believed this convinced the jury that Ken Dodd was not interested in accumulating wealth. He lived to work and worked endless hours without calculating the financial benefit of such work. It was unimportant to his way of life.

George's decision to have the inside of the Knotty Ash house reflected in a video was very inciteful. He was able to show the jury evidence of the chaos in which Ken Dodd lived and his total disregard for any order or system.

George was very flattered when Ken named one of the Diddymen after him. He was fond of him as a client and considered him a comic genius. During his subsequent shows, Ken frequently made jokes about the Inland Revenue. He continued to work for many years in his usual way, overrunning every show. He loved his audience and valued them even more after his acquittal.

Following the case, Anne telephoned me and said that Ken would like to take George to dinner to thank him for representing him successfully. She wanted to know George's favourite restaurant in London. I told her it was Le Caprice. The following week, the four of us ate there. Ken was so thankful to have been acquitted and to have avoided prison. Despite his love for his fellow man, I'm not sure he could have survived it.

When the waiter presented us with the bill, Ken seized it and began to search in all the pockets of his jacket and trousers for a credit card. But, in his usual chaotic way, he had forgotten to bring one. George smiled and took the bill from Ken's hand…

CHAPTER SEVEN

SONIA SUTCLIFFE V. NEWS OF THE WORLD

'She danced on the graves of her husband's victims.'

George Carman

In the years that followed the May 1981 conviction of Peter Sutcliffe – the monstrous 'Yorkshire Ripper' – the notoriety that followed the man who murdered thirteen women and attacked many others also seemed, in no small part, to also attach itself to his wife, Sonia.

Although Sonia had not known about her husband's heinous crimes, she was pursued relentlessly by the press, desperate to get an exclusive insight into what it was like to be married to Britain's worst-ever serial killer.

She would not talk, no matter how large the payment on offer, and she continued to stay married to Sutcliffe for thirteen years, finally divorcing him in 1994. Perhaps it was this doggedness in not turning her back on the man she had first met when she was only sixteen which led some newspapers to speculate publicly about what she might have known about her husband. And if they were pursuing her relentlessly, she responded in kind with the help of her lawyers and an array of libel writs. By 1990, she had amassed more than £300,000 in damages against newspapers, including the *Bradford Telegraph and Argus*, the *Daily Express* and the *Yorkshire Post*, among others.

One such publication that was ordered to pay Mrs Sutcliffe substantial damages was *Private Eye*. In January 1981, just after her husband's arrest, the magazine claimed she had struck a deal with the *Daily Mail* for £250,000 for her story. This was not true and in May 1989, when the case finally came to trial, the magazine admitted its mistake. It also suggested she had knowingly provided false alibis for Peter Sutcliffe. This, too, it admitted was untrue.

There was one payment she admitted had been paid; this was £5,000 lent to her by John Rodgers, of the Fleet Street News Agency, in return for the first option on her story. She used the money to pay off her mortgage and maintained that John Rodgers was 'a family friend'. The money, she said, had been paid back within two years.

A veteran of libel disputes, the *Eye* knew it was bound to lose and offered to print an apology and to pay a substantial sum – not to Mrs Sutcliffe, however, but to her husband's victims. Her lawyers advised her that she could do rather better than this.

She did. When the *Eye*'s barrister asked her where she got the money to pay off all her debts, she said it was a 'private person' and the judge, Mr Justice Michael Davies, amazingly, told her she was not compelled to name them. In his summing up, the judge sympathised with Sonia for having to be in the witness box for three days, under the scrutiny of the jury, the press and the public. It might be thought that since she had brought the case, it was a self-inflicted ordeal. This does not seem to have troubled the jury who, after less than two hours' deliberation, awarded Sonia Sutcliffe £600,000 damages.

Private Eye was left reeling. The award was £100,000 more than the previous record British libel sum and the very existence of the *Eye* was now in jeopardy. Sonia Sutcliffe received £25,000 of the award immediately and the rest was pending the appeal, which was lodged immediately by the *Eye*'s lawyers.

Ian Hislop, then and now the *Eye*'s editor, said the magazine would be appealing to its readers for financial assistance. He pointed out the award was 100 times larger than that awarded to three of Peter Sutcliffe's victims, before making a comment that would go down in legal history. On the steps of the court, he said, 'If that's justice, then I'm a banana.' In typical *Eye* fashion, the subsequent appeal to readers for help was dubbed 'Bananaballs'.

If any newspaper had any future ideas of printing anything even mildly critical of the Ripper's wife, its plans would have been aborted at that very moment. Crime may not pay, but a libel win of this magnitude certainly paid off. The *Daily Star* paid her £35,000 and the *Daily Express* £75,000, just to stay out of court.

The *Eye* appealed and was saved from extinction by a stroke of luck. A journalist, Oliver Duke, had lived for eleven years with Barbara Jones of the *Mail on Sunday*. She had befriended Sonia Sutcliffe in 1987 and offered to pay her £25,000 for an exclusive interview. The paper said it could not pay money to the Ripper's wife, but instead they paid it to Oliver Duke. He paid it to Jones and believed she passed it on to Sonia.

At the appeal by *Private Eye*, on 19 October 1989, Sonia's legal team knew they were in trouble – the original trial judge had said that if the £25,000 donor had been a newspaper, that would have been 'relevant to the highest degree'. On the basis of this, the Appeal

Court judges ordered a retrial on damages. Neither side wanted the expense of this, so a figure of £60,000 was agreed between them.

Yet the writs kept coming. In late 1990, the Royal Courts of Justice hosted Sonia Sutcliffe in the compact confines of Court No. 13 as she began a libel action against the *News of the World*. 'The News of the Screws', as it was known to one and all for the amount of sex-related stories it managed to produce each week, had accused Mrs Sutcliffe of having what they inevitably described as a 'sizzling' affair with a Greek travel agent. Given her fearsome reputation, the paper wasted no time in hiring George Carman as its counsel for the defence.

For Carman, this case, presided over by Mr Justice Drake, would point the way for the branch of law that made him famous – the notoriously unpredictable field of libel. It was to be the case that made his reputation as the pre-eminent libel lawyer of his generation, raising his stock among wealthy individuals and organisations facing such troubles accordingly.

The *News of the World* had run a story saying Sonia had gone to Greece with Barbara Jones and met a man called George Papoutsis, who had come back to Bradford to stay with her. 'Sonia Loves a Ripper Double' and 'Killer's Wife in Sexy Fling' screamed the headlines. Sonia sued and, after the *Private Eye* £600,000 award, the *News of the World* quickly offered a correction and to pay her £50,000 in damages. But this was not as much as Mrs Sutcliffe's lawyers thought she could get in court.

Sonia rejected the offer and the case went to court. She engaged Eileen Pembridge as her solicitor and although they had brought the case, they obtained permission not to walk through the main doors of the court like any other client. Sonia was driven in a van with dark windows into the central courtyard. She was accompanied by two minders, who made sure that no one saw her as she emerged and went down a maze of corridors to reach the back entrance of Court No. 13. She was even allowed to use the lavatory which was reserved for female barristers.

However, in what proved to be a masterstroke, the *News of the World* applied to 'join Barbara Jones as co-defendant to the action', as she was responsible for supplying them the story of Papoutsis. If Sutcliffe won, the newspaper would have been able to claim indemnity damages and costs from Jones.

Carman realised that to secure victory for his client, he needed to cast doubt on Mrs Sutcliffe's claims that she shunned all publicity. He listed what he believed to be the payments made to her since her husband's conviction: £5,000 from the *Bradford Telegraph and Argus*, £35,000 from the *Daily Star*, £75,000 from the *Daily Express*, £25,000 from the *Yorkshire Post* and then a further payment of £7,500 and £26,500 from News Group Newspapers, along with *Private Eye*'s £60,000. His tactic was to show that she was a serial pursuer of newspapers which said something slightly adverse about her – and not only in relation to her husband.

To Carman's suggestion that she had collected all this thanks to the serial murders carried out by her husband, Sonia was offended. This was not income; it was compensation, she said.

Carman wondered if she had given any of this money to the relatives of her husband's victims. The reverse was the case. Sonia had once called these people 'grasping' when they attempted to enforce a judgment for damages against the Ripper.

She said before the jury, 'I wasn't responsible for what happened – directly, indirectly – not at all.'

'You were prepared to keep those victims out of their money, weren't you?' pressed Carman.

'I was fighting to protect what was my own,' Sonia retorted.

'Forget about the legal niceties,' Carman said, 'just concentrate on basic human morality. Do you think you should seek to keep your husband's half of the house from his victims and their relatives?'

'I had worked and slaved in the house. I did not see anything immoral about wanting to keep a roof over one's head. I haven't harmed or murdered anyone,' she replied. 'I have not sought to profit from the murders, but if wrong aspersions are being cast on me, I think I have a right to put those matters right.'

'I'm not talking about putting right. I'm talking about profit – money,' Carman clarified.

'Profit is something of the business world,' Sonia replied.

Carman handed her two documents: one referred to a £15,000 payment, the other to £10,000. He suggested they were in connection with a book about her husband.

Mrs Sutcliffe denied this. 'Not to my understanding.'

'May I put the following suggestions to you? First, that you took a conscious decision to lie on oath to the *Private Eye* jury about that £25,000.'

'I did not lie on oath,' Sonia replied.

'Second, that the nature of your lie was to mislead the *Private Eye* judge into believing that the money was no more, or no less, than a charitable loan from a personal friend of the family,' Carman said. 'Whereas the truth was that it was money advanced by a working journalist, in connection with a potential book about Sutcliffe – Peter Sutcliffe – and/or yourself.'

'It was a charitable loan,' Sonia interjected.

'And that you concealed from the jury that there were documents in existence in your possession, two documents which gave details of that advance or loan of the £25,000, and the two documents I have produced in this court today you kept back deliberately from the *Private Eye* jury.'

'I knew of the one document, and this was the spirit in which I answered all my questions.'

'And that you did it because you were deliberately evasive, although the judge himself had asked you if there was any connection with a newspaper and the judge himself had reminded you that it might be important if the *Mail*, for example, had lent you the money,' Carman continued.

'And the judge had also said that I did not need to answer who gave or loaned or whatever the money if I did not choose to,' Sonia defended.

'Oh, correct, but when you were asked whether there were any documents, was it recorded in writing? And then you descended into lies, didn't you? Because you had to? Oh, what a tangled web we weave when Sonia Sutcliffe practises to deceive.'

Commenting on these exchanges, the *Daily Express* observed that Carman had performed a cross-examination of 'inquisitorial proportions. He is a man whose hands are so delicate they could be the subject of a Fairy Liquid commercial. He clasps them before him as he questions, seeking with his eyes.'

Forty-year-old Sonia Sutcliffe remained a mysterious presence in court. She was a petite woman, always dressed in black, with her hair brushed back but her face virtually hidden behind an oversize pair of tinted spectacles. It was the same outfit she had worn during the *Private Eye* trial where Peter Cook thought she behaved in the witness box like an angry schoolmistress, aloof from the murky allegations that others were making about her.

But now, for the first time in any of her libel trials, she became incoherent and confused. She knew she had been rumbled and was on the run. She could give no convincing answer as to why she had not revealed at the *Private Eye* trial that the money had come from a journalist. Flimsy excuses that the receipt for £15,000 had been made out to her mother, who hadn't initially shown it to her, or that she had only signed for the £10,000 because 'Barbara told her it was a nonsense' would have convinced nobody.

The following day, George Carman produced more incriminating documents. She had completed an application form for housing benefit from Bradford Council in which she wrote she had no money in a building society. Carman then showed her a letter from her solicitors, telling her they had put £23,800 in her account in the Newcastle Building Society some weeks before the housing benefit application.

Again, Sutcliffe was scuppered. 'I truly believed I didn't have it. I thought it was a trifling amount. I don't actually know what I knew.' She said the loan from Barbara Jones was nothing to do with a book, just a loan from a friend.

'You were trying to pull the wool over the *Private Eye* jury's eyes, weren't you?' Carman asked.

Mrs Sutcliffe, more unconvincing now than ever, tried to deny this.

Barbara Jones, anxious to prevent herself from going bankrupt should Sutcliffe win the case, represented herself, as she couldn't afford a lawyer. She swore on oath that she had told Sonia that the £25,000 had come from the *Mail on Sunday*.

With regard to the *News of the World*'s allegation that Sonia had an affair with George Papoutsis, Sonia maintained it was nothing more than a 'peck on the cheek and an arm round the shoulder'. Sonia had telephoned Peter Sutcliffe, to whom she was still married, in Broadmoor to assure him that this was the case, after the story came out.

Carman asked her if she thought Papoutsis, who looked somewhat like her bearded husband, was a 'charming man'.

'He did not seem a polished sort of person,' she replied.

'Do you think your husband is very polished?'

'When I first met him, I thought he was an uncut diamond.'

'What about the time he was committing these murders? Did you think he was polished then?'

'I did not know he was committing these murders,' Sonia replied.

'After nine years, is it not important to publicly divorce yourself from this man by law – this man who perpetrated such atrocious crimes? Then you might have a better argument to say to the press "Leave me alone,"' Carman said. 'But while you remain his wife, you on occasion use that position with the press.'

'I do not use it,' Sonia denied.

She further distanced herself from the jury when she said:

> My husband believed he killed these women humanely. When he took a hammer to the back of their heads, they died immediately. He did not torture them while they were alive. My view is that when my husband killed these people – some were prostitutes – he was in the belief that those people were immoral, and he had a mission. He was saving their souls.

It did not take Carman long to address the jury and capitalise on these words:

> Is it not a most ironic fact that this lady, who seeks to excite your sympathy, shows no sympathy at all for the unfortunate victims of her husband's monstrous crimes and the relatives of the dead victims? And those feelings have been terribly bruised and

> wounded in this court by the chilling words of Sonia Sutcliffe. That those monstrous killings were a humane termination of life will linger long, and perhaps for ever, in your minds.

He pointed out:

> She was a witness to be treated with the greatest possible caution. She has motives of her own richly to serve. She is a lady who has obtained around a third of a million pounds, by way of damages over six years and that averages £50,000 a year tax free, so she may regard libel as a very fruitful source of income.
>
> Mrs Sutcliffe has said that the *News of the World* article was the most degrading thing ever written about her. One might have thought that, in her scale of priorities, the most degrading thing would be that she was still married to Peter Sutcliffe. She has not sought to distance herself from him, in the way that normal people might be entitled to expect. She still lived in the same house, remained close to him, visited him and has attempted to dismiss, as unfair, the description of him as the Yorkshire Ripper.
>
> She is no shrinking violet and has used the press when it was to her advantage and has vilified and condemned the press when it suited her purposes. The concept that her feelings have been gravely wounded by this article is something that, when you look at the rest of her character, her attitude and feelings, you will very much doubt.
>
> If she is entitled to any damages at all, it should be no more than a single ticket to Bradford.

This last comment was quoted in a number of the following day's papers as one of George Carman's classic put-downs. *The Observer* wrote: 'Mr Carman's closing speech was a tour de force. His genius is that he combines a fine forensic mind with that rare ability among lawyers, the gift of speaking in ordinary English. The single ticket to Bradford remark rang through the courtroom like a rifle shot.'

But then Carman delivered the coup de grace.

'She danced on the graves of her husband's victims,' he said of the claimant. 'She is a clever, confident, cold and calculating woman. She has sought to excite sympathy at every possible opportunity in the witness box. The truth and Sonia do not make good bedfellows.'

Carman had shown scant interest in the primary reason Sonia Sutcliffe had brought this particular libel action: namely, that her reputation had been damaged by the newspaper's revelation of her affair with Papoutsis, whether 'sizzling' or not. The QC wanted to establish that she had no reputation, save that of a woman wishing to make a living out of libel damages.

In Mr Justice Drake's summing up, it was fairly clear where his sympathies lay. He underlined Sutcliffe's dishonesty in the *Private Eye* case. She had said she had never received money and the £25,000 was a private loan, whereas in this case the receipts showed that at least £10,000 was payment for information.

On the fourteenth afternoon of the trial, the jury of six men and three women retired to consider their verdict. Nothing was resolved that afternoon, but on the following day, after six and a half hours of deliberation, the jury filed back into court. None of them were smiling; none of them even glanced at Sonia Sutcliffe. She knew her game was up. A well-built young woman in a print dress had been elected foreperson and she uttered the fatal words: 'We find for the defendant.' They were unanimous.

Sonia Sutcliffe sat unmoving and seemingly unmoved as counsel debated costs. They would come to around £300,000, effectively wiping out all her previous libel gains. Carman asked for a court order that £150,000 of her money, in banks and building societies, should be paid immediately, in case there was any danger of her moving it abroad.

After the verdict, Carman went across to Barbara Jones, took her hand and told her how skilful she had been in presenting her own case. With a little more training, she might be able to join his chambers. 'I think you could be an asset, my dear,' he told her.

Barbara, Sonia's former 'friend', rubbed salt in the wound:

> She is a cold, greedy woman who has never, in all the years I have known her, shown the slightest moment of compassion for those poor women whom her husband murdered. She has ridden the gravy train on libel actions for years and now that train has run into the sidings. And if I have had anything to do with it, I'm glad.

'After the *Private Eye* case,' James Dalrymple wrote in the *Sunday Times*, 'Sonia Sutcliffe felt she was an experienced witness, capable of holding her own under any kind of cross-examination, but this time, facing her across the court, was the dapper but menacing figure of George Carman QC.'

After their win, the *News of the World* executives, Barbara Jones and employees from *Private Eye* went on to a champagne celebration. Carman slipped out of the court, largely unnoticed, for a drink at his regular, Daly's Wine Bar. In the years to come, he would sit there and muse upon some of the most extraordinary libel trials ever held in British courts – trials that would cement his reputation as the man who could get almost anyone out of dire trouble.

CHAPTER EIGHT

SPORTING LEGENDS

TESSA SANDERSON V. MIRROR GROUP NEWSPAPERS

'If people damage their own reputation by their own actions, then it's rather uncomfortable for them when they come to court and seek money from a newspaper.'

George Carman

By any standards, Tessa Sanderson was (and is) a remarkable person. One of Britain's finest track and field athletes, she took part in no less than six Olympic Games, winning the gold medal for the javelin event at the 1984 Los Angeles Olympic Games – the first Black British woman to achieve such a feat. She won gold medals at three Commonwealth Games events and set numerous records throughout her sporting career.

Her successes and engaging personality made her an extremely popular figure both on and off the field. She appeared numerous times on TV and founded an academy in her name which helped to locate and train future Olympians. She was awarded an MBE (1985), an OBE (1997) and a CBE (2004).

Sanderson had few of the privileges that many of her white counterparts took with them into sport at the highest level. She was born in Jamaica and until the age of six was raised by her grandmother while her Windrush Generation parents worked to make a new life in England. She then joined her parents, growing up in the Midlands, where her athletic potential was spotted at school. Even so, she was regularly a target of racist remarks, both in school and during her career. Nevertheless, her determination to succeed took her to the very top.

In short, Tessa Sanderson's story and achievements were the stuff of legend in a way that often bestows upon those legends the status of 'national treasure'. In the late 1980s, there was no doubt that Sanderson was heading for such an honour, until a story appeared in an edition of the *Sunday Mirror* (repeated in *The People*) that the athlete had 'stolen' a man from his wife of nine years. The man in question was no shrinking violet; his real name was Derrick Evans and he ran hugely popular exercise classes in the London area. Inevitably, these would bring him a much wider audience and eventually Evans became TV's 'Mr Motivator', a popular TV fitness guru who appeared regularly on breakfast TV. In 1989, his wife, Jewel, told the papers that, while he was still living with her and their three children, he had betrayed her by having sex with Miss Sanderson on at least two occasions, one of them in Jamaica.

To say this gave Tessa Sanderson's reputation a knock is something of an understatement. She didn't deny knowing Evans; both Jamaican by birth, they had a common heritage, and she had been keen to invest in a gym he had started in Neasden in north London. Both, however, denied having sex in February 1989 while he was still with Jewel, and Tessa Sanderson sued *The People* and the *Sunday Mirror* over this slur on her reputation.

In this instance, George Carman was engaged by Mirror Newspapers to defend it. When the case was heard in February 1990, the papers had already paid £20,000 into court in damages. Newspapers (and other defendants) sometimes do this to protect themselves where costs are concerned. They try to estimate an amount higher than the damages awarded, so that the plaintiff pays the costs. In this case, if the jury found for Sanderson but awarded her less than that sum, she would be liable for costs that might run into six figures.

The crux of the case was simply 'Did they or didn't they?' By the time of the case, they certainly did, but that was not the question.

Richard Hartley QC, for Tessa Sanderson, told Mr Justice Michael Davies that the articles were 'very vicious and unpleasant'. Miss Sanderson acknowledged she now lived with Mr Evans, but she denied wrecking his marriage after meeting him by chance outside his fitness club. The pair had formed a management company and gradually their friendship developed. In March 1989, they learned that Mrs Evans had been touting her story round Fleet Street. She had said that she could understand if her husband had been seduced by someone like the glamorous US sprinter Florence Griffith Joyner, 'But he has been seduced by a ten-stone machine with more rippling muscles than him.' She alleged that Sanderson had stolen her husband, destroyed her nine-year marriage and left her struggling with the three children.

As the only issue in the case was one of timing, Carman was quick to reject Sanderson's claim that she had not had sex with Derrick Evans before the first week of February 1989.

'I'm putting to you that it almost certainly began earlier,' he said.

'That's not true,' she replied.

However, it emerged that both Sanderson and Evans had shared a double bed in January 1989, but again, any hint of sexual activity was firmly denied. Carman told the jury that it was impossible to believe that the javelin champion had not had some sexual contact with the fitness trainer then.

'Why did you do it?' he asked incredulously. 'It is not something you would do lightly.'

'I don't know,' Miss Sanderson replied.

'You would not call committing adultery with a married man being a role model for young people, would you?'

'I did not set out with the aim to go out with a married man or to steal Mr Evans away from his wife. It just happened.'

'You decided, did you not, to carry on this relationship and let it become close and sexual even though you knew he was married?' Carman questioned.

'Yes, yes, probably yes,' Sanderson said.

'Then why didn't you leave this one alone, however bad the state of it was?'

'I got close to Mr Evans, and Mr Evans more or less pursued the fact. I don't know why we didn't leave it alone. What happened just happened.'

Carman urged the jury to consider why Sanderson and Evans strained so hard to date their sexual relationship as late as possible. The answer was plain. 'If they were engaged in a sexual relationship while Mr Evans was still living in the same house as his wife,' he said, 'it makes it just a little bit more sordid, that little bit more unacceptable, does just that little bit more damage to Tessa Sanderson's image.'

Carman said the love affair would have emerged irrespective of when Mrs Evans went to the press. He added that if a glamorous woman became involved with a married man, she had to take the consequences.

'If people damage their own reputation by their own actions, then it's rather uncomfortable for them when they come to court and seek money from a newspaper,' he added.

In his final address to the jury, Carman told them Miss Sanderson had fallen from her 'high moral pedestal' by committing adultery and her reputation was 'in tatters'.

Sanderson, having turned down the Mirror Group's offer of £20,000 in compensation, ran the risk of having to pay all the costs if she lost or if the jury did not award her more than £20,000 damages.

The judge was not particularly helpful in guiding them on the amount of money they could award if they found for her. It could be enough, he said, to take a group of friends out for a Chinese meal, go on a first-class holiday to Jamaica (this was a not-very-funny dig at their night in a double bed) or buy a new car or even a house.

It took the jury two and a half hours to reach their verdict. Tessa Sanderson had been libelled and they awarded her £30,000 in damages.

In truth, it was a difficult and hopeless case to defend. Miss Sanderson's reputation was evidently not in tatters and by even suggesting that, Carman was aware that it was somewhat likely to have the opposite effect, convincing the jury that this sporting heroine was indeed telling the truth. And so it turned out.

IAN BOTHAM V. IMRAN KHAN

'It has been a time-honoured tradition to break the laws of cricket without labelling the breacher of the laws a cheat.'

GEORGE CARMAN

The game of cricket, an apparently sedate and determinedly genteel affair, has, over the years, attracted its fair share of controversy that has regularly seen its protagonists appear in court. In the late 1970s, a breakaway international league, called World Series Cricket (WSC), was launched by Australian TV magnate Kerry Packer. Many star players from a variety of countries, including England, signed up for Packer's dollar and the cricketing Establishment reacted with outrage, banning players from Test and county matches if they took part. This ended in a landmark court case brought by three WSC players which saw a ruling brought against the International Cricket Conference (ICC) for inducing the players to break their contracts with the WSC.

Several well-known cases have involved amateur cricket clubs and their proximity to houses, with legal action being launched as a result of cricket balls striking properties. The case of *Miller v. Jackson* (1977) saw the plaintiffs obtain a ruling that stopped a club from playing on its own ground, close to the plaintiffs' property. This provoked the horror of Lord Denning (a former Master of the Rolls) who, during an appeal, gave a famously whimsical judgment that began, 'In summertime, village cricket is the delight of everyone. Nearly every village has its own cricket field where the young men play and the old men watch.' The appeal was predictably upheld. Happily, women and girls now also play, and since 1998, there have been female members of the Marylebone Cricket Club after 211 years!

One of the best-known cricket-related cases was heard in the summer of 1996 and featured two of the game's biggest names: all-rounders Ian Botham and Imran Khan. In the 1970s and '80s, 'Beefy' Botham was the often-controversial hero of English cricket, delighting crowds with his exemplary, fiery batting and bowling performances. Khan was cut from a different cloth: suave, cool and sophisticated, yet no less a formidable player than Botham. Whenever England faced Pakistan, the intense rivalry between this legendary pair was obvious for all to see.

They were, and remain, very different men. Born into a wealthy Pashtun family in Lahore, Imran Khan was educated at the Royal Grammar School in Worcester and Keble College, Oxford, and played county cricket for Worcestershire. He gained a reputation as a playboy in London, taking famous young women to nightclubs such as Annabel's and Tramp, and in 1995 he married Jemima Goldsmith, daughter of the flamboyant billionaire Sir James.

Ian Botham came from far more humble beginnings. He grew up in Yeovil, Somerset, and attended the local comprehensive school, where he excelled at both cricket and football. Botham didn't attend university; instead, he joined the ground staff at Lord's, cleaning windows and rolling the wicket while dreaming of knocking sixes right out of the hallowed ground. At eighteen, he was a regular with Somerset and two years later made his international debut in a limited overs match against the West Indies. The following year, he played his first Test match against Australia.

In subsequent seasons, Khan and Botham came up against each other many times during county and international matches. In Khan's last match, the final of the one-day cricket World Cup in Melbourne in 1992, he was caught by Richard Illingworth off Botham's bowling but not before he had hit a match-winning seventy-two; Botham was out for a duck.

Their less-than-cordial rivalry might have ended there, had Imran Khan not given an interview to *India Today* in April 1994. 'There is a lot of racism here,' he said:

When Bob Willis or Fred Trueman were tearing the heart out

> of Indian or Pakistani batsmen, we never heard an outcry about short-pitched bowling. How come the noise started when the West Indian and Pakistani bowlers started winning matches with their fast bowlers? How come we never heard about slow over rates until the West Indies fast bowlers came along? Australians can get away with anything because they are white. There is a lot of racism in this society. A lot of people such as Lamb and Botham making statements like 'Oh, I never thought much of him anyway and now it's been proved that he's a cheat.'

Later in the interview, Khan was asked about his belief that English cricket had a class problem. He was quoted as saying, 'Yes, look at Tony Lewis, Christopher Martin-Jenkins and Derek Pringle. They are all educated Oxbridge types. Look at the others, Lamb, Botham, Trueman. Differences in class and upbringing make a difference.'

Botham was outraged and instructed his solicitor to write to Khan to demand a retraction of his comments and a public apology: 'It is totally unjustifiable to allege publicly that Ian Botham is a racist motivated by hatred … Your comments on Ian's class, education and upbringing are grossly insulting, not only to Ian but to his parents and family.'

There was no satisfactory reply received, so on 21 July, Botham issued a writ for libel to Khan, and the next day, Allan Lamb followed suit. Both were convinced that Khan would apologise, but he didn't, and more than two years later, on 15 July 1996, the case came to court.

Botham was also suing Khan over a report in *The Sun* which, he claimed, accused him of ball-tampering – something he said he had never done. Khan, who denied libel, said his words were taken out of context. In this instance, ball-tampering consisted of lifting the seam of the ball with the fingernail to give the bowler an advantage. Khan freely admitted he did it himself, on one occasion with a metal bottle top.

Khan engaged George Carman to defend him. The onus was on the plaintiffs, Botham and Lamb, to establish that Khan's words were defamatory – i.e. that they would make a reasonable person think worse of them.

Opening the defence case, George Carman QC said it was 'a thousand pities that these great warriors of sport could not have made their peace and shaken hands'. He told the jury that Khan had written letters to Botham and Lamb, offering them in July 1994 a 'golden opportunity' to set the record straight. This, Carman said, would have made the vital points that Khan had been seriously misquoted in the *India Today* article and never suggested Botham and Lamb were racist and would also have made it plain that he had never accused Botham of cheating. Furthermore, Khan had intended to express regret if he had been misunderstood by others and caused distress to anyone.

Carman added that the trial was emotionally charged, with issues of race, class and country. However, he urged the jury to put aside 'all preconceptions of prejudice, all sympathies, all emotions', to keep cool heads and use 'the searchlight for the truth'.

Botham, represented by Charles Gray QC, was first in the witness box. Rolling a cricket ball in the palm of his hand, he told the court he had first read Khan's accusations in *The Independent*. Gray asked him what his reaction was. 'Anger,' Botham replied. 'I was just very screwed up inside. I couldn't understand what this was about. I thought we'd got rid of the days of amateurs and professionals. To me, cricket is open to anyone. It is not an elite sport.'

He went on to say he was 'very proud' of his background and

appreciated the sacrifices his parents made on his behalf. His mother would be very upset to hear the exact nature of the accusations – 'and rightly so'.

Racism was something he had fought all his life. He wasn't bothered whether a player was 'green and yellow with red spots and comes from Mars'. He recalled a time he had intervened, when Viv Richards, the former West Indian captain, was called a 'black bastard' and explained how he left his home county club of Somerset in protest over its treatment of Richards and Joel Garner, both Afro-Caribbean players. Also, he had shared a room with people of colour on many occasions.

Regarding ball-tampering, Botham denied he had ever done it. During the case, many famous players were questioned about their views on ball-tampering and whether it was regarded as cheating. Mike Atherton said it was 'part and parcel' of the game. Others, among them David Lloyd, the England coach, said he did not accept the practice. Derek Pringle said that using a fingernail was 'fair play'. David Gower had never seen Botham tamper with a ball. Brian Close had been warned on this matter before. On the ninth day of the trial, Carman advised his client to withdraw the specific allegation of cheating, which Khan did.

A moment of amusement was provided when Geoffrey Boycott was called into the witness box and asked to give his address. He did so, ending 'Yorkshire WF4 2JQ. That's in England.'

'It hasn't declared a state of independence, then?' Carman observed.

If the wasted days on ball-tampering had not been enough to boggle the minds of the jurors, Carman now wanted to let them know that Botham, however great a cricketer, was no angel when it came to his behaviour on foreign tours. Had he a reputation that could now be damaged by a quote in an Indian magazine which Imran Khan said was taken out of context?

Carman questioned Botham about previous newspaper allegations made against him regarding smoking cannabis and having sex with women in Auckland and a dalliance with a Miss Barbados on a West Indies tour. Carman wondered why Botham had not sued on those occasions. Botham said he hadn't enough money, so he did not wish to incur the costs. Carman suggested to him that the reason was that the allegations were true.

'Are you a truthful man?' asked Carman.

'Yes, sir, I'd like to think so,' Botham replied.

'Always?'

'As often as you can be. We are not all saints. I once broke a window at school. We all do something wrong.'

Regarding the sex and cannabis allegations, Botham agreed he had issued a writ for libel and had told a press conference that he had never smoked marijuana in his life.

'That was a lie, wasn't it?' questioned Carman.

'No, as I had to take legal advice. I was confronted by journalists and when you do that, you tend to freeze. It was a natural reaction.'

'It was a lie, wasn't it?' pressed Carman.

'Yes, sir,' Botham relented.

Botham took issue with Carman over his claim that he made a joke during a radio programme that Pakistan was 'the kind of place you sent your mother-in-law for a month with all expenses paid'.

'No,' replied Botham tartly, 'I said for two weeks.' The court erupted into laughter but was silenced by Carman.

'That was a disgracefully offensive observation to the people and cricketers of Pakistan,' he said.

'If that's the way you look at it,' Botham replied. 'I think I've been more offensive about Australia than Pakistan.'

Botham later wrote in his autobiography:

> For three long and boring days, Carman raked up the past, throwing any mud he could lay his hands on in the hope that some of it stuck. He went through the whole menu: Miss Barbados, sex, drugs, rock and roll. Carman's performance was a tour de force. Snarling, sarcastic and bullying, it was obvious he was trying to provoke me into losing my temper. But I refused to let him.

Charles Gray told Mr Justice French and the jury that it was a 'vile and defamatory' slur to say that cricketers who had spent their careers competing against teams from all over the world were racist. It was a particularly insidious allegation to make against South African Allan Lamb. And ball-tampering was 'cheating, according to anybody's right-thinking definition of that word', he added.

He claimed Khan was motivated by malice and went 'gunning' for the England players, because of his horror at the publicity given to his confession about ball-tampering.

Khan, Carman insisted, had not accused either man of being racist but had criticised the section of the tabloid press which referred to 'Paki cheats'. Khan also denied calling anyone – and specifically Botham – a cheat in *The Sun* article.

Khan told the jury, 'Sport was meant to unite and not divide.'

Carman told the jury that Botham and Lamb seemed to hold grievances against the English cricketing authorities. Botham's was apparently that they treated him differently from Khan, and Lamb's that he was fined when he broke his contract to speak out in the press about ball-tampering. Carman asked the jury to consider whether they approached the case with 'some kind of personal agenda'.

He added that the action Botham and Lamb had brought against Khan was 'contrived and hollow'. He concluded, 'We now know that from the village green to Lord's, it has been a time-honoured tradition to break the laws of cricket without labelling the breacher of the laws a cheat.'

In his own summing up, Charles Gray described this as 'absolute bunkum'.

The jury, after its first deliberation, returned to report that it had failed to reach a unanimous verdict. The judge told them that a majority decision of 10–2 would be acceptable. The jury then deliberated for almost a further five hours before returning the decision in Khan's favour, that he had not libelled Botham and Lamb.

At the verdict, the former England stars looked stunned while Khan grasped the hand of his pregnant wife, Jemima, and whispered, 'We've done it.'

As he left the courtroom, Khan said, 'I thank the Almighty.'

Botham and his wife remained stony-faced in their front-row seat. Botham once looked across at Khan's delight – and hastily looked away.

Khan said:

> We are overjoyed by the verdict. This backs what I have been saying about ball-tampering over the years. I have never called anyone a racist or low class or a cheat. I am sad this had to come to court. I hope that once and for all, the issue of ball-tampering will now be dealt with by the ICC.

Minutes after the verdict, Khan appeared live on CNN and said he would have been bankrupt had he lost. 'A complete exercise of futility,' he added. 'I mean a ridiculous situation to be involved in a case like this when I have something much more important in Pakistan.'

Asked what difference the verdict made, he said, 'The only difference this is going to make is that finally I can concentrate on our justice movement. I have been really tied up with this case for the past two years and for the past month, really involved in it.'

Khan's solicitor, Howard Cohen, said he was 'absolutely delighted' and that Khan would pay only a 'very small proportion' of the costs, which for Botham and Lamb were estimated at around £500,000.

In a brief press conference held outside his solicitor's offices shortly after the case ended, Botham expressed feelings of astonishment over the result.

'I'm a little confused as to how it went against us,' Botham said. 'If you had been there for two-and-a-half weeks, then I think it's a conclusion you are entitled to come to and it's one I came to.' Botham said he had fought for his dignity and honesty and added that he did not feel that the verdict had affected his reputation.

'Imran Khan had to withdraw justification and therefore had to admit I was not a cheat, which is why I'm finding it confusing. I'm sure other people will find it confusing as well,' he added.

On the issue of the costs, Botham said he had not had time to think about the implications, but he added, 'Life goes on. I'll just have to do a couple more road shows to pay for it.'

The veteran cricket commentator Henry Blofeld wrote:

> Mr Carman's mood of doubts, despair, predatory anticipation when he had cornered a witness and resigned irritation when a witness failed to answer the question, all hit home.
>
> The cunning old silver fox had been at his inimitable best.

Bouncy, abrasive, lightning fast to spot a weakness and always moving at his own pace. He never missed a trick.

CHRISTOPHER BRASHER V. CHANNEL 4

'As soon as they know it's me, they'll settle.'
GEORGE CARMAN

When Chris Brasher, the runner, told a legal friend he was going to see George Carman about his long-running libel case against Channel 4, the advice came back: 'Don't ask him about the weather. He'll charge you a fortune.'

Keep on Running, a programme in a series Dispatches transmitted in March 1991, alleged that Brasher and his friend and business partner John Disley had enriched themselves personally from the London Marathon event, which they founded in 1981. To uphold their reputations, they knew they had to sue the broadcaster, but negotiations on a settlement were as long running as the annual race, going on for almost five years.

Disley was the lesser known of the two. Brasher was a national figure through athletics and it is worth looking at the reputation he sought to preserve.

It could be said he established it in four minutes when he was only twenty-five. It could also be said that he was one of the few athletes in history who sprang to international fame by not winning a race.

In the early 1950s, British athletics was in the doldrums. The runners had returned from the 1952 Helsinki Olympic Games with only one medal – a bronze for John Disley. Something had to be done to restore the country's reputation for middle-distance running.

Athletics were dominated by young men from Oxford and Cambridge, the cream of whom were invited to join the Achilles Club. It was there that Brasher met the old Harrovian Roger Bannister, the fastest miler in Britain. Bannister had failed in Helsinki and after the games wrote to a fellow Achilles man, Chris Chataway, saying he intended to attempt to break the mythical four-minute mile and wanted Chataway as his pacemaker.

'Doctors and scientists said that breaking the four-minute mile was impossible, that one would die in the attempt,' Bannister, himself a medical student, confirmed.

Chataway was working for the brewing company Guinness, while training with Brasher under the legendary Viennese coach Franz Stampfl. Bannister joined them and Stampfl pointed out the fairly obvious statistic that to break the four-minute barrier, you needed to run each of the four laps of the track in sixty seconds. Brasher could lead for the first two, Chataway for the third and then Bannister would go for it alone.

On 6 May 1954, the three men went to their jobs in the morning as usual, then took the train to Oxford for an Amateur Athletic Association match against the university. The mile was scheduled for 6 p.m. Brasher, after a false start, led the first half mile in one minute and fifty-eight seconds, but when Chataway took the lead, the time for three laps was three minutes and 0.4 seconds – just behind schedule. Bannister, as planned, ran like the wind for the last lap.

The men waited anxiously for the time that the four stopwatches would record. Norris McWhirter, the representative for *The Guinness Book of Records*, announced through his megaphone that Bannister had broken the track record, the British record and the world record in a time of 'three...' and at that point his words were inaudible due to the cheers of the crowd. It was, in fact, three minutes and 59.4 seconds, making sporting heroes of all three men.

Chris Brasher only scraped on to the British team for the 1956 Melbourne Olympics but was first past the post in the steeplechase final. Initially, he was disqualified for interfering with another runner, but after three hours, the judges' decision was overturned and the following day, in a postponed ceremony, he was duly awarded the gold medal.

He remained in the public eye, whether as a journalist on *The Observer* – 'Are you so big-headed because you won an Olympic gold medal, or did you win the gold medal because you were so big-headed?' the editor is reputed to have asked him – or a BBC executive or a prominent sports organiser.

It was wearing the last hat that he proposed to the Greater London Council (GLC) that there should be a London Marathon, as there had been in Boston since 1897 and New York since 1970. The GLC agreed, providing it was a charitable event with the money raised by entry fees and sponsorship being used to fund sport in the local boroughs. In March 1981, 7,000 runners started in Greenwich Park, including Brasher himself who, at the age of fifty-two, ran the twenty-six miles and three hundred and eighty-five yards in under three hours. Within a few years, it became the biggest marathon in the world. Millions were raised for charity via runners' sponsorship.

However, there was controversy. Brasher was later to concede it was possibly unwise to send out with the entry forms an advertisement for a running shoe company which he partly owned with John Disley. Undoubtedly, the take-up was to make him and Disley rich men. In 1983, the turnover in Fleetfoot was £1.7 million. By 1988, it had grown to £34.5 million.

At the same time, much of the money raised from entry fees

that was charitably promised to be given to sports in London was instead diverted to bringing in big international names in the marathon world.

Moreover, Brasher had gained a reputation for verbal bullying, sometimes reducing people on his staff to tears and causing several resignations. He even fired his assistant race director (and former friend) David Griffiths. Griffiths appealed to the marathon's board of governors. He was the fourth senior member of staff who had been fired or quit.

Duncan Campbell, who advised the GLC on civil defence, was a runner and a journalist on the *New Statesman*, was not a fan of Brasher and wrote a memo to the GLC leader, Ken Livingstone, to find out what had happened to the marathon money.

He backed this up with an article in the *New Statesman*:

> On Monday the governors of London Marathon Limited, a registered charity founded by the Greater London Council in 1980 to provide recreation and sports facilities in London, met to give their verdict on the leadership struggle at the top of the race organisation. The growing row has helped bring to light allegations of deliberate concealment of profits, improper financial payments, lavish hand-outs to athletes and their agents and reticence about 'honoraria' paid to officials, like the ex-Olympic runner Chris Brasher, now sixty-two, founder and Race Director of the Marathon … The row was the culmination of a ten-year-long history of dissatisfaction with Brasher's stewardship.

Campbell went on to point out that a former press officer, Mike Butcher, who had left after a row with Brasher, called him 'truculent and abrasive'.

In the event, the governors backed Brasher and agreed to terminate Griffiths's contract. But Campbell's company, IPTV Limited, went ahead with the Channel 4 documentary which was to repeat allegations of fraud and dishonesty.

A preview of the programme in the *Evening Standard* noted: 'What emerges is truly disturbing. Brasher's critics say that his insistence on dominating every facet of the Marathon with an imperious, irascible style is now sapping the organisation's strength.'

Brasher and Disley made an application for a High Court injunction for the programme not to be shown. It was delayed, but Channel 4 assured Mr Justice Morland that everything in the documentary could be shown to be true and it went out on 20 March 1991.

Nick Pitt summarised the main points in the *Sunday Times*:

1. Disley and Brasher used their position in the London Marathon to promote their business distributing running shows.
2. Monies which should have been paid directly to charity were retained by the London Marathon Company.
3. Consultancy payments were made by the London Marathon to a company controlled by the wives of Brasher and Disley.

The programme prompted the Fraud Squad, the Inland Revenue and the Charity Commissioners to investigate Brasher. It also prompted him to sue Channel 4 for libel.

Negotiations between solicitors for both sides went on for three years. Neither party wanted the huge expense of a court case, and it seemed that by 1993, the action had become dormant. But Brasher, whose reputation had been badly sullied by the programme, was determined to revive it.

In this instance, fortune favoured the brave. Unlike the BBC, Channel 4 had libel insurers, which would cover any award made against the TV company. During these protracted negotiations, the channel fired its solicitors, Richards Butler, and changed its libel insurers. But the original two were obliged to be responsible for the Brasher case. However, they now had no great loyalty to the channel and perhaps wanted to settle the case as cheaply as possible, regardless of whether the allegations were true or false.

An important step in any libel case is the production and exchange of witness statements, which show each party the strength of the respective cases. There was a deadline for this in mid-January 1995. By then, Brasher's solicitors had prepared thirty-five witness statements. Richards Butler had prepared none. On instructions from its libel insurers, all it had done was to pay £40,000 into court – effectively an offer to Brasher to drop his case.

This seemed strange, as Channel 4's lawyer had cleared the programme for transmission on the grounds that there was no libel in it. But the fired solicitors and insurers no longer had any ongoing obligation to the channel and nobody at Channel 4 seemed interested in fighting this distant problem.

However, Duncan Campbell and IPTV did. Fearful, perhaps, that they might take action against the people who were supposed to be representing them, the solicitors applied for a further two weeks in which to provide their statements. They managed to put together five, three of which were from the men who made the programme.

A date for the trial had been set some time earlier for June 1995, with an estimated duration of six weeks. Were Channel 4 to lose, the cost to the insurers could run into the millions. Brasher's solicitors, sensing they had the defendants on the run, demanded a craven apology that all of Campbell's allegations were untrue.

On 19 December 1994, Channel 4's solicitors paid £100,300 into court – £85,100 for Brasher, £10,100 for Disley and £5,100 for the London Marathon Company. It wasn't accepted. So they upped it to £220,100, £150,100 and £10,100, respectfully.

It was at this point that Chris Brasher went to see George Carman. He had read the papers and was happy to take on the case. 'The trouble is', said George with a smile, 'that as soon as they know it's me, they'll settle. Which is good news for you but bad news for me, as I won't get my daily rate in court.'

He was right. On Tuesday 23 May 1995, the opposing parties went before Mr Justice Waller in the High Court. Carman saw no reason why John Disley should not have parity with Brasher, so the agreement for the judge's approval was £380,00 each for Brasher and Disley. Channel 4 and the *New Statesman* were also faced with a costs bill which brought the total settlement package to more than £1.1 million.

Carman told the judge:

> The two men who founded the marathon in 1980 were caused serious distress and damage by the magazine publication in July 1990 and the broadcast in the Dispatches series in March 1991. It was alleged that they had been consistently guilty of fraud, deception and dishonesty, but this was entirely untrue.

Brasher said afterwards:

> As a former sports editor of a national newspaper, my normal inclination is not to rush into libel action against the media. However, these allegations were so outrageously untrue and hurtful that we had no choice but to seek retribution through the courts.

> Now our reputations have been completely cleared. I am only sorry that it has taken four years – four years of hell for us and our families – for the *New Statesman* and Channel 4 to admit that the allegations made were completely unfounded.

Chris Brasher bought himself a racehorse with his winnings, named Dangerous Precedent.

Duncan Campbell's reputation was not harmed by the settlement. He had continued to remain chairman of New Statesman Publications and in the early 2000s exposed the police shortcomings in Operation Ore, which accused more than 7,000 Britons of downloading child pornography.

CHAPTER NINE

JANI ALLAN V. CHANNEL 4

'You saw a bottom. What colour?'

George Carman

In the unpredictable world of libel, it is occasionally the fate of not those bringing a case but those associated with it to become the inadvertent star of the show. Such was the position of Eugène Terre'Blanche, the charismatic South African leader of that country's biggest white separatist militant movement, the Afrikaner Weerstandsbeweging (AWB).

Terre'Blanche was a notorious racist who could not and would not accept that in the late 1980s and early 1990s, the tide was turning away from his kind as apartheid ended. For a while, it appeared that Terre'Blanche and his supporters might pose a real – and armed – threat to the emerging African National Congress (ANC) government. It was not to be, yet there was no doubt that for a few years at least, Terre'Blanche was a menacing bogeyman who epitomised all the ills of South Africa's past.

Until, that is, a libel trial at the High Court in London during the summer of 1992. A prominent South African journalist, Jani

Allan, accused Channel 4 of alleging that she'd had an affair with Terre'Blanche, arising from a documentary about the AWB leader made by British director Nick Broomfield. She had interviewed Terre'Blanche several times, memorably stating in one article that she had been 'impaled on the blue flames of his blowtorch eyes'. Yet she was adamant she'd never had an affair with him.

Unfortunately for her – and arguably even more so for him – these denials were examined forensically in court in a case which, among other things, examined evidence about Terre'Blanche's underpants (green, full of holes) and his bottom (large and white). If humour, intentional or otherwise, is the best weapon against tyranny, this was a masterclass in cutting a would-be tyrant down to size.

At the time of the trial, Jani Allan was forty years old, based in Cape Town and writing for various South African newspapers and magazines. Her good looks (she was a former model) and breathless prose style impressed both editors and readers alike, and in 1987 she was named as 'the most admired person in South Africa' by the country's *Sunday Times*. She was certainly no intellectual slouch; a trained concert pianist, she made her debut with the Johannesburg Symphony Orchestra at the age of ten and was an accomplished artist and photographer. As a journalist, she interviewed the prominent political voices of the day, including Winnie Mandela and Zulu leader Mangosuthu Buthelezi. And, of course, Eugène Terre'Blanche.

Following the 'blowtorch eyes' interview, Allan attended several AWB rallies and was filmed and photographed with Eugène, fuelling the rumour that they were having an affair, which they both denied. This was belied by the fact that a year later, an acrimonious battle ensued in the press resulting in Allan taking legal action against Terre'Blanche, because of his repeated 'nuisance contact'. What nuisance could he be causing her? We never found out, as the case was settled out of court.

However, when Broomfield, an incisive documentary-maker, made a film about Terre'Blanche for Channel 4 entitled *The Leader, His Driver and the Driver's Wife*, the subject of Jani Allan surfaced again, this time for the British public. Broomfield used snaps of Jani's modelling days and mentioned the rumour that she had had an affair with the AWB leader.

Allan was outraged and managed to obtain £40,000 in out-of-court settlements from the *Evening Standard* and *Options* magazine, for repeating the allegations.

However, Channel 4 itself was not so nervous, and when, in 1992, Allan sued it for presenting her as 'a woman of easy virtue', it decided to fight the case. Allan was represented by Peter Carter-Ruck, with Charles Gray as her QC. Channel 4 instructed George Carman QC. His junior was Adrienne Page; his solicitor was Susan Aslan. Mr Justice Potts heard the case in the presence of a jury.

Allan was at pains to emphasise her distaste for Terre'Blanche – a volte-face from their initial meeting. Indeed, she went as far as calling him 'a pig in a safari suit'. For some reason, though, he kept pestering her, even turning up at her house. Charles Gray QC did not enquire why this happened or whether there might have been earlier encouragement from her. For herself, Allan said she would never have an affair with a married man – a statement that would be disproved in strange and dramatic circumstances.

On the second day of the trial, a motorcycle dispatch rider delivered a paper parcel addressed to George Carman at the Royal Courts of Justice. In it was Jani Allan's private diary, written eight years previously. There was no indication as to who had sent it. Allan had noted explicit details of sexual acts between her and a man named Ricardo, a married Italian airline pilot.

According to Jan Tomalin, solicitor for Channel 4, and Susan Aslan, the diary was like a teenager's book, with red lip stickers over it. It referred to sexual encounters while stoned and drunk. Rumours abounded as to where this diary had come from – it later emerged it had been left at the home of a couple Allan had once stayed with in London.

To say that it was embarrassing is an understatement. Allan later described Carman's reaction to the diary's appearance: 'Like an amateur magician producing a rabbit from a hat, he triumphantly brandishes a hard-cover notebook. Electricity runs through the court like a silent fuse.' For her part, Allan claimed that the acts she'd described were nothing but 'fantasy'.

The diary, of course, was manna for the defence. Carman reminded her that she had once said that she 'would never commit adultery with a married man, because it would be against her moral principles'.

'Yes, I have said so,' she confirmed.

'But you would commit sexual foreplay with a married man?' Carman questioned.

The judge intervened, to find out if she now admitted to an affair.

'I suppose you would call it an affair,' Allan said. 'There wasn't absolute sexual intercourse.'

'It is with regret, one has to say, you would never have revealed you had sexual foreplay with this man, until you were confronted with these documents,' Carman noted.

'I am aware there is something deeply hypocritical about saying I didn't have an affair because I didn't have intercourse. I am aware that is why I'll be viewed as somebody not telling the truth,' she said. 'I'm not sure if actual intercourse is the only thing that makes it an affair or whether foreplay and flirtation is an affair.'

'Not only do I suggest that you are a liar but you are a hypocrite because you tried to portray yourself as a woman who would not have a sexual affair with a married man,' Carman stated.

'I understand,' Allan replied. 'I was a lot different then than I am now.'

'You have lied about your sexual relationship because it is easy to lie – because you think that is the way to obtain more damages.'

'Whatever award is given for libel, being cross-examined by you would not make it enough money,' she replied, adding to the list of memorable soundbites emanating from the trial.

Then she landed a rare custard pie of humour on Carman when she told him, 'You have milked this diary so much it is practically mooing.' He acknowledged the effectiveness of the jibe before turning to the evidence of some of Allan's friends, who were by now very much in the 'former' category.

Carman said that Marlene Burger, a friend and news editor at the Johannesburg *Sunday Times*, would testify that Allan entertained Terre'Blanche at her flat.

'He would arrive and you would make a meal for him out of an Afrikaner speciality sausage, called a boerewors, with scrambled eggs,' Carman stated.

'That is not true,' Allan insisted.

'This caused some amusement, making this sausage, because there has been graffiti on the walls of Johannesburg saying "Jani Allan Loves Boerewors". It had crude sexual connotations as it also meant a man's sexual organs,' Carman said.

'It caused me tremendous pain and upset,' Allan replied.

Giving evidence, Marlene Burger told the court how Allan had hoped Terre'Blanche would marry her and how her attitude to him changed dramatically after his decision to stay with his family. 'She became extremely and increasingly vitriolic about him,' she said. She also alleged that Allan had attacked Terre'Blanche with a riding crop and that he rang Allan at her flat to say he was leaving his wife, in order to marry her.

Charles Gray QC countered that the claims were 'utterly unfounded and wholly untrue'.

Later, another 'friend' and flatmate of Jani Allan, Linda Shaw, a Welsh-born journalist, said that Allan saw sex as a 'trump card' in which she fancied herself as a future First Lady of South Africa, under the presidency of Terre'Blanche:

> She was incredibly excited and babbling about how wonderful Eugène [Terre'Blanche] was and how she had never met such a devastating man and how charismatic he was. I initially thought she was joking, but it soon became clear she wasn't. She said she was in love with him and that she wanted to marry him ... Jani was obsessed with finding a husband and preferably a wealthy, powerful husband ... One time, she told me, she was going to let him kiss her. They kissed in a parking lot. She said he had a flat in Pretoria and she had had sex with him in the flat. She said he was 'a great lay but a little heavy'.

Carman then asked about a claim that Shaw looked through a keyhole and saw Allan and Terre'Blanche having sex.

'I saw this huge man standing in my room undoing his shirt buttons,' Shaw said. 'He claimed that Jani said I liked sex and I was a whore and he had come to have sex with me.'

'What did you do?'

'I thought he was going to rape me. I told him that I'd call the police. He called me a whore. I tried to get rid of him. Eventually, he left. I sat up, got dressed, locked the door and sat there shaking,' Shaw replied. 'Then I heard the stomping of feet past my bedroom door. They went into Jani's room. Then I heard this incredible noise, like she'd turned on every electrical appliance in her room, there was the TV, radio, scrambled music and noise.'

'When you heard this, what did you do?' Carman asked.

'I was absolutely petrified. I thought he was hurting Jani and using the noise to cover up the sound of her screams. I crept along and tried calling her name. There was no response,' Shaw remembered. 'I tried knocking. I called out. I turned the handle and it was locked. It was then that I looked through the keyhole.'

'And what did you see?'

'I saw Jani's feet. Her knees were up. This large white bottom was on top of her.'

'Could you recognise Miss Allan's feet?'

'Yes,' Shaw replied. 'She was very neurotic about her feet. She thought she had a gnarled toe and she was always asking me to reassure her.'

'You saw a bottom. What colour?' Carman enquired.

'White.'

'Sex and shape?'

'I didn't see the genitals. It was a large bottom. It was on top of Jani, rising up and down,' Shaw said.

'Indicating sexual activity?'

'Yes. From what I had seen of Terre'Blanche, the bottom was the right size and shape for him.'

According to Shaw, Allan later said to her, 'Sweetie, you've had a nightmare.' Indeed...

Jani Allan later commented that 'one of Carman's gifts as an advocate is to plant a lasting image or phrase in the minds of the jury'. That of Terre'Blanche's 'lilywhite, Aryan bottom' was one that the media would pick up on worldwide.

Allan's QC, Charles Gray, dismissed Shaw's 'wildly unlikely' testimony and stressed the physical impossibility of her claim. He continued to express that her field of vision through the keyhole would not be sufficient to support her claim.

He produced from a brown paper bag a replica lock and keyhole, which he proposed to ask the jury to inspect, to see whether the spectacle would have been visible.

George Carman immediately leapt to his feet to object and the jury was sent out while legal argument followed. Carman was able to illustrate that the exhibit bore no resemblance to the real one. Therefore, it was not admissible. The judge ruled in his favour.

Later, Terre'Blanche's former aide Kays Smit was called to give evidence for Channel 4. He was interviewed in London by Jan Tomalin and Susan Aslan. Smit was leader of a white supremacist movement that considered the AWB rivals. They described him, following a meal at Rules restaurant, as 'a cultured man, very charming, possessing an extreme mindset, but had the sense to keep his political views to himself'.

Smit said he was telephoned at 3 a.m. one day by Jani Allan and was told to come to her Johannesburg flat. He believed that Terre'Blanche and Allan were having an affair, having observed both their cars parked outside her flat on various nights.

When Smit arrived on this occasion, Jani wanted to get rid of her lover. Terre'Blanche was asleep on a couch, snoring loudly and clasping a wine glass to his chest. He was naked apart from a khaki jacket around his shoulders and a pair of underpants.

George Carman innocently enquired what the underpants were like.

'They were green, and they had holes in them,' Smit replied. 'He had a pair of khaki slacks which he could not get higher than his knees because they were too small.'

Allan had told Smit she wanted Terre'Blanche out of her flat before someone else arrived. Smit dressed Terre'Blanche and took him back to his own home.

Having been handed the gift of the moth-eaten underpants, Carman was now playing to the jury. He asked Smit where he was when he got Allan's call.

'I was in bed,' he replied, 'with my wife.'

There was laughter in court as Carman let slip the audible aside, 'A rare species, sir.'

Jan Tomalin said the evidence of Smit was 'a game changer'. He was the only witness who did not emanate from the journalistic community; he was credible. Therefore, it was difficult for Jani Allan to dispute his independent evidence. Susan Aslan said that he was very believable and had a charisma about him.

Terre'Blanche himself did not attend court, despite some persuasion to do so. Instead, he submitted a sworn statement denying that he had had an affair with Allan:

> All these attempts to exaggerate the extent of my relationship with Miss Allan will ultimately be seen for what they are – a pack of lies. I have not had a sexual relationship with Miss Allan. I have never proposed marriage to her, not even in jest. I do not know Linda Shaw.

After ten days of evidence, Carman gave his closing speech to the jury of six men and six women.

'Is this woman, Miss Allan, an innocent woman, as she would claim, unjustly wronged by a television programme?' he asked the panel.

It was Channel 4's submission that Allan's case was 'so seriously flawed in so many respects' that on analysis it was 'really unworthy of belief'.

The documents and tape recordings produced to support the defence case cast 'a flood of light' on where the truth really lay. 'They really portray Miss Allan as having been, sadly, gravely untruthful in the witness box,' Carman said.

Carman told the jury they should consider the 'compelling weight' of evidence from six defence witnesses, five of whom had spoken out in front of them:

> The case may have proved an entertainment for others but not for the witnesses involved – and above all, not for Miss Linda Shaw.
>
> You, and you alone, will decide which witnesses deserve from you a seal of approval for truthfulness. You will decide where sits the enemy of truth in this courtroom.

In his closing speech for Allan, Charles Gray QC said:

> On the one hand, we have Jani Allan saying adamantly and repeatedly to you that she never had any kind of sexual relationship with Terre'Blanche. Equally, on the other hand, we have a band, a planeload of witnesses from South Africa, each of whom, when they came into the witness box, grabbed every opportunity to assert or imply sex had taken place between Terre'Blanche and Jani Allan.

He reminded the jury they did not decide these things by adding up the witnesses on each side. He asked whether they really believed that if, as Channel 4 asserted, Allan had had a passionate fling with Terre'Blanche, she would have had the 'gall' to start the action 'founded upon a lie'.

Gray said Channel 4 had to prove Allan had sexual intercourse with Terre'Blanche. Her sexual conduct, which would normally be a private matter, had become an issue for public debate, because Channel 4 chose to drag her into the film 'quite unnecessarily and quite gratuitously'.

Of Shaw's 'keyhole' evidence, Gray said, 'I don't know what the female equivalent of a Peeping Tom is, but it must be a fair description of Miss Shaw.'

Shaw's evidence was 'wildly unlikely', he said. She could never have seen through the keyhole what she said she had seen. Her field of vision was not big enough, he added.

Gray said the jury should award Allan a substantial sum in damages. It should reflect the damage to her reputation, her indignation and upset, her anxiety awaiting the trial, her embarrassment, the harrowing ordeal she had undergone in court and the physical effect of the case.

On 5 August 1992, the judge ruled that Channel 4's allegations did not, in themselves, defame Allan. She had brought the case against the channel for presenting her as a woman of 'easy virtue'.

It took the jury less than five hours to decide that she was of easy virtue. She lost not only the case but her reputation and was faced with legal costs that would have soared to over half a million pounds.

Many years later, Jani told Nigella Lawson (who had had a drug allegation brought up in a court case):

The first mistake I made was to take the advice of the leading libel lawyer in the land, one Peter Carter-Ruck. He told me that I had been severely libelled and that I would have no future in the UK if I didn't put the record straight. I didn't take cognizance of the fact that if you are suing for libel, you are putting yourself in a legal contest with someone. The more forceful QC or the one with the best jokes will win. The truth has nothing to do with it. Also, suing for libel, I now realise, puts a kind of perverse credibility to that which you consider libelous. Thus, by my denying that I had an affair with the 'pig in the safari suit', even if people did not necessarily believe it, they thought: where there is smoke there is fire.

Nigella, you had Anthony Metzer tormenting you; I had George Alfred Carman QC, the most feared criminal barrister in the land. He subjected me to humiliation of a deeply personal kind. The kind from which one may never quite recover. Finally, grasping at straws, he suggested that I had brought the action to make money.

Jani Allan had, in a curious way, made her case a battle between Carman and herself, less so than a libel action. When he reminded her that on her first encounter with Eugène Terre'Blanche, she wrote, 'I'm impaled on the blue flames of his blowtorch eyes,' and this implied she had fallen for his charms, Allan replied, 'Mr Carman, his eyes bore into me in much the way your eyes are boring into me.'

'I'm not sure I welcome that comparison,' Carman replied.

Sandra Barwick, commenting for *The Independent*, observed:

Certainly Mr Carman's eyes are blue. There are not many other obvious similarities between him and Mr Terre'Blanche who,

> by all accounts, has a mock-heroic, military air suited to a man surrounded by neo-Nazis calling themselves the Aquila or Eagle Guard. He kept a model eagle on his desk. Mr Carman, by contrast, is an unheroic figure: a small man, tubby waisted with a small beakish nose. His eyes, and any fire, are usually concealed behind large gilt spectacles whose glass thickens in the lower half. Sometimes he peers over them.

As the session ended, she noted, 'George Carman went out into the corridor, swiftly lit up a cigarette and was surrounded by his team. The wings of his gown flew out behind him and then fell at rest. The hearing continues, but the Owl, for this moment, has landed.'

The *Daily Mail* sent along its theatre critic, Jack Tinker, for his assessment of the drama. 'ENTER THE STAR IN SILK, PLAYING COURT JESTER WITH SUAVE SUBTLETY' ran the headline. Tinker began:

> Mr George Carman QC is to the courtroom what Sir John Gielgud is to the stage, or Spencer Tracey is to the screen. He is a star performer of infinite subtlety and variety who knows that farce can be funnier and drama more dangerous than deadpan delivery.
>
> He was at his most politely silky when he gently headed the bulky Mr Kays Smit into the realms of slapstick, trouser-dropping comedy while planting ticking time-bombs beneath the reputation of the plaintiff who sat, nun-like in black, a little to his left.
>
> This was South Africa's ongoing answer to the sex-and-politics soap operas, and it was building up to its biggest scenes. Mr Carman – known as Killer Carman to his colleagues backstage – was about to demonstrate how to share a scene, while stealing the entire show.

We had the hilarious descriptions of South Africa's right-wing leader sprawled naked except for green underpants 'with holes in them'. We had the horror of hearing how Miss Jani Allan was alleged to have urged the men of his neo-Nazi party to wear khaki instead of business suits because 'it doesn't matter how expensive the suit; you can't look any better than a Jew from Rosebank.'

Not for a minute did Mr Carman indicate anything but gracious concern for all of this.

CHAPTER TEN

THE VIRGIN KING: TWO CASES INVOLVING RICHARD BRANSON

'These words cannot be misinterpreted.'

George Carman

RICHARD BRANSON V. BRITISH AIRWAYS

In 1967, Richard Branson left school at sixteen to start his own business. Fifty years later, *Forbes* magazine estimated his fortune was worth five billion dollars.

Admittedly, Branson's alma mater was Stowe, a leading English public school; he came from a distinguished lineage of lawyers and his mother, Eve, was a successful entrepreneur.

Richard ran a magazine, *Student*, which attracted so many advertisements for records that it led him into selling pop records. He undercut shop prices and eventually joining the high street with his own Virgin record store.

He saw a greater profit in actually making records, so he set up a studio near Oxford. His first release, *Tubular Bells* by Mike Oldfield, went to the top of the UK charts and then became a worldwide phenomenon when it was used on the soundtrack of *The Exorcist* in 1973, one of the biggest grossing Hollywood films of its time. It made Oldfield and Branson rich men, and Branson began to expand his business horizons beyond the world of music.

He entered the airline industry after he and his future wife Joan had their flight cancelled to Puerto Rico. Stranded on a small island airport with the other passengers, Branson managed to charter a plane there. He divided the cost of the plane by the number of seats and charged his fellow passengers $39 each to continue their journey. At that moment, Virgin Atlantic was born.

In 1984, it expanded into a competitive international airline. The obtaining of slots and flight timetables, initially from Gatwick, proved a little more complicated than his Puerto Rico charter. Worse still was the opposition to the upstart newcomer from the major American airlines and especially the newly privatised British Airways (BA).

In March 1991, Virgin Atlantic's fortunes took a turn for the better when the government finally allowed it to operate from Heathrow (much better than Gatwick, since it could pick up passengers arriving from the major European airlines) and nominated it to operate two extra flights to Tokyo. Branson was overjoyed, but Lord King, the chairman of British Airways, wasn't. He told *The Observer*:

> It seems that every time we build up a profitable route, someone comes along and says 'I'll have some of that' and the government obliges. The two extra flights to Tokyo will cost BA £250 million a year in lost revenue. That's £250 million lost to our public shareholders which has gone straight into Richard Branson's back pocket.

This was a gross exaggeration. In fact, Virgin's airline finances were precarious, with Lloyds Bank pressing them to pay back a £45 million loan. The only thing Branson could do was to sell his interest in Virgin Music to Thorn EMI, which he did for over £390 million.

It solved the airline's financial problems, but it was still haemorrhaging passengers to BA. A journalist informed Branson that BA was waging a dirty tricks campaign against them, led by their adviser, Brian Basham. There were reports that the Virgin gay nightclub Heaven was a venue for drug dealers, and there were rumours that one of its planes would 'fall out of the sky'. More tangibly, its booking system was being hacked. Passengers were offered BA Concorde flights to New York instead of their Virgin upper-class ticket. Yvonne Parsons, a regular Virgin passenger, got a call from someone 'purporting to be from Virgin reservations' saying her flight was overbooked and would she mind changing to BA? Ronnie Thomas, who ran Virgin's free limousine service for first-class passengers in New York, reported that when he and his drivers dropped them off at JFK, British Airways staff would meet them and offer them 'incentives' to fly BA instead.

In an open letter to BA's non-executive directors, dated 11 December 1991, Richard Branson claimed that an internal task force had been set up within BA, sanctioned at the highest level, with a remit to wage a 'dirty tricks' campaign against Virgin, designed to discredit and damage its business.

He claimed that smear stories were being peddled around the press by Brian Basham, questioning Virgin's financial standing and Mr Branson's other business activities.

Former BA staff also came forward and volunteered affidavits allegedly describing how they had been ordered to shred files referring to Virgin. Virgin claimed these sworn statements detailed the lengths to which BA employees were asked to go to undermine the smaller, rival airline by introducing selective fare cuts and refusing to handle Virgin long-haul passengers needing to connect to BA's European network of destinations.

Meanwhile, according to Virgin, the BA dirty tricks campaign was advancing on other fronts. In October 1991, a 48-page 'dossier' on Virgin, compiled by Basham, began to circulate among the press.

In 'Operation Barbara', a team of private detectives convinced some of BA's senior management that Branson was running an undercover operation investigating their airline. This was not true.

Branson contacted Sir Freddie Laker, who claimed his own airline had been put out of business by BA. Laker gave him the advice, 'Sue the bastards.' So Branson called George Carman.

In his autobiography, Branson wrote, 'With his white hair and impeccable manners, George seemed like everyone's favourite uncle outside the courts. Inside, he had the subtlety, tenacity and killer instinct of a praying mantis. People went to extraordinary lengths to avoid him.'

The case was set down to be heard in the High Court in January 1993. But, on 7 December 1992, Carman contacted Branson. He had been negotiating behind the scenes with BA's lawyers.

'BA have collapsed,' he told him. 'They've paid £485,000 into court. In effect, they've admitted they're entirely guilty as charged.'

It later transpired that BA's lawyers had told them they had no hope of winning. If Lord King and his management wanted to avoid the humiliation of having to stand in the witness box and be cross-examined by Carman and seeing all their activities written up in the press, their only option was to make a payment into the court and start negotiating an out-of-court settlement.

Branson had tasted blood and was of a mind to put King and

his directors in the witness box to savour his victory. But Carman counselled restraint.

'You've got to remember why you brought this case,' he said. 'You wanted the dirty tricks to stop and you wanted to clear your name. BA have admitted that you are totally right. You have cleared your name. If you persist with the case, then two things may go wrong.'

Carman outlined the first potential issue. 'The jury may award you damages, but they might think that you are such a rich man that you don't need £500,000 and just award you £250,000. That would be seen as a failure for you and a victory for BA.'

On the other hand, he said, 'If the jury were to award you less than they have paid into court, then you will have to pay both sets of costs. That could come to £3 million.'

Branson could see the logic in his counsel's advice. 'So, what do we do?'

'You have twenty-one days to take the money out of court – if you accept it.'

'So, we'll do that?' asked Branson.

'Good Lord, no,' George replied. 'I'm going to get them to give us at least £600,000. Every extra £100,000 makes an inch bigger headline.'

Carman spent the next week negotiating further with the BA lawyers and on 11 December 1992, they agreed the terms of the highest uncontested libel payment ever made in British legal history: £500,000 to Branson to compensate for the personal libel and £110,000 to Virgin Atlantic to compensate for the corporate libel.

Although the corridor was crowded outside Court No. 11 of the Royal Courts of Justice, notable by their absence were Lord King, Sir Colin Marshall and Robert Ayling, the three men at the top of British Airways. Brian Basham had 'gone abroad' and although his lawyers argued his name should be removed from the statement of apology, the judge ruled that it should remain.

Branson stood proudly with his father as Carman made public for the first time what the agreed statement was:

> British Airways and Lord King now accept unreservedly that the allegations which they made against the good faith and integrity of Richard Branson and Virgin Atlantic are wholly untrue. They further accept that Richard Branson and Virgin had reasonable grounds for serious concerns about the activities of a number of British Airways employees, and of Mr Basham, and their potential effect on the business interests and reputation of Virgin Atlantic and Richard Branson. In these circumstances, British Airways and Lord King are here now by leading counsel to apologise and to make very substantial payments to the plaintiffs by way of compensation for the damages and distress caused by their false allegations. They also seek to withdraw their counterclaim against Virgin Atlantic Richard Branson.
>
> In addition, British Airways and Lord King have agreed to pay Richard Branson and Virgin Atlantic's legal costs in respect of the claim and the counterclaim and have undertaken not to repeat the defamatory allegations which are the substance of this action.

After a theatrical pause, Carman revealed the record-breaking £500,000 in damages to Branson and £110,000 to his airline. There was a mini-uproar in the court and Carman had to raise his voice to state, 'In the light of the unqualified nature of the apology and the payment of a very substantial sum by way of damages, Richard Branson and Virgin Atlantic consider that their reputation is publicly vindicated by agreeing to settle the action on those terms.'

The only blot on Branson's horizon was the agreement that BA's counsel could say the directors of the airline were not party to any concerted campaign against Branson and Virgin.

'Let them leave it in,' Carman advised him. 'People will see exactly what it really means. We haven't heard the last of the word "concerted".'

Outside the Royal Courts of Justice, Richard Branson raised his arms and shook his fists in triumph before the hordes of photographers.

'I accept this award not only for Virgin', he said, 'but also for all the other airlines: for Laker, for Dan Air, Air Europe and British Caledonian.'

That night, every television bulletin led with the news of British Airways' humiliation.

RICHARD BRANSON V. GUY SNOWDEN

Branson was to need Carman's professional services again in January 1998 for a defamation case he brought against a rich American businessman, Guy Snowden.

The matter had its origins in Prime Minister John Major's announcement in 1994 that the UK was going to have its own National Lottery. The money spent on tickets each week would be distributed in a pre-ordained way: 50 per cent would go to the prize fund; 28 per cent to good causes (which ranged from £50 being spent to mend a broken trumpet to more than £2,000,000,000 going to the 2012 London Olympics); 12 per cent to the government in duty; 5 per cent to retailers in commission; 4.5 per cent to cover the operating costs of whoever won the franchise; and a final 0.5 per cent to the same company as profit.

Branson's eyes lit up at the opportunity for further publicity for Virgin, as the winning numbers would be chosen at prime time on BBC One. Moreover, he came up with what looked like a cast-iron bid. Virgin would not take any profit out of the money raised. All of it would go to good causes.

He sent a colleague, John Jackson, on a fact-finding mission to learn how to run a lottery and, late in the day, Jackson discovered that the king of American lotteries was Guy Snowden, the self-made billionaire son of a bulldozer driver, whose company, GTech, managed twenty-seven lotteries in the US and a further fifty worldwide. He employed 6,000 people and had patented a system which could process 90 million transactions a week.

Naturally, Branson needed Snowden on board and made contact with him. Unfortunately, knowing of the likely event of a lottery, Snowden had not only set himself up in business in the UK but even formed a consortium under the leadership of Cadbury Schweppes, which he reckoned would have as good a knowledge as any firm of the British retail outlets where the lottery terminals would be placed. GTech, as well as providing the expertise, took a 22 per cent stake in the bidding company, which was called Camelot.

When he related this to Branson, it looked as if the stable door was closed, but the Virgin boss was never one to give up easily. He later got his secretary to invite Snowden to lunch at his Holland Park house the next day.

They were joined by John Jackson for baked salmon and salad with Chablis and Branson confidently told Snowden that Virgin would win the franchise, as it was going to make the Lottery Board an offer it couldn't refuse: it wouldn't take any profit from the scheme, everything that was left over would go to good causes. After listening to Jackson and Branson and realising that they knew very little about how to run a lottery, Snowden doubted that Virgin was such a certain winner.

'If you read the government's outline prospectus, you'll see that you'll need to provide a lot of requirements to win,' he said. 'The government's regulator, Peter Davis, needs to be certain that the winner will be capable of organising the National Lottery's technology, guaranteeing its security and accurately forecasting the amount of money raised.'

Nevertheless, Branson exuded confidence. His bid – the UK Lottery Foundation – was certain to win and GTech would benefit if it was to provide its expertise to Virgin.

Snowden had no intention of helping Virgin, not least because it was too late. But at the same time, he could do without a candidate like this (there would be eight contenders) and realised that the 'no-profit' element would cause Camelot to cut down on its own projected profit.

Then the following exchange took place, or Branson and Jackson said it did; Snowden remembered it a little differently and has always denied that he attempted to bribe Branson.

'I don't know how to phrase this, Richard,' said Snowden, in Branson's account of the tale. 'There's always a bottom line. In what way can we help you, Richard? I mean, what can we do for you personally?'

'What on earth do you mean?' Branson replied.

'Everybody needs something in life.'

'Thank you,' Branson said. 'I'm quite successful. I only need one breakfast, one lunch, one dinner a day. The only way you could have helped is providing services for our bid.'

Branson then excused himself to go to the loo, but what he really wanted to do was to make a note of the American's words. It was to become known in court as the 'loo note'. Branson was convinced that Snowden was trying to bribe him, and Jackson, not unexpectedly, agreed.

This was underlined by the fact that when he came back, Snowden was preparing to leave – and no pudding. And, according to Branson, later that day – in fact, it was four days later – Tim Bell, a PR man for Snowden, called and said something to the effect, 'Guy may have said something he might regret without going into details. You're not going public, are you, Richard?'

Branson didn't exactly go public, as in making the allegation known in the press, but he told friends, his solicitor and even Peter Davis when he met him, although Davis was later unable to recall this. Its significance, evidently, was not great.

It was more important actually to win the lottery franchise. On 25 May 1994, Branson threw a champagne breakfast for staff who had worked on the Virgin bid. The announcement would arrive via a fax at 9 a.m. It was on time. Lord Young (the former Trade Secretary and his bid figurehead) lifted the piece of paper from the machine. 'Camelot', it read.

There were reporters eagerly waiting outside the Holland Park house. Branson went out to meet them. 'It's a nasty little fax,' he told them. 'Possibly the most crass move made by any government department. It's absolutely wrong. I've lost the chance to do the most important thing in my lifetime. There will be nothing else in my life that could equal this.'

In fact, he lost fair and square. But never one to go down without a fight, he had an appointment to see Peter Davis, thinking he would then have his decision overturned by the courts on the grounds of negligence and maladministration.

It was revealed that Camelot planned four times more retail

outlets to sell tickets, the regulator had found Virgin's IBM terminal and computer systems unreliable and, worse, its retention fund for administrative costs was the sixth highest of the eight bidders. An independent audit found Branson came overall fourth out of the eight.

And there the matter might have rested, had not Branson's publicity spokesman, Will Whitehorn, received a phone call in July 1995 from Mark Killick, a BBC producer. A *Panorama* researcher in America had uncovered that there were at least three indictments against GTech for bribery to secure lottery contracts. Killick had also heard the rumour that Branson had also been offered a bribe. Would he appear in the programme?

Initially, Branson responded, 'No one will believe me. I've left it two years.' But he went on the programme and asserted that Snowden had said, 'In what way can we help you, Richard?' Branson added, 'I just couldn't believe it. Nobody's tried to bribe me before in my life.' He continued, 'Later that day, I had a telephone call from one of his PR agents wishing us well … trying, I suspect, to offer us, you know, quite a considerable sum of money to move away from bidding.'

The programme was transmitted on 11 December 1995. Snowden's public reaction was, 'Mr Branson's allegations are grossly defamatory and untrue.'

Branson's reaction was to get hold of George Carman.

The case came to the High Court on 13 January 1998, four years and four months after the fateful lunch. George told the jury Branson's version of what Snowden had said at lunch, concluding:

> There is no shilly-shallying about this, no room for doubt, misunderstanding or misinterpretation. It is as plain as a pikestaff that

> what Guy Snowden was about that day was floating a bribe in front of Richard Branson in order to get him out of the bidding and pave the way for GTech and Camelot to go on without this dangerous rival.

The judge, Sir Michael Morland, had privately warned Branson not to mention *Panorama*'s allegations about GTech's US corruption, since he would have been unaware of them in 1995. Of course, Branson ignored him and outlined *Panorama*'s findings in order to prevent similar bribery in Britain.

Morland ordered the jury to ignore this part of Branson's evidence, but he was too late; the damage had been done. Richard Ferguson QC for Snowden leapt on this. 'You are trying, Mr Branson, to inject into this case every piece of dirt which you can rake up … You are seeking to expand the prejudice as much as possible.' He called Branson a 'crass amateur', a 'bitter man' and a 'fabricator of embellishments' with regard to his notes.

Snowden pretty much agreed with Branson's account of their lunch but insisted he had never used the word 'personally'.

Carman asked Snowden to agree he had said, 'In what way can we help you?' Snowden did and Carman pronounced, 'These words cannot be misinterpreted. Mr Snowden has shut the door on there being room for a mistake.'

Snowden was also forced to agree he had made payments to lobbyists in London to help Camelot's bid. He admitted, 'The whole thing looks a bit awkward.'

Peter Davis, the regulator and a witness for Snowden, stated that the presence of the Branson bid had caused the others to 'sharpen their pencils', so that more money was raised for good causes as a result.

Branson had said under oath how he had told Peter Davis about Snowden's 'bribe' the day after Davis had awarded the lottery to Camelot. Davis testified that this was not true.

But under questioning from Carman, Davis admitted he secretly confided to Sir Ron Dearing, the chairman of Camelot, that he had been concerned about GTech's methods of obtaining contracts in America.

'Are you sure Richard Branson did not tell you about his experience?' Carman pressed him.

'I'm afraid you have put doubts in my mind,' Davis conceded. This was to destabilise Snowden's case considerably.

Carman told the jury that Snowden 'did not have the courage to say that Richard Branson has lied'.

He continued, 'The defendant's case is one of complete intellectual disarray. Mr Ferguson seemed to lurch around from opening to closing, walking on a tightrope, willing to wound but afraid to strike.'

Another unspoken fact that might have had an effect on the jurors was that Richard Branson looked fresh-faced and honest, whereas the thick-necked Guy Snowden had the misfortune to look like someone who could play a member of the Mafia in an American movie.

After only two and a half hours' deliberation, the jury found for Branson, awarding him £100,000 in damages.

Once again, thanks to Carman, Branson was punching the air on the steps of the High Court. 'I don't lie and I can't stand liars. My parents always told me to tell the truth.'

CHAPTER ELEVEN

ELTON JOHN V. MIRROR GROUP NEWSPAPERS

'When you come to award exemplary damages, to punish the newspapers, you are entitled to wipe the smile off the board of directors of the Mirror Group of Newspapers.'

George Carman

In December 1992, the singer and musician Elton John was stunned to read in the *Sunday Mirror* that he was on 'a diet of death'. Playing on the fact that he'd previously admitted to being a recovered bulimic, the newspaper reported that the superstar had told 'friends' at a Christmas party in Hollywood thrown by his manager that he had a policy of chewing but not swallowing his food, an act which kept him slim and trim. He had then apparently demonstrated this to two female party attendees by chewing up a shrimp and spitting it into a napkin.

These latest set of revelations came as a complete surprise to Elton John – not least because he'd been in Atlanta on the night of the party.

A flurry of letters then ensued between Elton's solicitor, Frank

Presland, and Mirror Group Newspapers. The latter claimed that the story had been published 'in good faith' and that the paper's Los Angeles reporter had interviewed the two witnesses who were convinced that the man at the Christmas party was Elton John. Nevertheless, the paper agreed to accept Elton's version of events and were prepared to print an apology and pay damages to a charity of the singer's choice.

An apology was printed, but it was half-hearted at the very least. Presland had wanted to see a statement that admitted the story was a work of pure fiction. The paper wouldn't agree to this, and so the stage was set for a court battle.

As he prepared the case, Presland wondered which barrister he might instruct to lead the libel action. Then he remembered a case in which George Carman had been instructed and that he made a mental note then that he could use him in any future libel cases.

There was, however, an issue of coincidence to deal with first. Some years previously, I had befriended Renate John, then married to Elton. She told me that her marriage was going through a bad patch and later asked me to represent her because she and Elton were going to divorce. I sympathised with her, pointing out that I didn't do much matrimonial law and had, of late, mainly practised at the criminal Bar.

At that time, there was no direct access to barristers; all work was sent to us via solicitors. Nevertheless, she insisted that I handle it as she needed someone whom she could trust and rely upon for absolute discretion. I said that I could help her by introducing her to a matrimonial solicitor. To do this, I asked her for some details.

Renate said she thought Elton would agree to an amicable settlement and that she didn't want a penny from him. I advised that she needed to have a home and some financial stability.

Eventually, she instructed David Bultitude, to whom I introduced her as I knew he was the soul of discretion and good at keeping his clients out of the newspapers. We prepared the divorce papers and met with Elton's barrister, Robert Johnson QC. He found our suggested modest settlement unacceptable. This was based on a statement by Elton's accountants that their client wasn't well off and therefore could not provide Renate with a home of any great value or any significant maintenance.

We couldn't agree with this, and as Elton had instructed a silk, I asked George Carman to lead me for the final financial stage. He was instructed by Bultitude. We appointed an independent accountant to study the accounts and came up with a very different figure from the previous firm Elton had instructed. In the face of this, the singer's lawyers conceded that this was nearer the mark. Despite newspaper speculation that Renate received tens of millions, this was not the case. She was far from greedy. The details of the November 1987 settlement remain privileged.

Bultitude described Carman as 'having inevitably some arrogance but also magnanimity and a willingness to pause, listen and consider, even when ultimately he dismissed the points made by others'.

So, it may have come as a surprise to Elton to learn that George Carman – the man who secured his ex-wife a much better settlement than initially offered – was in the frame to represent him against Mirror Group Newspapers. Nonetheless, he accepted the lawyer's instructions and the case opened at the High Court on 1 November 1993, before Mr Justice Drake. Lord Williams of Mostyn was instructed on behalf of the *Sunday Mirror*.

During his opening, Carman made it plain to the jury that he was going to argue, as part of his case on exemplary damages (i.e.

damages aimed at punishing the defendant for the manner in which they committed the wrong against the claimant), that parts of the article were pure invention by the *Sunday Mirror*'s reporter, Tony Brenna, and/or the newspaper's editorial staff and that the newspaper was legally responsible for the former's recklessness.

It was alleged that two women who had gatecrashed the party thrown by John Reid, Elton John's manager, had first seen the star then spoken to him about his eating habits. Brenna claimed that his sources were reliable and that he had their comments about the party on tape and in writing.

Unfortunately for the *Sunday Mirror*, the tape of the pre-publication interview between Brenna and his two sources (together with the transcript of the tape) had been lost or destroyed. A transcript was available, however, of the telephone conversations which Brenna had with his two sources on 7 January 1993 and of the report which Brenna sent to London on the same day.

According to this transcript, the two women had arrived at the party by mistake and saw a man 'who looked exactly like Elton John' and who was referred to by other people as Elton. The man was eating shrimps and spitting them out into a napkin. They asked him what he was doing and he told them that it was a way of staying slim. Both claimed they thought the man was Elton John.

Carman argued that the *Sunday Mirror*'s editor would have known about Elton John's previous medical problems and should have verified the information in the freelance news story. He charged that the *Sunday Mirror* had benefited economically from publishing the story, saying that the article was 'a commercial advantage for the *Mirror* and helped to increase the circulation of the paper'.

Elton John, who attended the second day of proceedings, told the court his treatment for addiction was one of the best things he has done.

'The single most worthwhile and difficult thing I have done in my life was to admit that I had a problem with food, drugs and alcohol and begin the recovery process,' he said.

'My recovery means more to me than anything, because my life since I've been clean and abstinent has been the best three years of my life,' he added.

Worst of all, he said, his mother had read the article and thought he was going to die.

John Reid told the court that he did not know the two girls whom the *Sunday Mirror* had relied on for its information. They were gatecrashers who were on their way to another party. Whoever they claimed to have witnessed and spoken to that night, it was certainly not Elton John, who was 2,000 miles away in Atlanta.

Frank Presland said that the *Sunday Mirror* had insisted it would have been easy to settle the case.

'But it is not easy to settle with a newspaper. The problem is that when an apology is being considered, their view as to where an apology should be placed and mine are very different,' he said. 'They would have a front-page splash on the original story and then they think the place for an apology is in very small print on page seventy-two underneath the greyhound racing results.'

The judge was amused and after this case, the phrase 'under the dog results' became a term of usage.

Carman could not see the *Sunday Mirror* coming up with a scintilla of justification, but, pointedly, he kept repeating to the jury, 'It will be very interesting to see what the editor of the *Sunday Mirror* is going to say' – never more forcefully than when he concluded the evidence on behalf of Elton John and determinedly sat down to await it.

He did not have to wait long. The lawyer for the *Sunday Mirror* rose to his feet and announced, 'We shall not be calling any witnesses.'

If the jury were shocked, they were outdone by George Carman. Frank Presland recalled:

> There then ensued the most theatrical moment I have ever seen in court when George, taken by such surprise, pretended to faint and then leaned dramatically backwards, in mock surprise and horror.
>
> We knew they could not put up any witness at all; the editor would have been torn to shreds. Whenever he could, George would turn to the jury and say, 'It will be very interesting to hear what the editor has to say,' knowing that they would never dare call him.

When asked by the judge if he was ready to proceed, Carman said he was surprised the *Sunday Mirror* did not have the courage to call any witnesses. He told the judge, 'I shall need a few minutes to compose myself and to prepare for my speech, as I have not had much time.' He could, of course, have continued straight away, but he wanted to give the jury more time for the facts to sink in.

Frank Presland was amused by Carman's Oscar-winning performance. 'We went out for twenty minutes to have a cigarette and a chat,' he recalled:

> On his return to court, he gave a devastating final speech, a marvellous descriptive passage to the jury; it was a mastery of jury

advocacy. It all turned on exemplary damages. Looking straight at them, George said, 'I want you, members of the jury, to imagine a large boardroom. You will have seen one on television or may have been in one. At Mirror Newspapers, all the directors will be there, smartly dressed. The chairman asked, "How much did libel cost us last year?" The accountant states how much they have paid in libel damages. A look of gloom passes across the faces of the board of directors. The chairman then says, "How much did our circulation and advertising revenue increase last year?" The figure is revealed by the accountant. A smile spreads across the board's faces.

'When you come to award exemplary damages, to punish the newspapers, you are entitled to wipe the smile off the board of directors of the Mirror Group of Newspapers.'

According to Presland, George had told him he had heard of this tale years ago in a libel action he had read when he was a student and had waited all those years for the appropriate occasion to use it.

Lord Williams said the *Sunday Mirror* had offered to apologise and pay damages. Quoting one of Elton's songs, 'Sorry Seems to Be the Hardest Word', he said. 'It wasn't the hardest word for the *Mirror*, and they said it a long time ago.'

In his summing up, Mr Justice Drake said there were three issues for the jury to consider: (a) whether the words were defamatory; (b) if so, compensatory damages; and (c) exemplary damages.

He asked the jury to keep a sense of proportion in assessing damages and resist the temptation to put a 'nought or two on the end'.

After a retirement of four hours, the jury returned with a unanimous verdict for the plaintiff on liability: the words were defamatory. They awarded Elton damages of £75,000.

After a further hour's retirement, they returned with their award of exemplary damages, by a 10–2 majority. This time the figure was £275,000, in order to punish the *Sunday Mirror* for outrageous conduct.

Clearly, George Carman's verbal portrait of a greedy Mirror Group boardroom had made a mark on the jury – well, at least ten of them. Frank Presland had no doubts that they would win, but even he was surprised at the size of the figure they reached. Elton John was mainly relieved that his reputation had not been unfairly damaged. It was his intention to give the money to his AIDS Foundation.

Elton told George he was delighted with the award of £350,000 and refused to speak to reporters before he signed autographs for fans who had gathered. He said, 'They printed a story which wasn't earth-shattering, but it wasn't true. I would have accepted an apology much earlier if they had accepted it was fiction.' Later, he sent a case of champagne to George to thank him.

However, the AIDS Foundation was not fortunate enough to receive the large award. The Mirror Group appealed and the learned judges in the Court of Appeal – Sir Thomas Bingham, Lord Justice Neill and Lord Justice Hirst – reduced the sums in a historic judgment which was to change libel damages from then on.

They deemed that in the case of defamation, the paper had not attacked Elton's integrity, nor damaged his reputation as an artist. They felt that damages for hurt feelings should not be comparable to those for personal injury. The time had come for the presiding judge to draw the jury's attention to this comparison and have the power to suggest a reasonable sum. So, they reduced the £75,000 damages to £25,000.

With regard to the £275,000 exemplary damages, the Appeal Court ruled:

> The fact that a libel is committed in the course of business carried on for profit, for example the business of a newspaper publisher, is not by itself sufficient to justify an award of exemplary damages.
>
> In our judgment, this sum is manifestly excessive and goes well beyond the minimum sum needed to meet the two relevant requirements. We think that those requirements will be fully met by an award of £50,000 exemplary damages, making a grand total of damages under both headings of £75,000, which will ensure that justice is done to both sides and will also fully secure the public interest involved.

The Court of Appeal then laid out recommendations for future awards; the guiding hand of the judge could now deter juries from coming up with disproportionate sums. Ironically, this was due to Carman's success in convincing a jury to recommend some very disproportionate damages.

CHAPTER TWELVE

GILLIAN TAYLFORTH V. THE SUN

'A coarse and lewd exhibitionist.'

GEORGE CARMAN

In the world of TV soap operas, there has been no shortage of stars attending court to either deny criminal allegations against them or bring actions against media outlets which have printed salacious stories about them. Back in the days when newspaper editors knew that celebrity stories sold by the truckload, most weeks seemed to bring an entirely new set of gossipy revelations about 'blonde stunners' and 'soap studs' to public attention.

One such 'stunner' was Gillian Taylforth, the *EastEnders* actress who, as Kathy Beale, seemed to have more than her fair share of drama going on within the confines of Albert Square. 'Kathy' made her appearance in the very first episode of the show, on 19 February 1985, and was at the centre of many of the show's early dramas, including a memorable storyline that saw her raped by a slick ne'er-do-well by the name of James Willmott-Brown. This was followed by a series of tempestuous relationships that seem to ensnare Kathy right up to the present day.

With Taylforth, art seemed to mirror life and by the early 1990s, she was in a relationship with businessman Geoff Knights, a character of dubious reputation who could have come straight from the pen of the *EastEnders* scriptwriters. And in 1992, not long after the birth of their daughter, Jessica, Taylforth and Knights would discover just what was involved in cocking a snook at the law.

In June of that year, Taylforth and Knights joined friends for a day at the races. Although Knights had promised to drive home, he spent the day drinking, so it was down to Taylforth to take the wheel of the couple's Range Rover before heading along the A1 to their home in Highbury, north London.

What happened next was open to question. Taylforth said that Knights told her to pull into a slip road near Trotters Bottom, Hertfordshire, as he had developed an attack of pancreatitis as a result of drinking too much champagne and he was going to be sick. He undid his seat belt and the top button of his trousers to relieve the pressure. Taylforth leaned over and asked him if he was going to be all right.

At that moment, however, the enquiring face of Police Constable Terry Talbot appeared at her window. Taylforth wound the window down and Talbot said, 'I saw what you were doing. You were committing an act of gross indecency.'

Knights got out of the car and was sick.

Taylforth pointed to the vomit and told the police officer, 'You can see he's not well.'

Knights then became belligerent towards Talbot, who summoned assistance. Four police officers arrived to take him to the station and Taylforth drove home to collect her baby.

The following day, *The Sun* and the *Daily Star* called the *EastEnders* studio to pass on to Taylforth what the police had told them. Knights had evidently been abusive at the station and signed a caution admitting an offence of indecency (which he would later claim he was too drunk to remember signing). Taylforth gave them her version of the story, but, nevertheless, the next day's tabloid headlines were 'TV KATHY'S SEX ROMP FURY'.

Taylforth then contacted a solicitor, William Garnett, who managed to get an offer of a few thousand pounds' compensation from the *Star*. But Garnett's firm thought Taylforth had a good chance of winning a libel action against *The Sun*. So, Taylforth declined the *Star*'s offer and a libel action was commenced against, initially, *The Sun*.

Some days later, Garnett rang Taylforth with a warning. *The Sun* had engaged George Carman, he informed her. She was told that Carman's history of winning cases was excellent and that to take the action further, she would need an equally capable operator, which would be costly. Step forward the Hon. Michael Beloff, who had an Eton and Oxford background and was one of the best silks in the country, who would be tasked with convincing the jury that there had been no oral sex in the Range Rover that day. Taylforth may have to sell her flat and empty her bank account to pay the lawyers, but, if successful, she would probably get all the money back – and much more.

Beloff told the couple they had to be entirely honest about anything they had done in the past, as Carman was famous for unearthing skeletons in people's cupboards, thereby discrediting them. Knights told him about his fights and his time in prison, but Beloff thought that they weren't particularly relevant since it was Taylforth's reputation that they were protecting. Unfortunately for her, one such skeleton was already lurking.

On Wednesday 12 January 1994, Gillian Taylforth entered Court No. 13 of the Royal Courts of Justice on the Strand. Like her *EastEnders* character, Taylforth retained her dignity despite knowing that she would be subjected to an inquisition of the most deeply personal nature and at first it appeared that the judge, Mr Justice Drake, recognised this. He refused to allow George Carman to introduce articles from other newspapers alleging that Taylforth was something of an exhibitionist.

Beloff went on the attack, describing *The Sun*'s report as 'serious, scandalous and unwarranted'. He made the point that PC Talbot was mistaken because 'you cannot get an erection when you are about to throw up'. He even quoted *Macbeth* to substantiate the point, 'Drink provokes the desire but takes away the performance.'

On the second day of the trial, Knights was instructed to park his Range River in the complex behind the court. The judge, the jury – eight men and four women – six barristers and some chosen journalists assembled around the car. Knights sat upright in the vehicle – the judge told him he did not need to undo his trousers. And Taylforth, keeping her seatbelt on, demonstrated that it was impossible for her to lean over the brake to put her head on his lap. No photographers were allowed and Taylforth's solicitors held up umbrellas to prevent long-lens shots from the gate.

Then, in the interests of fairness, a man and woman from *The Sun* took the places of Knights and Taylforth. PC Talbot took over direction and showed them what positions to get into for the act of oral sex which he claimed to have seen. The woman giggled in embarrassment, but the judge was unable to declare silence in court in that setting. Carman said to those assembled, 'The jury must realise this reconstruction is not quite correct. A vital component is missing: an erect penis.'

The next day's edition of *The Sun* carried the headline: 'Yes, you can do it in a Range Rover'.

Taylforth gave her version of the race day to Beloff. She pointed out that 'an indecent act would have been the last thing on my mind. I had had a baby four months earlier and I didn't fancy sex for a long time afterwards.' She admitted that she was very annoyed with Knights for his behaviour at the races; they had hardly spoken and she was most certainly not in a passionate mood.

Beloff put it to her bluntly, 'Were you committing oral masturbation? True or false?'

Taylforth replied, 'Utterly false … When *The Sun*'s story came out, I didn't want to leave the house. People had shouted, "Any chance of a blowjob, Kathy?" … I didn't want Jessica to grow up and read this sort of stuff about me in the paper.'

Carman stated that the pancreatitis story was a complete invention, a sham from start to finish. He wanted to establish that Taylforth was putting on a performance and reminded her that when Kathy Beale was raped by James Wilmott-Brown on *EastEnders*, she had to act out how cheapened, disgusted and humiliated she felt.

He went on, 'I suggest that your performance this morning in the witness box was similar to what you had to say when playing the part of a rape victim.'

'No, Mr Carman, that was Kathy Beale. I am Gillian Taylforth.'

'I suggest that Geoff Knights dared you to give him a blowjob on the A1,' said Carman. 'I suggest you had your mouth engaged around his penis and you were moving your head up and down, backwards and forwards, in order to masturbate him. You had both had a merry day and had some drink. It was a silly indiscretion that went wrong.'

Taylforth denied this. She also denied that she had brought the libel case for the money she might get in damages. 'It has never been about the money. It is to clear my name,' she said.

Knights was put in the box and asked to list his criminal offences. 'What? All of them?' he replied, provoking laughter in court. They began when he was fourteen and stole some alcohol from a shop. He was now thirty-eight and his earlier crimes hardly seemed precursors to the one of which they were now accused. He admitted to signing a caution in the police station but said he was too drunk to see it, so admitted to an act of indecency. He further denied that after his arrest, he said to a police officer, 'You know how it is, you just get the urge.' What Knights did admit was that he had challenged two police officers to come outside for a fight.

PC Talbot then gave his version of events. He said:

> The light was perfect, with still some sun. I got out of my Panda car. I put on my hat and walked up the offside of the Range Rover in the road. I could at first see only one person in the passenger seat, just the top of his head and shoulders. I looked through the driver's window and saw a woman with blonde hair lying across him with her head in the man's lap and her head was moving up and down. The man had his eyes closed. I tapped on the window. He turned and I saw, for a fleeting moment, an erect penis in his right hand and then he was trying to put his penis into his trousers. I have no doubt that I saw an erect penis. I have no motive to make that up.

Notwithstanding the officer's seeming honesty, by the end of the first week, there was a general feeling that he was mistaken and Gillian Taylforth had been unjustly maligned. She seemed, if not prim, a very proper person and concerned mother.

Now, Taylforth had trained as an actress at the Anna Scher Theatre School. It was unlike the famous colleges such as the Royal

Academy of Dramatic Art or the London Academy of Music and Dramatic Art and was subsidised by Islington Council. Classes were held in a large room in a block of flats in Canonbury in north London. Integration through improvisation was Anna's philosophy and she fed a steady stream of actors to television soaps including Kathy Burke, Gary and Martin Kemp, Linda Robson, Patsy Palmer – and Gillian Taylforth.

In 1988, the school held a party to celebrate its twentieth anniversary. With news of the Taylforth trial all over the papers, one of the former students who had shot a video at the party remembered that it included some humorous but salacious scenes with a drunk Taylforth. He took it to *The Sun*, whose editor, Stuart Higgins, was happy to part with a paltry £2,000 for the tape. It was, in fact, worth pure gold.

The question was: was the video relevant to the case and therefore admissible evidence? It was shown in private to Mr Justice Drake and the lawyers for the defence. Beloff had no doubts that it was not. 'It should be put in a rubbish bin and sunk to the bottom of the sea,' he said. But the judge could see that Taylforth had spent so much of her seventy minutes in the witness box protesting her good character that the jury should be allowed to see it to help them make up their own minds.

The video ran for thirty-five minutes and was pretty shocking. Somebody produced a large German sausage, which Taylforth sucked and told the camera, 'I give good head; I give very good head.'

'What, in street language, do the words "I give good head" mean?' Carman asked her.

'I think we all know,' Taylforth replied. 'Giving a man a blowjob.'

'What was the relevance of asking for a battery for the sausage?' Carman innocently enquired.

'I was joking that it was a vibrator. The whole afternoon was just a joke.'

In the video, she had pressed a wine bottle to her bottom with the words, 'Come on up your cracksie, give it loads.'

George asked her, 'What part of a woman's anatomy does the word "cracksie" refer to?'

'I was very drunk.'

'You were simulating an act of anal intercourse.'

'It was just a bit of fun between friends.'

It was not Carman's job to join in the fun. 'By anyone's standards, for a young woman in a public place, in daylight, to put a wine bottle near her vagina after placing it near her bottom and then simulating masturbation is pretty disgusting behaviour,' he commented.

During the video, somebody suggested they go to a wine bar, but they hadn't enough money. Taylforth jokingly replied, 'I should go sell my services on the way; I should make £2.50.'

For Taylforth, the footage changed everything. She may have put a German sausage in her mouth, but George was not going to miss looking at the gift horse in his. The previous week, it seemed as if it was the actress's word against PC Talbot, and Carman sensed the jury would give her the benefit of the doubt. Strategically, he had tried to persuade them that she was putting on an act; it was, after all, her profession. His tactic hadn't worked, and she had come out of the witness box with her head held high.

Now Carman went for the jugular. Po-faced, he suggested that her words plainly suggested that she was prepared to prostitute herself for £2.50. He said she was 'no lady when in drink', implying she had no reputation to lose and therefore was likely to have behaved on the A1 in the way described by PC Talbot.

It was time to plunge in the dagger:

> The whole impression of your evidence, the clothes worn, the tears shown, the language selected, the expressions of outrage and disgust you have shown the jury, I suggest all that has been a great show, misleading the jury, and the true Gillian Taylforth, when in drink, emerges on that video – a coarse and lewd exhibitionist.

Further, Carman reminded the jury of PC Talbot's evidence, 'An open mouth over an erect penis going up and down, up and down.' He suggested she had done this as a dare, egged on by Knights. In his final speech to the jury, Carman tried to emphasise that Taylforth's story was fiction:

> Her baby [Jessica] was weaved in and out of the script as if Miss Taylforth was president of the Mothers' Union. We are not a court of morals, but do we believe her performance in the witness box or her performance in the video? The words 'I give good head' may describe what happened that evening on the A1 and may be her epitaph. She and Knights hoped *The Sun* would back down and pay up.

Beloff, in his summing up, could do little more than attack Carman and his 'magician's tricks'.

'He is the past and present master in the art of distracting juries from the evidence,' he said:

> He's the Torvill and Dean of advocacy rolled into one. But with this important difference: straight sixes for style; straight zeros for content. Mr Carman's final speech in a libel action is always a source of entertainment, especially if you are hearing it for the first time. But I would sooner take lessons on family values from Cinderella's Ugly Sisters.

Commenting on George's habit of producing a 'so-called' vital piece of evidence at the eleventh hour, Beloff compared him to Perry Mason:

> Perry Mason would produce a firework, but Mr Carman has produced a damp squib …
>
> Any man who wants sex will open his trousers, but not all men who open their trousers want sex. Has any credible explanation been advanced by *The Sun* as to why this couple should have sex beside the A1? It is not exactly lovers' lane, is it? With the exception of Wembley Stadium, Hammersmith Palais or Parliament Square, it's about the last place in the country anyone would select for love-making. A jape? A dare? As John McEnroe used to say, 'You cannot be serious.' This is not a whodunit but did they do it at all.

In his summing up, Mr Justice Drake suggested:

> It is possible the video may assist you by helping you to judge the truthfulness and the reliability of Miss Taylforth's evidence. It is what lawyers call evidence as to credit or credibility. Its only use in this case is to help you judge Miss Taylforth's truthfulness. It does not affect her reputation.

The jury could hardly have had a broader hint as to who the judge believed was telling the truth. But they took longer to make up their minds. The foreman eventually asked the judge, if the fact that Knights had signed a caution form at the police station, knowing it to be an admission of guilt on the part of the couple of outraging public decency, would they still have been able to bring a libel case, or could he just sign it to get out of the police station?

Carman said, 'If the jury finds for the plaintiffs on that basis, I will demand a retrial.'

This was a little naughty, as the secrets of the jury room are sacrosanct. However, when the foreman came back the following day and asked pretty much the same question, it was Mr Justice Drake's turn to indicate to the jury which way to decide: 'Members of the jury, if you do find for the plaintiffs, on this basis, I will want to know why and I will have to decide whether to have a retrial or bring Mr Knights to court for perjury.'

Even then, not all of them were convinced. Juries don't like to find against soap stars. But when Drake agreed to a 10–2 verdict, this tradition was overthrown.

'Have you reached a decision?' he asked.

'Yes, we have,' replied the foreman. 'We find for the defendants.'

What happened next was, if anything, more dramatic than an episode of *EastEnders*. Taylforth's legs went from under her and she collapsed into the arms of Knights. She lay lifelessly on the floor while someone who'd been in court actually punched her in the chest to get her breathing again. But she wasn't dead; instead, she made for a lucrative target for the crowd of photographers and film crews outside the court who pictured her being carried by paramedics into an ambulance.

Gillian Taylforth's personal wealth was devastated by the case she brought, although her career appeared unaffected. She returned to *EastEnders*, followed by a continuing career in *Footballers' Wives*, *The Bill* and *Hollyoaks*. If anything, she became even more of a celebrity, appearing on *Celebrity Big Brother*, *Loose Women* and *Strictly Come Dancing*.

Her relationship with Knights continued and they went on to have a son, Harrison, but separated in June 2009 after twenty-three years together. Knights died of stomach cancer in 2013, aged fifty-eight.

For George, the whole case was about overcoming the odds. Later, he admitted that he was extremely lucky to have the evidence of the video, as it showed Taylforth in a totally different light. For her part, Gillian Taylforth complained in the press about being 'Carmanised'.

Reflecting on the experience of advocating opposite George, Michael Beloff commented:

> I have certainly never heard a better jury advocate and I have appeared against most of the leading libel silks. The precise way in which George articulated Geoff Knights's alleged words to the arresting officer, 'I got the urge,' sticks in my mind to this day.
>
> I know the tabloids depicted the case as a contest between an intellectual academic lawyer and a street fighter, which I always felt was a little unfair to me! As ex-president of the Oxford Union and hardly reputed to be lost for words, I wouldn't pretend in a million years to have had the same forensic affinity with any jury as did George.
>
> Somehow, George exploited his own lack of height to his advantage in his style of advocacy. His presentation of the case was, as usual, notable in itself for the introduction of new evidence in the shape of a video tape; I know George has a history of last-minute evidential bounty in his cases.

Beloff reiterated in his memoir, *MJBQC: A Life Within and Without the Law*:

> The impact of the video evidence at the time it surfaced was, of course, far greater than it would have been had our team

> known of it in advance, when we could have softened its edges in examination-in-chief. It has often been suggested that George deliberately, and unethically, in this and indeed in other cases, kept such material under lock and key until the moment when it would have been maximum effect. In the signature phrase of Francis Urquhart, 'Others might think that, but I couldn't possibly comment.'

Beloff added:

> I used to speculate that George quite deliberately sloughed off his legal knowledge in order to attune himself to the thinking of the jury. What is certain is that the case gave me far greater publicity than all my other cases rolled into one: and it was some comfort that neither my client nor my solicitor blamed me for the outcome.

CHAPTER THIRTEEN

JONATHAN AITKEN V. THE GUARDIAN

'We'd better get Carman – before Aitken gets him.'

Alan Rusbridger

On Monday 10 April 1995 (and just in time for the early evening news), the Rt Hon. Jonathan Aitken MP, a Cabinet minister in John Major's government, called a press conference at Conservative Party headquarters in London's Smith Square.

Stung by allegations made by *The Guardian* and ITV's *World in Action* investigative programme that Aitken had accepted financial favours from the Saudi government and of being involved in a secret arms deal with Riyadh, the MP was about to summon up all the high-mindedness and self-righteousness that only an Eton and Oxford education, plus a well-connected and privileged background, can afford.

Puffing out his chest in front of assembled journalists and TV crews, Aitken denied any wrongdoing, describing the allegations as 'wicked lies' and threatening to sue as a result. Then he declared, 'If it falls to me to start a fight to cut out the cancer of bent and twisted journalism in our country with the simple sword of truth and the trusty shield of British fair play, so be it. I am ready for the fight.'

And with that, he marched the 100 yards back to his Westminster home, accompanied by his wife Lolicia, daughter Victoria and his ever-present and unshakeable confidence that his cause was just. Four years later, Jonathan Aitken was in prison, a convicted perjurer and inveterate liar. As former *Guardian* editor Alan Rusbridger put it, Aitken had 'impaled himself' on the very sword of truth he had once wielded so mightily.

George Carman was engaged to represent *The Guardian* against a libel action brought by Aitken as promised at the gathering in Smith Square. As a rattled Rusbridger watched Aitken making the infamous speech live on TV, he immediately contacted Geraldine Proudler, the newspaper's solicitor. He wasted no time on seeking her advice; instead, he told her, 'We'd better get Carman – before Aitken gets him.'

He wasn't wrong. Had he not moved so quickly, there is more than a likely chance that Aitken would've got there first, with what might have been a wholly different verdict when the case finally came to trial in the summer of 1997. This was because George Carman had previously assisted Jonathan's sister, actress Maria Aitken, and he and the QC had struck up an acquaintance as a result. Had Aitken been quicker off the mark in 1995, he and Carman would've made a formidable pairing in court, but it was not to be.

Ironically for someone determined to 'cut out the cancer of bent and twisted journalism', Aitken started his career as a journalist, reporting from the Vietnam and Biafra wars in the 1960s. Ink was in the blood – Aitken's great-uncle was Lord Beaverbrook, who owned the *Daily Express* and became a minister in Churchill's wartime Cabinet.

Like Beaverbrook, young Aitken had a hankering for politics and entered Parliament as a Conservative MP in 1974. During the Thatcher years, he sat firmly on the back benches – it is said that he fell foul of the Prime Minister after ending a relationship with her daughter, Carol. However, Aitken wasn't content to wait out his time until Mrs Thatcher had gone. Instead, he embarked on a series of business affairs, one of which included a directorship of arms manufacturers BMARC. Aitken became embroiled in controversy when, in the mid-'90s, it was revealed that as a minister he'd signed 'gagging' orders relating to the supply of arms to Iran by BMARC.

Aitken also forged links with several prominent Saudis, including Prince Muḥammad bin Fahd, the son of the Saudi king. Money from Arab sources went into the launch of a financial services group and the ITV breakfast show *TV-am*.

Predictably, perhaps, Aitken's various extra-parliamentary dealings fell under media scrutiny, especially when he was promoted to Minister for Defence Procurement following John Major's 1992 election success. There were allegations in *The Guardian* that he had spent a weekend in the Paris Ritz Hotel and that the room had been paid for by a Saudi business associate, in breach of ministerial guidelines.

Aitken fought back, firstly by approaching the Cabinet Secretary Sir Robin Butler and telling him – falsely, as it turned out – that the bill had been paid by his wife. He also kept up correspondence with Peter Preston, then *Guardian* editor, denying allegations against him until he felt everything had blown over. *The Guardian*, however, kept digging away at links between the person who had paid the bill and the Saudi royal family, wondering if it spoke of anything more concerning than mere friendship.

By this time, Aitken was Chief Secretary to the Treasury and there were whispers that, one day, he could be in line for the top job. But fresh thunderstorms were brewing. In May 1994, *The Guardian* published an article questioning Sir Robin Butler's clearing of Aitken and followed up in October of that year with direct allegations about the stay at the Paris Ritz.

Then in April 1995, the newspaper and Granada TV's *World in Action*, in a documentary called *Jonathan of Arabia*, repeated the Paris accusations – in defiance of Aitken's performance on the steps of Conservative Party HQ – and also claimed that Aitken had procured prostitutes for Arab clients at the Inglewood Health Hydro in Berkshire. In addition, the media investigation questioned his directorship of BMARC, a company which sent weapons to Iran in breach of a UN embargo.

Aitken was in Switzerland when the articles were faxed to him in the early hours of Monday. They didn't come as a total surprise: *The Guardian* had been running a campaign against him, not least regarding the hotel bill. But the allegations of organising defence contracts and obtaining girls were the last straw. Aitken later recalled that his twelve-year-old son, William, was in the room with him and had asked, 'What's a pimp, Daddy?' although, in fact, the word was not used in the article. Nevertheless, the former Cabinet minister recalled, 'It was almost the equivalent of having a heart attack in terms of the shock and pain I felt in reading it.'

He flew back to London that morning, drafting a passionate speech en route. The press conference was called for 5 p.m. and the die was cast.

Aitken seemed intent on spearheading a campaign against British media, not the sensation-seeking popular tabloids but both a newspaper (*The Guardian*) and a television programme (*World in Action*), whose reputations relied on truthful and accurate reporting.

To conduct his libel action, Aitken enlisted the services of one of his Oxford contemporaries, Charles Gray QC, who had made a reputation as a top libel silk.

There were an unusually high number of people working for the defendant in the case. Geraldine Proudler was a senior partner of Olswangs, the solicitors. She brought in two junior barristers, James Price and Alexandra Marzec; the latter's sole task was to coordinate documents. *The Guardian* had the investigative reporters and David Pallister, plus the editorial backup. *World in Action* had its producer, David Leigh, his assistant, Quentin McDermott, and executive editor, Ian McBride.

The team met Carman at his chambers in the Temple. They already had mountains of research documents to substantiate their allegations. But now that war was declared, they were in a position to obtain more. To defend themselves against Aitken, they drafted more than 500 pleadings to obtain bank statements, property deeds, travel receipts and numerous other documents from the plaintiff.

After Carman had painstakingly worked his way through these files, he informed the defendants that this was a classic case to settle. On the question of who paid the bill at the Ritz, Carman noted that Aitken faced formidable problems, but he wasn't convinced of the strength of the evidence on the other allegations. And the costs were going to be enormous. Alan Rusbridger was persuaded of this and tried to set up a meeting with Aitken to sort things out, using businessman Maurice Saatchi as an envoy. However, Aitken was not going to drop the case without an apology, and *The Guardian* was not going to apologise.

Battle lines were drawn, and the first victory went to Aitken. Charles Gray appeared before the trial judge, Mr Justice Popplewell, and made an application that since the case was so intricate, it was too complicated to be heard by a jury but should be decided by the judge alone. To Carman's surprise, Popplewell agreed.

Aitken was pleased. He believed he would have done well with a jury; however, he preferred a judge, as it would take less time and incur fewer fees. And he prepared his case carefully. 'Time spent in reconnaissance is never wasted,' he said. He went to observe Carman in court, to see how he performed and to pick up as many hints as possible. He concluded that Carman was 'a real bruiser'.

Back at Carman's new chambers in Gray's Inn, there was dismay among the lawyers and journalists. The reason Rusbridger had engaged Carman was for his legendary skill in dealing with juries. The image of Aitken as an old Etonian who made his money through dodgy deals with Arabs was much more likely to turn twelve people against him than it was to influence the judge. The team decided that they had to get the ruling overturned.

Six days later, Carman went to the Court of Appeal, where Lord Chief Justice Bingham sat with two other judges. 'The ordinary layman and the media will say, "This is a bit of a whitewash, it should be left to a jury,"' Carman claimed to the judges. 'There will be criticism which will diminish public confidence in the administration of justice.'

Bingham, however, chose to stand by Popplewell. 'I do not believe that public perception is a reliable guide,' he pronounced, dismissing the appeal.

It was considered that *The Guardian* had come at Aitken from too many directions, potentially weakening the case. Two days before the trial, it withdrew the allegations of Aitken procuring prostitutes. It had emerged that one of its main witnesses was a woman whom Aitken had fired from Inglewood Health Hydro (of which he was a director) and thus had reason to be hostile to him.

All parties arrived at Court No. 10 of the Royal Courts of Justice on the Strand on the morning of Wednesday 4 June 1997. After taking the judge through *The Guardian* articles and the Granada videotapes, Gray said:

> It is no exaggeration to say they have butchered Mr Aitken's personal, political and professional reputation … They have pursued their case against Mr Aitken on the basis of particulars that are nothing more than assertion and flannel. This total dearth of evidence has not prevented the defendants from pursuing Mr Aitken remorselessly and oppressively for documents relating to his private financial affairs in the hope of being able to make out the case of dependency. This they have manifestly failed to do.

Aitken took the stand, and for two days, Gray gently took him through the 'truth' of what really had happened. Predictably, Aitken was relaxed and confident in his responses, knowing that he only needed to convince one person of injury to his reputation, not twelve.

Then it was George Carman's turn:

> If in this courtroom, in the course of these proceedings, My Lord has eventually to make the melancholy decision that you have lied to the Cabinet Secretary while a Cabinet minister, that you lied to your own Prime Minister as a Cabinet minister, that you have lied to the House of Commons as a Cabinet minister and that you have lied to this court on all occasions to do with your stay at the Ritz, if that were to be so, would you accept that such a series of lies would prove you totally unfit for public office?

It was quite an opener, but one which Aitken fielded with eloquence.

'I don't accept any of these melodramatic, hypothetical allegations you are putting to me,' he countered. 'But if his Lordship were to make those dramatic judgments, it would obviously be a shattering blow to me, yes.'

'It would butcher your reputation,' Carman stated.

'My reputation has already been butchered.'

'It would butcher it again.'

'It would,' Aitken agreed.

Carman questioned Aitken about his dealings with the Saudis and he admitted that he had accepted a 'magnificent watch' from a member of the Saudi royal family. 'I think I gave it to my wife – or one of my secretaries.'

Carman then moved on to his strongest suit: who paid the £1,000 bill for the minister's stay at the Ritz Hotel in Paris on 19 September 1993? Aitken said that his wife, Lolicia, usually settled hotel bills in cash due to her dyslexia and had paid a sum to the Ritz Hotel for his stay.

At that moment, Lolicia Aitken was sitting in court. Carman countered that the hotel cashier had stated that the bill had been paid by a brunette European lady, speaking French. He then pointed at the blonde Lolicia. 'Mrs Aitken's hair is not dark.'

'She's not this week,' Aitken calmly replied. 'At the risk of getting into trouble at home, I can tell you that the natural colour of her hair is not blonde.'

Carman shook his head. 'Manon Vidal, secretary to the treasurer of the Saudi Prince Muhammad bin Fahd, was a French-speaking brunette. She paid.' Again, Aitken was asked if he had paid the bill for the two-night stay.

The truth was that Lolicia had gone to Switzerland with their sixteen-year-old daughter, Victoria, to enrol her in a new school.

Telephone records from the Ritz showed that Aitken had telephoned the Hotel Bristol in Villars on Sunday lunchtime. The time of this call meant Lolicia would not have been able to get to Paris that afternoon. Carman put this to Aitken and awaited an explanation.

Observing proceedings, junior barrister James Price said that Aitken's skill in his evidence was in picking apart this point. Aitken stated that he had rung to speak with his mother-in-law in the hotel in Villars, as she had travelled there to see her granddaughter off to school the previous day. Furthermore, he claimed that she had occupied a double room with her daughter for one night, before Lolicia had left for Paris. In the mass of documentation, the record of his telephone call from the Ritz was time stamped and attached to his hotel bill. This added a plausible explanation for being able to speak with someone at that time, in the hotel bedroom, in Switzerland, when Lolicia was supposed to be in Paris.

In an attempt to strengthen his account, Aitken had also persuaded his daughter to sign a witness statement that her grandmother, Madame Azucki, was the person he spoke with at the Hotel Bristol. This meant Victoria would have to go into the box and testify to Carman that this was the truth. Carman had no desire for this to occur, as he knew that behind the scenes, concrete evidence was being assembled to prove this was not the case. He determined that he would intervene with the judge to prevent Victoria committing perjury. Alan Rusbridger later said of Aitken, 'We always wondered how low he would stoop. This was the moment we knew.'

Then Geraldine Proudler, *The Guardian*'s lawyer, appeared in court with an envelope containing the evidence that George had been desperately waiting for. It had been dug out following hours of painstaking detective work on the part of *The Guardian*/*World in Action* team.

Carman said:

> My Lord, before any further evidence is called by my learned friend, I am in a position to provide the plaintiff's solicitors, Mr Gray and your Lordship with a signed witness statement of a lady called Wendy Dawn Harris, who is employed by British Airways. I think, my Lord, if I may say so, it might be very important for Mr Gray and your Lordship to read it immediately.

The air ticket microfiche records showed that Lolicia and Victoria had travelled directly from Heathrow to Geneva on 17 September 1993, and that Lolicia had flown back to London from Geneva on the night of Monday 20 September. She couldn't have paid the bill because she had never been in Paris in the first place.

A look of bemusement and then of stone came over Aitken's face as he read the document. In a later interview, he commented that 'until that point, we were winning the case. However, when the evidence was produced to my legal team, I knew my life was over.'

Mr Justice Popplewell looked over at the plaintiffs. 'No doubt, Mr Gray, you will want to consider the position overnight,' he said. 'I shall be ready to see counsel in chambers tomorrow morning.'

When he met with his lawyers, Aitken was downbeat. 'I'm afraid this is a mortal blow,' he said. 'We will have to surrender.' Gray agreed, but his solicitor, Richard Sykes, felt they should fight on to get a judgment on the other issues, especially the arms-dealing allegations. But Aitken had no stomach for this, saying his reputation was now ruined in the media and in politics. That said, Aitken's team felt *The Guardian* had not proved any arms-dealing charges and so felt they were entitled to costs from the defendants in respect of that charge. But Alan Rusbridger was unbending. He wanted

Aitken to pay the costs in full. 'Why should we back off when we have our foot on his windpipe?' he asked, not unreasonably.

Carman, however, was more experienced in these matters and felt Aitken was more likely to agree to 80 per cent of the costs. He was right; Aitken did agree to the percentage.

The following day, the surrender would be announced in court but not by Jonathan Aitken, who had gone to ground. Charles Gray announced, 'I am instructed by my client to ask for the action to be withdrawn on terms, which subject to your Lordship, have been agreed on costs.'

The headline of the *Evening Standard* on Friday 10 June said it all: 'THE RUIN OF AITKEN'. *The Guardian* devoted five hostile pages to the surrender and Alan Rusbridger wanted more blood. He wrote to the Director of Public Prosecutions saying there had been 'a well-laid and carefully co-ordinated conspiracy to pervert the course of justice'.

The Crown Prosecution Service (CPS) agreed. Almost two years to the day of the collapse of the libel case, Jonathan Aitken admitted perjury and perverting the course of justice. He received eighteen months' imprisonment for both counts, to run concurrently. At the Old Bailey, Mr Justice Scott Baker told Aitken, 'For nearly four years, you wove a web of deceit in which you entangled yourself and from which there was no way out unless you were prepared to come clean and tell the truth. Unfortunately, you were not.'

After serving seven months of his sentence, Aitken was released and returned to Oxford to study theology. He was eventually ordained into the Church of England as an Anglican priest.

An intriguing question about this case is why Aitken lied about who paid his hotel bill. This was a far less serious allegation than illegal arms dealing. The bill had, in fact, been paid from the account of Mohammed Said Ayas, an old friend of Aitken and godfather to one of his children, so Aitken could have easily explained his generosity.

In an interview with me, Aitken said that he 'invented the story of my wife paying the bill, because *The Guardian* thought that I was a corrupt arms dealer, and they were up the wrong tree.' He joked, 'I wish I had made all that money from arms dealing. I had to nail that point and I felt *The Guardian* legal team had no evidence regarding the Ritz bill. The problem was I denied the facts the first time around.'

As regards the involvement of his daughter, Victoria, and his using her to support his perjured version of events, Aitken said, 'She was very keen to give evidence in support of me … She didn't realise the significance, in the great game of what was happening.'

Reflecting on the case, Aitken said:

> I had no complaints about what George Carman said, or did, in the trial. He had an intuitive feel for when someone was on weak ground … The word 'persistent' was nowhere good enough to describe him – he was mega persistent.
>
> I didn't have any feelings of hatred towards George and don't feel he had any towards me.

Sometime after his release from prison, Aitken met Carman at a party given by Charles Gray QC. The conversation was affable. Carman said he was delighted that Victoria had not been pursued by the prosecutors for perjury.

Privately, Carman said he'd felt quite sorry for Aitken, as he had totally trapped him, despite Jonathan's feeling that evidence would never be adduced to substantiate his lies.

And who was it that informed *The Guardian* of Aitken's stay at the Ritz, the place where his tangled web of deceit would eventually come apart? In fact, it was none other than Ritz owner Mohamed Al Fayed, who was, at that time, pursuing a one-man campaign against what he saw as a government-led plot to refuse him UK citizenship. As we will see, Aitken's was not the only political scalp that the vengeful Fayed would have a hand in taking…

CHAPTER FOURTEEN

RUGBY AND FOOTBALL: THE CASES OF LAWRENCE DALLAGLIO AND BRUCE GROBBELAAR

'You are a goalkeeper who keeps moving the goalposts in the sense that you are playing with the truth.'

George Carman

In the dying days of the 1990s, George Carman was involved in two cases where two popular sportsmen were fighting allegations of, respectively, drug-taking and match fixing. The pair were Lawrence Dallaglio, the golden boy of English rugby union who captained the national team for two years from 1997, and Bruce Grobbelaar, the flamboyant South African-born goalkeeper best known for his appearances with Liverpool FC.

Carman himself enjoyed watching sport occasionally on television if time permitted, which was rare. But he wasn't much interested in playing sport. He had pursued such an intense academic life that there wasn't time for the playing fields. Besides, at 5ft 3in., his stature was hardly that of a footballer or a rugby player.

Among the papers he left behind was a pale-yellow card on which he had grouped the cases he might include in his autobiography – and these two were included among them.

At the top of the list was Lorenzo Bruno Nero Dallaglio, better known as Lawrence, who was born in London in 1972 to an Italian father and Irish mother. He went to the leading Catholic school, Ampleforth College in North Yorkshire, whose alumni include characters as diverse as Rupert Everett, Brigadier Andrew Parker Bowles, the Duke of Norfolk and Baron Julian Fellowes, author of *Downton Abbey*.

Dallaglio was to bring further credit to the school by being made captain of England's rugby team. He was the only player in Martin Johnson's squad of 2003 who played in every game in Australia until that memorable last-minute drop goal from Jonny Wilkinson secured the World Cup for England.

However, this was a career that could easily have been brought crashing down just a few years earlier when, in May 1999, the *News of the World* produced a story alleging he had taken hard drugs and had even once been a dealer in them.

Dallaglio was caught in the kind of newspaper 'sting' that the *News of the World* specialised in and thrived upon. A blonde reporter posing as a representative of a company interested in a sponsorship deal secretly captured him on tape, bragging that he was a drug dealer before he took up rugby – and that he took ecstasy and cocaine during the 1997 Lions tour of South Africa.

When the story broke, Dallaglio vehemently denied the allegations but stepped down as England captain the next day. The day after that he bravely spoke to the press at Twickenham and seemed badly shaken by the allegations and the resultant publicity. He did his best but at various points was close to tears as he tried to sidestep the issue. His demeanour perhaps wasn't helped by some scathing observations from England coach Clive Woodward, who described his charge as 'a complete prat' and 'naïve and stupid'. Even so, Woodward believed Dallaglio was innocent of the main allegations in the *News of the World* and he was supported in that by rugby union's bigwigs who decried the tactics used to trap the hapless player.

Wisely, Dallaglio secured the services of George Carman to represent him at an inquiry panel and, later, during a disciplinary procedure.

Lawrence Dallaglio relayed to me the amusing story of how he retained Carman through his fellow Amplefordian and excellent lawyer Gerrard Tyrrell. Lawrence highlighted that it was the same week the Liverpool striker Robbie Fowler had appeared before the FA disciplinary commission in Birmingham. Fowler was ordered a four-match suspension for his goal celebrations against Everton, where he mimicked snorting cocaine, and handed a record £32,000 fine for this and one other misconduct charge. He was also given a two-game ban for his bust-up with Graeme Le Saux, where he wiggled his backside at the Chelsea defender, taunting him and questioning his sexuality. This hearing had been in private; Dallaglio's would not be!

Tyrrell had introduced Dallaglio to Carman, as he felt it was very important to instruct a QC as the RFU had retained one. Dallaglio's mother Eileen had tried to secure Carman's services previously for the inquiry into the *Marchioness* disaster – a tragic incident in which two ships collided in the Thames and resulted in the loss of fifty-one lives. Eileen's daughter and Lawrence's sister Francesca was among the dead. Eileen was desperate to secure a verdict at the inquiry of 'unlawful killing', rather than 'accidental death'. However, Carman could not help her as he was instructed on another case. This time, however, Carman was available to help her son. He charged Dallaglio a meagre fee – 'probably the fee for drafting a couple of letters', Dallaglio told me – partly in recognition of the fact that he had been unable to help Dallaglio's mother. She, like Carman's mother, was Irish and Catholic and he felt empathy in respect of her grief.

At this time, Dallaglio was told that Carman was not well but that he would see him on a Sunday evening privately at his home, to avoid the press. Dallaglio told me that when he arrived, Carman had sensed his distress:

> Carman said go and help yourself to a decent bottle of wine. I selected one, noticing there were two more, in case they were required! We both lit a cigarette and discussed the *News of the World* article.
>
> Carman said, 'What happened? Don't bullshit me, you have done this.'
>
> I said, 'Yes, we are in a spot of bother.'

Dallaglio told me, 'Carman made me feel at ease. It was good to be going to the hearing with Carman on my arm, very comforting.'

Carman advised him initially not to sue the *News of the World* but to wait for the outcome of the inquiry by the Rugby Football Union (RFU) that was commissioned to look into the matter.

Two RFU officials were to sit on the panel under the independent chairmanship of Sir John Kay, a High Court judge, whom, the RFU stated, was 'independent of them and had no formal connection with Twickenham'. However, a little digging would have revealed that his son, Ben, had been in the second row of England's

World Cup-winning team. The panel took no less than ten weeks to complete the very lengthy report – Sir John was a stickler for detail.

One such detail that particularly stood out involved a tragic incident that affected Dallaglio deeply. On 20 August 1989, not long after Dallaglio left Ampleforth and just ten days after his seventeenth birthday, two vessels collided in the Thames. The *Marchioness*, a pleasure boat, sank and fifty-one people died. Lawrence Dallaglio's sister, Francesca, was among the losses.

Dallaglio suffered terribly following the loss of his sister. He played no rugby for over a year. He sat for his A-levels and enrolled in Kingston University to study property development. He moved out of his parents' home and went to live on a houseboat on the Thames. He later joined Wasps and began his rise to rugby fame.

Fast-forward to 1999, and the *News of the World* sought a story that would fly off the newsstands. It decided that subterfuge was the way forward. A meeting was set up via Dallaglio's agent, who believed he had been contacted by a representative of the Gillette company. The agent was told that Gillette was thinking of offering the player £250,000 a year for four years to promote its products. Very tempting, and Dallaglio was lured into two drunken evenings in hotel rooms with *News of the World* reporters Phil Taylor and Louise Oswald, who pretended to be managing and marketing director of Gillette.

They steered the conversation onto the subject of cocaine and ecstasy and Dallaglio agreed that he had used drugs before he became a professional rugby player. They were recording the conversation and, fatefully, to impress the couple, he boasted, 'I tell a lie actually. I know I can tell you things in confidence.' And he went on to describe how during an all-day party in the presidential suite of the InterContinental Hotel in Johannesburg, to celebrate the 1997 Lions series victory over South Africa, he and two other players took ecstasy and cocaine. 'We got absolutely mullered.' And with that, the *News of the World* had its scoop.

Facing the panel with George Carman by his side, Dallaglio agreed that much of what he read in the transcripts was correct. But Carman said that he and his client had not seen or heard the video and tape evidence made by the *News of the World*. The paper had declined the panel's request to provide even copies of the original video and tapes. The panel or Dallaglio could see them at the *News of the World*'s offices.

Dallaglio was extremely reluctant to go into that particular lion's den and his lawyers considered that it would not assist them to go without their client. At the time when Dallaglio was attending to answer questions, the requested full transcripts were still not available, although partial transcripts of some of the more important passages had been provided.

Carman told the panel that at any disciplinary proceedings, reliance would be placed on a breach of the rules of natural justice in respect of Dallaglio not seeing the videos before he was questioned.

In response, Sir John countered:

> The panel is not a decision-making body but an investigative body. Just as there is no requirement for the police to show a suspect all the material in their possession before conducting an interview, so there is no requirement upon us, so long as Mr Dallaglio and his advisers fully understood the nature of the allegations against him.

Carman told the panel that if this were a criminal investigation, having regard to the way in which Dallaglio came to say what he did, the Crown Prosecution Service would drop it in five minutes, as the absence of corroborative evidence that what he said when drunk, along with his motives for doing it, was true.

He said:

> If criminal charges were brought, the judge might well exclude the evidence pursuant to the discretion given to him under Section 78 of the Police and Criminal Evidence Act 1984 to exclude unfair evidence. The Act states: '(1) in any proceedings the court may refuse to allow evidence on which the prosecution proposes to rely to be given if it appears to the court that, having regard to all the circumstances, including the circumstances in which the evidence was obtained, the admission of the evidence would have such an adverse effect on the fairness of the proceedings that the court ought not to admit it.' If there was support from an independent source, the position might be different. But there is none.

However, Dallaglio's questioning did reveal a few significant pieces of evidence – that the player claimed he didn't even know there was an InterContinental Hotel in Johannesburg or that it had a presidential suite and had certainly never been there. He made this up in his drunken boast to impress the 'Gillette executives' that he had taken drugs there celebrating the Lions' victory.

The panel tracked down a Virgin air hostess in whose name the suite was booked on the night in question. She told them that some of the Lions had returned to it with her after the match. They included Lawrence Dallaglio. They had had a good party and a great deal of alcohol had been drunk, but she insisted no drugs had been taken at that party. She had been trained to recognise those who were affected by drugs as part of her flying duties, and she was satisfied that Dallaglio had not been taking drugs.

Sir John's panel's recommendation was that if the future disciplinary panel was satisfied that Dallaglio had lied, they may conclude that there would be a prima facie case to answer. This was the main disciplinary charge that should be considered possible. The other was Dallaglio's boast during the 'sting' that he had indulged in both drug-taking and drug-dealing activities, so that he might thereby secure financial gain for himself.

Sir John noted:

> The decision whether to institute any disciplinary proceedings is not for us and is for the independent judgement of the disciplinary officer. We would only wish to record that we have no doubt that Mr Dallaglio has already suffered considerably as a result of the publicity given to this matter. When we saw him, we were very conscious of the strain upon him from these matters and he clearly, genuinely became emotional when mention was made of the effect of the matter upon his parents and his immediate family.

At this stage, Carman and the prosecutor, Richard Lissack, discussed the drugs charge and as a result of persuasive negotiation, the charge of taking drugs was dropped. Sir John's lengthy report was then submitted to the RFU, albeit that Dallaglio still had to answer a charge that he brought the game into disrepute when he went before the Rugby Football Union's disciplinary panel.

Dallaglio later confessed to the panel that, in fact, he had gone to the InterContinental Hotel in Johannesburg. Yet nobody in rugby wanted to see Dallaglio suspended as a result of the honey-trap tactics of the two reporters. It was considered that he'd suffered enough, and behind the scenes, George Carman had forcefully put this point to a receptive Rugby Football Union.

On Wednesday 25 August 1999, Dallaglio was summoned to Twickenham for the disciplinary hearing to decide whether he had brought the game into disrepute. It was presided over by the High Court Judge Sir Oliver Popplewell.

Richard Lissack QC presented the case for the Rugby Football Union, recounting to Sir Oliver how the *News of the World* had obtained its story.

Although Dallaglio had pleaded guilty, Carman publicly argued that his client had suffered enough. 'The damage caused came from the *News of the World*, not Lawrence Dallaglio. He didn't make anything public. He was speaking in private and in confidence. In many ways, he was the victim,' he said.

He pointed out that the player and his agent had been advised to do everything to humour the couple, so eventually he talked about his previous use of drugs. 'Lawrence Dallaglio was making it plain that in his position, it was inappropriate for him to now take drugs. He talked about an earlier involvement with drugs,' Carman said. 'It was a gross, elaborate and unfair entrapment of the worst kind, providing a circulation boost to a national tabloid.' There was no evidence to suggest Dallaglio had taken drugs while a professional player.

Sir Oliver deemed a fine of £15,000 was appropriate, plus £10,000 in costs. He then wished Dallaglio every success in the World Cup. So off he went to join the England squad. Dallaglio continued to enjoy a distinguished career, regaining the captaincy in 2004 and playing for England until 2007. The *News of the World* closed in 2011 amid a public backlash following the phone-hacking scandal.

Carman was impressed with Dallaglio as a person; he liked his humour and was genuinely convinced by his humility. He was also astounded at the size of Dallaglio's appetite on the occasion when they met privately and ate together. And as a favour to the lawyer, Dallaglio gave tickets to George to attend the next rugby international match at Twickenham. He gave them to his son and grandchildren as he couldn't afford the time to watch the match and knew they would really enjoy going in his place.

BRUCE GROBBELAAR V. THE SUN

To those outside of the law, it is often a puzzle to understand why a libel lawyer can, over the course of one case, aggressively challenge an organisation (a newspaper, for example) on behalf of their client, then, a week or so later, represent that same organisation when a libel action has been brought against it. 'Won't the newspaper hate that lawyer?' people ask. 'Isn't there a conflict of interest?'

The answer to both questions is 'No'. A lawyer with the standing of a George Carman will always be at the top of the list when an organisation is in trouble, no matter whether they have acted against it in the past. And a conflict of interest does not exist: the lawyer's job is to argue the law to the best of their abilities, no matter who the client is.

Such was the case in the early summer of 1999, when George Carman represented *The Sun* newspaper in a libel action brought against it by the goalkeeper Bruce Grobbelaar. As we've read, Carman would go on to act for Lawrence Dallaglio later that summer, facing the fallout from a 'sting' operation by the *News of the World* – *The Sun*'s stablemate.

Born in South Africa and raised in what was Rhodesia, now

Zimbabwe, Grobbelaar found fame in Britain as Liverpool FC's goalkeeper. From 1981, he played for the club 628 times over the next thirteen years, as it won six League Championships, three FA Cups and, in 1984, the coveted European Cup. He had an acrobatic style, often bordering on the dangerous, which endeared him to the fans.

A glorious career, one might think, but his reputation was badly tarnished by a former business associate, a fellow Zimbabwean and, supposedly, a friend, Chris Vincent, who offered him various sums of money to lose football matches on behalf of a betting syndicate. Vincent was paid by *The Sun* to videotape their conversations. The paper published them in a series of articles in November 1994.

The newspaper's lead headline on its front page was: 'GROBBELAAR TOOK BRIBES TO FIX GAMES' and its first paragraph read, 'Soccer star Bruce Grobbelaar is exposed by *The Sun* today for taking massive bribes to throw key matches.' On page two of the same issue, its headline read 'GROB: "I let in three goals and picked up £40,000"'. So the articles continued, with references, cartoons and jokes suggesting that the appellant had fixed matches, let in goals deliberately, saved goals by mistake and deliberately dropped the ball.

The most damning allegation was that Grobbelaar took £40,000 to make sure that Liverpool lost away to Newcastle in 1993. (They did: three-nil.) The beneficiaries of this pre-information were gambling syndicates in the Far East who bet heavily on English football.

The goalkeeper had been offered £125,000 in a key game against Manchester United in 1994 to make sure Liverpool lost. Ironically, Grobbelaar's instinctive talent overruled his alleged greed, and he made a sensational save so that match ended in a 3–3 draw.

Grobbelaar pleaded not guilty to criminal charges, claiming that he was actually gathering evidence against the syndicate that he intended to take to the police. He (and other co-defendants) faced two criminal trials in Winchester Crown Court in January and August 1997. On both occasions, they were found not guilty as the juries were deadlocked. In the first trial, they had held seven weeks of deliberation before failing to agree.

Nevertheless, the Football Association fined Grobbelaar £10,000 for breaking betting regulations.

Stung by this, and perhaps emboldened by his acquittal in Winchester, Grobbelaar was determined to clear his name and launched a libel action that came to trial in July 1999, accusing *The Sun* of waging a 'classic scam' to ensnare him.

Richard Hartley QC, the footballer's barrister, said that the newspaper conspired with Chris Vincent to trick Grobbelaar into making admissions while he was being secretly taped. Hartley also said that the footballer pretended to go along with the plan in a bid to expose corruption.

'It was a high-risk strategy and, most unfortunately, it did not have the result Mr Grobbelaar was hoping for,' said Hartley.

Hartley told the judge, Mr Justice Gray, and the jury that when *The Sun* confronted Grobbelaar about the allegations, his explanations and denials 'fell on deaf ears'. He said, '*The Sun* had its scoop, for which they had paid Vincent no less than £33,000, and it was determined to publish come what may.'

Hartley added. 'You may think that the fact Mr Grobbelaar is prepared to face a jury for a third time shows a certain amount of guts and that he knows he is in the right.'

The trial saw the appearance of two celebrated former footballers, goalkeeper Bob Wilson and midfielder Alan Ball. Both had attended matches that Grobbelaar was alleged to have 'thrown' and neither saw anything suspicious about his performance in any of those games.

George Carman, representing *The Sun*, was having none of it. He accused Grobbelaar of lying, telling him:

> If you can forgive the phrase, you are a goalkeeper who keeps moving the goalposts in the sense that you are playing with the truth in the witness box and trimming your answers to fit in with any new facts presented to you. I have to suggest to you your whole story is riddled with lies, evasion and deviousness.

Grobbelaar replied, 'That is simply not true.'

Carman asked the jury to consider whether Grobbelaar was 'just an innocent victim caught up in this black cloud of intrigue'. Or, he added, 'is he a man heavily involved in it, who lurches from one lie to another to try and extract himself when condemned by his own words and out of his own mouth?'

He said that it would be a dangerous mistake for the jury to rely on what they knew of the outcome of Grobbelaar's previous criminal trials, and that *The Sun* had taken the view that the case against the goalkeeper was 'overwhelming' by virtue of his own confession.

Summing up the case for *The Sun*, Carman said:

> If ever a man was the author of his own misfortune, it is Bruce Grobbelaar.
>
> It was the great American President Abraham Lincoln who said, 'You can fool some of the people all of the time and all of the people some of the time, but you can't fool all of the people all of the time.'
>
> Dare I say to you, members of the jury, are you all fooled?

> Our position is plain – that this man in all justice is not entitled to one penny of damages from you.

The jury disagreed and on 28 July, it was announced that Grobbelaar had won £85,000 in libel damages from *The Sun*. The jury was unanimous. As in the Dallaglio case, they did not like the idea of a sportsman, or anyone, being nailed by a tabloid sting.

The goalkeeper was cock-a-hoop as he stood on the steps of the High Court and declared that one of his objectives had been to restore the tarnished image of English football. As well as the sum of damages, *The Sun* would be forced to pay Grobbelaar's £400,000 legal costs, as well as its own bill of £500,000.

Grobbelaar's moment of triumph was, however, short-lived. *The Sun* subsequently appealed, and three High Court judges set aside the original decision, entering judgment for the newspaper.

Lord Justice Simon Brown said that he had 'some misgiving' about allowing the appeal on the defence of justification.

'That, however, is not because I entertain the least doubt about Mr Grobbelaar's guilt, but rather because, as I earlier observed, the court must inevitably be reluctant to find a jury's verdict perverse and anxious not to usurp their function.'

He said it would have been easy to reject the newspaper's challenge on the basis that the issue was one for the jury.

'Some, no doubt, will say that that is the decision we should have reached. I cannot agree. It is, I think, the experience of all of us that juries, from time to time, do arrive at perverse verdicts.'

He said the verdict was 'an affront to justice'. *The Sun*'s other ground for appeal, that the stories about a public figure should have been protected by qualified privilege, was rejected by the court.

George, sadly, did not live to learn of his victory. He died two weeks earlier on 2 January 2001.

On 24 October 2004, the House of Lords reversed that decision but awarded Grobbelaar a derisory £1 in damages, leaving him with costs of £500,000 – and bankrupt.

CHAPTER FIFTEEN

NEIL HAMILTON V. MOHAMED AL FAYED

'On the make and on the take.'

GEORGE CARMAN

Political life in the 1990s was marked by a series of scandals which came to reflect a country in which long-held values were changing as quickly as the fashions exploding out of the 'Cool Britannia' era. After the turbulent, iconoclastic 1980s, we were promised calmer waters. But anyone assuming that John Major's incoming government would be as grey as its Prime Minister was in for a shock.

It seemed that week after week, some Conservative minister or other was landing himself (and invariably it was a 'him') in hot water. In an attempt to reinstall old-fashioned values, Major launched a 'back-to-basics' campaign, which the press promptly used to expose even more political hypocrisy. Neither was Labour immune; after the party came to power in 1997, there were questions about donations from F1 boss Bernie Ecclestone and loans made to New Labour enforcer Peter Mandelson.

If all that wasn't enough, the royal family kept the nation entertained with tales of toe-sucking, illicit and intimate tape recordings and dalliances with dashing army officers, culminating, of course, in the tragic death of Princess Diana – the undisputed icon of the era.

Perhaps the biggest political scandal of the 1990s – the one that contained so many of the ingredients listed above and a dash of royalty for good measure – was a series of allegations that came to be known as the cash-for-questions affair. At its heart was a bitter dispute between two former acquaintances. In the blue corner stood Neil Hamilton, the right-wing Conservative MP for Tatton and, in the mid-'90s, a minister for trade in Major's government. Hamilton, it appeared, understood very well that MPs are constantly approached by lobbyists acting on behalf of individuals and organisations in the hope that they may use their influence in Parliament to get results. Indeed, Hamilton had a professional relationship with such a person, Ian Greer, a lobbyist who had an excellent reputation for getting his clients the results they wanted.

Emerging from the other corner, bursting with vim, vigour and more than a few half-truths about his colourful past, was Mohamed Al Fayed, the Egyptian-born owner of Harrods and, by the time of the trial, the grieving father of Dodi, who was killed alongside Princess Diana in Paris during the terrible events of 31 August 1997. Following the crash, Fayed vocally and publicly pointed the finger of blame at the British Establishment and certain members of the royal family for the deaths of the couple, claiming a conspiracy of the highest order.

If this wasn't colour enough, there was also the formidable presence of Christine Hamilton, Neil's wife. No shrinking violet, Mrs Hamilton had had a long parliamentary career as secretary to various Tory MPs, including her husband, and now stood resolutely by his side.

The tentacles of this case reach back into the mid-1980s, almost to the start of Neil Hamilton's career as an MP. In 1984, as secretary of the backbench Trade and Industry Committee, Hamilton had become involved in the hostile takeover bid for House of Fraser, which included Harrods. The bid was led by Lonrho chairman Roland 'Tiny' Rowland, disgruntled that his ambitions for House of Fraser had been thwarted by the government in 1981. Hamilton supported his government against Rowland's bid, and after a vicious battle between Rowland and Fayed, who had snatched the House of Fraser deal from under his nose, Hamilton's sympathies lay with the latter.

To regain a battered reputation, Fayed engaged Ian Greer, who asked Hamilton and others to place parliamentary questions on Fayed's behalf. Something of a relationship grew between Hamilton and Fayed; Hamilton asked various questions in Parliament on his behalf and in 1987, Neil and Christine stayed as a guest of Fayed's at the Ritz, Paris.

Cut to 1992 and John Major's election as Prime Minister. Hamilton became Minister for Corporate Affairs at a time when Fayed was in deep conflict with the Department of Trade and Industry, following investigations into his wealth and the House of Fraser takeover, which described him as a liar. Fayed assumed Hamilton would be on his side (and he was also keen to obtain British citizenship, which had been repeatedly denied to him), but after an exchange of letters, Fayed felt snubbed by his former associate. As Hamilton would discover, Fayed held grudges. In October 1994, *The Guardian* published an article stating that Hamilton and Tim Smith, another minister, had been paid by Fayed, via Ian Greer, to ask questions in the House of Commons. All hell broke loose, with Fayed claiming it was possible to 'rent an MP like you rent a London taxi' – a memorably sticky claim. The paper alleged Hamilton and Smith had each been paid £2,000 a time to ask such questions. Smith admitted he was guilty and resigned immediately. Hamilton vehemently denied any wrongdoing but was forced to resign four days later.

Two years later, as Hamilton and Greer prepared to sue *The Guardian* for libel, Greer decided to withdraw from the impending trial. In turn, this undermined Hamilton's case and he abandoned the action. Soon after, Fayed made allegations that he directly paid Hamilton cash in brown envelopes, claiming he had witnesses to prove it.

Hamilton lost his safe seat in the 1997 election in a memorable fight against BBC reporter-turned-independent politician Martin Bell. The battle gave birth to the image of Christine Hamilton as a good old British 'battleaxe' – a term she would quickly turn to her advantage, building a media career from it.

Sir Gordon Downey, the Parliamentary Commissioner for Standards, led an inquiry into 'cash for questions' which found against Hamilton, accusing him of lying to Michael Heseltine, then the president of the Board of Trade, in assuring him that he had no financial relationship with Ian Greer. Hamilton vowed to fight to clear his name and sued Fayed for libel, establishing a 'fighting fund' to underwrite what would be significant legal bills.

The case was heard before Mr Justice Morland in the confines of Court No. 13 of the Royal Courts of Justice, beginning on Thursday 18 November 1999. Jury candidates were questioned to establish if there was any possibility of prejudice. Two had previously worked for Harrods and were not eligible. They were asked if any of them were members of or supporters of Fulham Football Club (which Fayed owned). Silence. 'What? Not one?' exclaimed the judge in mock surprise, alleviating the tension in court.

Hamilton was represented by Desmond Browne QC, an Old Etonian and a silk with a reputation for guiding juries through complex matters in a low-key, forensic fashion. Browne had assisted Hamilton in the long lead-up to the trial proper, which included hearings in the House of Lords on technical points. In an interview for this chapter, Neil Hamilton said that Browne was an excellent lawyer whose style was perfect for the Lords. 'However,' he added, 'when dealing with a jury of average Joes, it is arguable he didn't quite have the touch of George Carman. I wouldn't want Carman representing me in the Lords on technical points, but you would benefit from him in front of a jury of ordinary people.'

That said, Browne didn't pull any punches in his opening address to the jury. He accused Fayed of portraying himself as the 'Fabulous Pharaoh of Knightsbridge' after his takeover of Harrods. '[Fayed] said that Harrods was a pyramid in which one day he would be buried,' Browne said. 'We say that when you have heard all the evidence in this case, you will see that the fabulous pharaoh of 1985 was really a phoney pharaoh of 1999. What is going to bury him is not the pyramid of Harrods but the sheer bulk of his lies.'

Warming to his subject, Browne highlighted three aspects of Fayed's character which, he said, gave the clue as to why he was telling such appalling lies:

> Firstly, Mr Fayed is a habitual liar – a man for whom lying has become a sickness. Secondly, he is a deeply vindictive man – a man ready to take his revenge on those who he sees as responsible for exposing the lies he tells. And thirdly, we say that he is a man

> who is a tyrannical employer – a man who is able to prevail over his employees by managing them through fear.

Browne's client, Hamilton, was 'a prime example of a man who dared to stand in the path of Mr Al Fayed's ambition'.

Then Browne moved in for the kill. If anyone on the jury thought that such a well-bred, eminent and erudite lawyer would shy away from bringing up the subject of Dodi Fayed, they were sorely wrong. The knife went in below the ribs.

'What Mr Al Fayed has said repeatedly is that to prevent the marriage of Dodi and the Princess of Wales, they were murdered by British intelligence on the direction of Prince Philip … and Prince Philip did that because he was motivated by racism – he was a German racist.'

Browne said he regretted having to refer to the tragedy but felt that Fayed forfeited the right to such sympathy. Having stunned the courtroom into silence, Browne introduced a final note of seasonal levity into the proceedings. 'I hope the case will finish in plenty of time for you to do your Christmas shopping,' he said. 'The only present Mr Hamilton wants this Christmas is to have his name cleared by you. Please be Father Christmas.'

In his opening speech, George Carman, representing Fayed, played one of his classic overtures – that of summarising Neil Hamilton's reputation into a sentence that would resonate with both the jury and the following day's newspapers. He said that Hamilton was a politician 'on the make and on the take' and followed up this right-hook (that did indeed land on the front page of the following morning's *Times*) with a series of expertly aimed jabs. Hamilton, he said, was someone who put 'pocket before principle and who, over the years, has shown his character to be deeply flawed by a degree of dishonesty, by half-truths and lies, disguising his financial activities'.

It has been argued by the Hamiltons that Carman's tactic, the one that caught everyone off-guard, was to divert attention away from Fayed's evident failings as a witness, choosing instead to steer the jury into the murky waters of politics, lobbying and deal-making that had gone on in Hamilton's past. Anyone in that court-room who hadn't heard constant media references to 'Tory sleaze' over the past seven years would have had to have been hiding under a rock, and Carman knew it. So to stir some of Hamilton's previous dealings into the pot, albeit that they weren't linked at all to the libel case, was a shrewd move that would plant the opinion in the jury's mind that all politicians, including the former MP now pursuing Fayed, were on the fiddle.

Carman put it to the jury that in 1989, Hamilton had been asked by Mobil Oil to see what he could do to get the Finance Bill altered in a way that would save oil companies £70 million. Hamilton tabled an amendment, but it was not carried. Nevertheless, Hamilton sent Mobil an invoice for £10,000 for 'consultancy services'. 'The company was more than surprised,' said Carman. 'They were flabbergasted, embarrassed and shocked.' However, since the company thought it was under some kind of moral obligation to the MP, it paid up. 'The demand for payment to Mobil made by Mr Hamilton in the summer of 1989', Carman stated, 'was corrupt – just as corrupt as the money he took from Mr Fayed for asking parliamentary questions.'

In an excruciating set piece that would humiliate the Hamiltons, Carman then focused on the six-night stay at the Paris Ritz in September 1987 on the largesse of its owner – Mohamed Al Fayed. The latter agreed that the couple would not have to pay anything to stay there, a deal prompted by Hamilton agreeing to do Fayed's bidding and ask questions in Parliament primarily targeted to help Fayed in his quest for British citizenship.

A lesser lawyer might only have shown the jury the size of the bill they ran up, but Carman calculated the devil was in the detail. With a flourish, he produced an itemised bill and, poring over it, revealed details of the couple's extravagance, all from Fayed's pocket. Four-course meals, champagne, full usage of the minibar – it seemed that the Hamiltons' tastes were expensive indeed, especially when they weren't paying.

Each night, they would dine in the hotel's Michelin-standard L'Espadon restaurant. They would have a four-course dinner with vintage champagne and wine. This cost £220 on 8 September 1987. In addition, they had breakfast in their room, ran up a minibar bill of £35 and then had lunch in L'Espadon, where the bill came to more than £100. 'No Big Macs or chicken sandwiches for them,' Carman observed.

The pattern was repeated over the course of their stay. On the last night, they had a meal which included 1979 Bollinger champagne. All their tips went on their final bill. Carman even produced a photograph of the luxury room the couple occupied, number 356. 'It's not like the sort of accommodation you would get on a package holiday to the Costa del Sol,' he said, waspishly.

'In today's prices, they spent £3,000 – or £500 a day,' Carman concluded. 'They must have thought Christmas had come early.'

In an attempt to repair some of the damage Carman had wreaked on the couple, Desmond Browne pointed out that Hamilton assumed he was enjoying the hospitality of a generous friend. He had repaid him by sending Fayed a warm thank-you letter and with the gift of a House of Commons coffee set. But even this wasn't enough.

The jury heard that Hamilton had failed to declare any of the free hospitality in the MPs' register of interests and had been castigated by the Commons Standards Committee for his omissions, described as 'casualness bordering on indifference or contempt'.

Having put Hamilton's reputation through the wringer, Carman gave it another hard squeeze. Turning to the meat of the trial – the cash-for-questions allegation – Carman said that when Hamilton worked for Ian Greer, he would go to Harrods himself and pick up cash from Fayed in plastic wallets straight from the bank containing £2,500 a time in new £50 notes. Sometimes he would pick up envelopes of cash from Fayed's offices in Park Lane. He even had cash couriered to his home in Cheshire. It was said that between 1987 and 1989, the payments added up to £30,000 in cash and £8,000 in gift vouchers.

Naturally, the provider of such generosity was required to give evidence. Into the witness box stepped Fayed, complete with funereal black tie, and swore his oath on the Qur'an. Knowing that Fayed had a habit of making speeches, Carman tried his best to keep his client's account of his relationship with Hamilton on track. It was not an easy task. Fayed was taken back to the Tiny Rowland affair and the questions around Fayed's takeover of Harrod's. In a bid to get his reputation back on track and curry favour with the politicians he considered he needed to assist with his citizenship bid, Fayed took the advice of Lord King, chairman of British Airways, and hired Ian Greer.

'Mr Greer came to see me', Fayed went on, 'and explained what he had done for several companies and all the MPs who could do anything for me. Number one on the list was Tim Smith and Neil Hamilton. All these MPs you could rent, exactly like you rent a taxi driver.'

Sensing another great opportunity to bring the jury round to his way of thinking, Carman asked him what his reaction was to this suggestion.

'Shocking!' Fayed thundered. 'It completely changed my perception of democracy in this country. These men are there to make money.'

Fayed claimed that in 1986 or 1987, Hamilton came to see him and had asked for cash payments. The Harrods boss always kept at least £10,000 in cash in his briefcase and would hand Hamilton money in bundles of £2,500 in £50 notes. He also gave him Harrods gift vouchers. 'It was four visits – two of £1,000 and two of £3,000. Hamilton said he has incurred other expenses and needed cash to pay some of his colleagues,' Fayed, said. 'All the time baloney excuses, because he thinks he has discovered the golden goose.'

Carman's line of questioning around the Hamiltons' stay at the Ritz prompted a furious tirade from Fayed, who accused Neil Hamilton of 'putting his hand in my pocket and taking out £5,000'. But as Fayed warmed to his theme and became worked up, the judge warned him to stop making speeches – a request which appeared to go unheeded after Carman told him it had been suggested he had made up the story about Hamilton's cash payments and had continued to lie about it as an act of revenge.

'Why I have to take revenge for him?' Fayed exploded. 'For me, he is nothing, not a human being, someone who will sell his mother for money.'

Cross-examining, Browne wondered how Fayed could talk about integrity when he had made corrupt cash payments to MPs. Once again, he stepped into the sensitive subject of the deaths of Dodi Fayed and Diana, bringing up the claim their deaths had been caused by British security services. Visibly upset, Fayed said he had the right to know how his son had died before appealing to the judge to tell Browne to stop asking about it. But the QC pressed on, aiming to undermine Fayed's protestations of honesty and integrity by airing his public accusation that the Duke of Edinburgh had masterminded the crash. Angrily, Fayed replied that he had the right to say what he felt.

Finally, after accusations by Browne that Fayed was vindictive towards those who had worked for him, which included threats to 'destroy' one individual, and that he habitually withdrew up to £120,000 in cash from his bank every week to 'lubricate' the wheels of business (to which Fayed rudely replied, 'My personal cash is my personal life. It's none of your bloody business. It's my business. Get on with it and don't waste everybody's time.'), the cross-examination was over. 'Thank you, Mr Fayed,' concluded Desmond Browne. 'For me, at any rate, it's been a memorable four-and-a-half days.'

During his cross-examination, Browne had alluded to there being no physical evidence to support Fayed's claim that Hamilton was paid by cash in envelopes, and when Carman re-examined his witness, Fayed claimed to have a 'definite memory' of paying Hamilton but couldn't remember how many times.

It was now down to two of Fayed's employees, Alison Bozek and Iris Bond, a reserved person who was nervous of public speaking, to put the finger on Hamilton. Bozek, Fayed's former long-time secretary and by now a practising solicitor, said she vividly recalled Hamilton's name on an envelope containing a large amount of cash. In her evidence, she said Hamilton visited frequently – she had noted twenty-one appointments for him in the diary, three of which had been crossed out and up to twelve of which had taken place at an office in Park Lane. Her evidence was backed up by Bond, who claimed to have witnessed three occasions when Fayed organised cash for Hamilton, and by Philip Bromfield, a security officer still working for Fayed, who said he'd physically handed over envelopes to Hamilton.

Browne suggested that all three had colluded in a conspiracy against his client. In response, Bozek said it had taken her nine years to become a solicitor. 'I wouldn't risk that for anybody. I wouldn't jump in and put myself into this sort of situation unless I was telling the truth. I do not fabricate evidence.'

On 8 December, Neil Hamilton finally took the stand. He dismissed Fayed's allegations as 'a pack of lies' from start to finish and said that they'd wrecked his political career. He also insisted that he believed he was acting as a paid consultant for Mobil and was not being paid to place questions in Parliament on the company's behalf.

So far, so good. Compared to Fayed's emotional performance, Hamilton was the epitome of cool, calm and collected. Carman, though, was a master of cross-examination. He played out each question to a witness like Sir John Gielgud on the stage, slowly, with deliberation and wasted no time in undermining Hamilton's case by getting him to drop one of his claims against Fayed. In fact, it took precisely twenty-two minutes.

Hamilton was emphatic that had it not been for Fayed, he would've been destined for a top role in the shadow Cabinet following the 1997 election. Carman then brought up the criticism levelled at Hamilton by the Commons' Standards and Privileges Select Committee:

> Are you seriously saying to the jury, 'Award me damages for the loss of my career prospects, which include the possibility that I'd be serving in the shadow Cabinet or as a frontbench spokesman now,' in the light of the fact that the select committee found in

1997 that, if you were still a serving member, you'd have deserved a substantial period of suspension?

Hamilton began, 'Well, Mr Mandelson is back in the Cabinet…'

'When was Mr Mandelson criticised by a select committee or threatened with suspension from the House?' Carman asked.

After a slight hesitation, Hamilton said, 'I am happy to exclude from any damages that I would be a frontbench spokesman.'

'Are you withdrawing that?'

'Yes,' Hamilton replied. 'I am quite happy to abandon that specific point.'

Scoring this hit put the wind into Carman's sails. In forensic detail, he questioned Hamilton on all matter of financial dealings and, using Hamilton's status as a qualified tax lawyer against him, began to paint a portrait of a man who knew his way round all sorts of rules and regulations. There was also more sport to be had by Carman on the subject of the Ritz stay.

'Looking back on what you and your wife spent, is it unfair to say you were somewhat greedy?'

'I don't like the use of the word "greedy" in this context, but we certainly enjoyed very lavish hospitality. After what we've been through in recent years, you do learn a little more humility,' Hamilton said.

'What has humility to do with greed?'

'I don't think "greedy" even now is a word I would attach, but I think we went over the top a bit.'

He and his wife were not proud of the 'depredations' into the food and wine and agreed he felt 'an element of shame'.

The acidic exchanges continued. At one point, Carman asked, 'Do you avoid paying attention to anything you find disagreeable?'

Hamilton replied, 'No, I'm playing close attention to you, Mr Carman... That was just a joke, Mr Carman.'

'Not a bad joke,' Carman admitted.

The laughing stopped when Carman focused on the £10,000 paid to Hamilton by Mobil. He put it to Hamilton that he had corruptly moved an amendment to the Finance Bill in exchange for the payment from Mobil, to which Hamilton replied:

> It was no part of my intention that Mobil should pay me for undertaking parliamentary work on their behalf ... I certainly wouldn't anticipate that a major international oil company like Mobil would have the slightest intention of engaging an MP for a fee to promote or amend a piece of legislation.

By getting Hamilton to agree with his suggestion that it would have been corrupt to ask for payment for promoting the amendment to the Finance Bill 'and corrupt if it had been offered', Carman watched his victim walk into a carefully laid trap. Unbeknown to Hamilton, Carman had suggested his instructing solicitor, Susan Aslan contact Mobil to discover its attitude. The response surprised even Carman when he received a sealed envelope with a witness statement and documents. This dossier had been compiled by a now retired executive of Mobil who, shocked by Hamilton's behaviour, had left the dossier behind in case anyone ever queried the matter.

It explained how the company had approached Hamilton about the Finance Bill's effect on it. It had not suggested any consultancy agreement but had approached him as an MP with an interest in taxation. Hamilton had subsequently moved an amendment to the Finance Bill which he presumably thought would help the company. To the company's astonishment and out of the blue, he submitted a bill for £10,000. The executive made clear his disgust, adding, 'I have been waiting for someone to ask about this.'

Carman now pressed home the advantage:

> Mr Hamilton, you are trying to clothe your demand for payment with respectability because you are saying to my Lord and the jury, 'I did offer my services generally to Mobil as a consultant and they did agree to pay me.' Whereas you know the truth of the matter is now that Mobil were embarrassed at your request, you put them under a moral obligation by requesting payment and the consultancy agreement was a mere expedient.

Hamilton's insistence that he did not ask to be paid for promoting an amendment, and that he had nothing to be ashamed of, cut no ice with Carman, who suggested he had not shown 'total candour' about the matter on seven occasions, including at a meeting with Michael Heseltine.

Carman asked whether, in May 1989, Hamilton believed he had a concluded consultancy agreement with the company. Hamilton said he had a 'clear understanding' to that effect from Peter Whiteman, the QC who approached him on the company's behalf to promote a proposed amendment to the Finance Bill. Carman then asked if he had ever made an agreement with anyone from Mobil, soliciting the response that he had not spoken to any of its people directly. He also agreed he thought Whiteman had the authority to broker such an agreement but not to fix terms. Hamilton said he did not raise the matter with Mobil but allowed it to drift until it occurred to him that it should be formalised and he asked Whiteman to make inquiries. He said he did not declare it on the register of members' interests within four weeks of May 1989, as required, because it was not yet formalised.

Pressed by Carman, Hamilton also agreed that he had not been completely candid about his intervention in the Finance Bill with the parliamentary select committee dealing with his case in 1997, saying the latter was not an independent process. Carman then suggested he was less than candid when 'self-preservation is paramount in your mind'.

Hamilton disagreed, 'I am here in this court today because I want to be here and I know that the full story of these allegations is to be played out before the jury in conditions which will ensure a fair trial. I am delighted to be here.'

Hamilton's days in the witness box had been long and taxing and – given the forensic exploration of financial dealings – sometimes difficult for the jury, one of whom was seen to be frequently entertaining himself with games of noughts and crosses. The following week saw Christine Hamilton take to the stand. To say that her defence of her husband was robust is an understatement; for once, Carman seemed to be at a loss as to know how to get under her skin, as she made compelling statement after compelling statement that Neil was no crook and hadn't taken a penny from Fayed. 'If he had had it, he'd have given it to me, because I empty his pockets of change every night,' she said. 'He just wouldn't have known what to do with it.'

After closing speeches, Mr Justice Morland warned the jury not to be 'over-sanctimonious or priggish' when considering Hamilton's admitted lack of candour. He said it was surprising, given Fayed's admitted propensity for placing 'crooked men' under surveillance, there was no videoed or taped evidence showing the former MP either at Harrods or the businessman's Park Lane residences.

Morland then asked the jury to consider Fayed's evidence:

> You may have come to the conclusion that Mr Al Fayed's evidence in detail is inconsistent and unreliable; that he has made many wild and unsubstantiated allegations about all manner of people and that, at times, he is vindictive towards those who he thinks have let him down or double-crossed him.

Fayed had admitted his memory was often 'defective', the judge said:

> All these matters mean, you may think, that Mr Al Fayed's appreciation of what is fact and what is fiction, and what is truth and what is fantasy, is warped. Therefore, I strongly advise you that it would be very dangerous to accept even those parts of Mr Al Fayed's evidence that you find credible – and indeed would be unwise to do so – unless you are satisfied on evidence, independent of Mr Al Fayed's evidence, which you find highly convincing.

To support the allegation that Hamilton corruptly accepted cash in return for parliamentary services, the judge invited the jurors to examine the testimony of Bozek and Bond, and of Philip Bromfield, but only if they rejected an accusation, made by Desmond Browne, that they had conspired to lie in the witness box.

Beginning with Bozek, the judge reminded the jury of her insistence, under cross-examination, that she would not risk 'for anybody' the nine years of hard work it had taken to become a lawyer.

Turning to Bond, the judge described her performance in the witness box as 'rather languid – almost distant'. He added, 'I don't know whether this struck you or not – there may be nothing in it – did she appear as though she might have been on tranquillisers or something of that kind?'

He pointed to inconsistencies in her evidence, asking the jury to consider whether at one point she had made a slip of the tongue or 'forgotten the lines of a dishonest story'.

For both Neil Hamilton and George Carman, the judge's pointed comments about Iris Bond's state of mind rang alarm bells.

Hamilton said:

> As soon as I heard that, I thought, 'This will be the basis for an appeal.' Carman challenged it, asking the jury to be sent out while the matter was discussed. The judge said he'd reflect on it, and on the Monday he came back without the jury being present to say he'd thought carefully about the words he was going to use. I was appalled because I thought it could kibosh the case. We couldn't have afforded to have a retrial.

After a day and a half of tense waiting, the jury returned at 2.35 p.m. on Tuesday 21 December. They had been deliberating for eight hours and now they would be home for Christmas. But would they deliver the seasonal present that Desmond Browne had asked them to give his client? When asked if they were unanimous in deciding Fayed had shown highly convincing evidence that Hamilton had acted corruptly, the female foreperson replied in a clear voice, 'Yes.'

In response, Mrs Hamilton emitted a strangled cry. The couple shook their heads in disbelief. The colour drained from their cheeks. They buried their faces in their hands. Neil Hamilton had vigorously pursued a long and expensive case in a bid to clear his name. It had failed and now he and his wife faced public shame and financial ruin.

Fayed was not in court to hear the verdict. George had advised him to stay away, fearing his client might let slip an indiscretion which would bring them back to court. But the news was immediately conveyed to Harrods, where the pharaoh announced, 'Christmas has come early. It's champers and hampers,' after which he hot-footed it to the steps of the High Court to revel in his triumph, mobbed by reporters, photographers and camera crews.

In a rare public statement, Carman said, 'I am very pleased indeed for Mr Al Fayed. I think this jury has given this case very great and careful consideration and it has confirmed my belief in the value of the jury system.'

From a personal point of view, George was always keen to pull rabbits out of hats and this case was no exception. He believed that the whole business of the Mobil Oil fee would plant a perception of Neil Hamilton's character in the jury's mind, deciding to go on the attack using this line following the discovery of the Mobil employee's note. In an interview for this chapter, Neil Hamilton admitted that the Mobil Oil line was 'a problem' for his legal team.

'It muddied the waters so much it diverted attention from the real issue, which was Fayed's cash,' he said. 'Carman knew that introducing an extra limb to the case would make it difficult for us to convince the jury there wasn't something fishy here. Carman decided to complicate our case as much as possible, like dropping bits of silver paper out of planes to baffle radar.'

George considered Hamilton to be a clever man and a prepared witness – certainly in respect of the main body of evidence. Yet he also liked to right what he felt was a wrong, and he considered the idea of 'cash for questions' taking place in the House of Commons immoral. He didn't like the idea that an MP might try to hide what he had done. 'Despicable', was his comment.

George's brilliant strategy in this case was to expose the greed of the Hamiltons as a diversion. It belittled them as people and made the jury dislike them personally. No one else but George would have had the patience to itemise every breakfast, lunch, tea, drinks, dinner and use of the minibar, highlighting the Hamiltons' progress through a stay at the Ritz which could very easily define the word 'freebie'.

Of course, we will never know exactly what it was that swayed the jury in Fayed's favour, though perhaps we might take an educated guess. Consider this extract from the judge's summing up:

> The evidence of Alison Bozek, Iris Bond and Philip Bromfield, if you find it highly convincing, is capable in law of confirming the thrust of Mr Al Fayed's evidence, being independent of his. Mr Browne, on behalf of Mr Hamilton, has put to each of Ms Bozek and Ms Bond and to a lesser extent Mr Bromfield the grave allegation that each of them is guilty of conspiracy to pervert the course of justice and conspiracy to commit perjury … If you are satisfied that Ms Bozek, Ms Bond and Mr Bromfield were not guilty of conspiracy to pervert the course of justice or of conspiracy to commit perjury and are highly convinced that they have told you the truth on essential matters, you may think, it's a matter for you, that their evidence provides cogent confirmation of the main thrust of Mr Al Fayed's evidence that Mr Hamilton received cash payment from him.

'A GREEDY, CORRUPT LIAR' ran the headline in the following day's *Guardian*, over a picture of a crestfallen Neil Hamilton with his broken wife. *The Times* wrote, 'The king of the libel silks has done it again.'

Mohamed Al Fayed said in interview that he liked and respected George Carman. He identified with George as an outsider, a bit like himself. George was not part of the Establishment; he fought for his client and was not worried about his own reputation.

Susan Aslan said, 'Mohamed Al Fayed was courteous and behaved well with the lawyers during the case. Yet it was difficult to get him to concentrate on anything for longer than a few minutes. When in the witness box, you did not know what he would say.'

George said that he liked his client, who was kind to him. As long as he could see he had a case to argue and didn't think the person he was acting for was a rogue, he was prepared to act for them.

Neil Hamilton told me that he became bankrupt as a result of the trial and therefore had no way of paying costs. I do not believe these were pursued by Fayed, in any event. Neil was not bitter about George Carman's triumph; in fact, he said he would have loved to have instructed him as his lawyer. He was in no doubt that George's advocacy was very powerful and lost him the case.

What no one knew was it would be George's final case. Remarkably, he had been attending the Royal Marsden Hospital for radiotherapy treatment early every morning prior to going to court each day.

CHAPTER SIXTEEN

RETIREMENT

The following year, on 29 August 2000, George Carman announced he was going to retire because of 'a little local difficulty'. The papers could only speculate why; he was seventy and at the height of his powers.

To the outside world and, indeed, inside the courtroom, George seemed a composed and unflappable character, seldom showing much emotion but with the ability to dissect his opponent's reasoning with a surgeon's knife and to turn around a jury with a persuasive argument delivered with the simplicity of a bedtime story.

But sometimes, more than sometimes, his stomach was a knot of nerves and he began to suffer physical symptoms. I urged him to go to the doctor (he and I attended the same practice in Sloane Street). Dr Hunt of course suggested he cut down on his workload (some hope!) and prescribed some medicine to alleviate the pain for the moment. But he also ordered a CT scan.

This was in 1996, when the scan showed a single bony metastasis in the pelvis, with no clear primary tumour seen with diverticular disease accounting for the abdominal pain. I remember George discussing the matter with his close friend Dr Veronica Varney, who was a consultant but was only giving George advice as a friend. He had had a biopsy from the area, but it gave no definite primary site. Veronica was always convinced it was prostate cancer. Extensive tests were performed, but no primary was confirmed, although the pelvic bony tumour persisted and was treated with local radiotherapy.

George seemed outwardly well and unperturbed. But, in fact, nearly every day at 8.30 a.m., he would go the Royal Marsden Hospital for treatment and then at 9.45 a.m. he would continue to the Royal Courts of Justice to spend the day in court.

He also underwent a great number of invasive tests and eventually further prostate biopsies proved positive. His treatment was changed accordingly.

He continued to work and at the end of 1999, on 23 December, after five weeks in the High Court trial, his client Mohamed Al Fayed won against the former Tory MP Neil Hamilton. George was incredibly brave at this time and managed to continue with the case without anyone knowing how demanding this time was personally for him. He did not allow the physical drain he was enduring to be obvious to the legal team, his client or the press.

The millennium year was not a good one for George. In public, he seemed his normal self, but the medication began to take its toll and the prostate cancer started to spread. Standing up in court all day became an ordeal.

Nevertheless, he insisted we go to Venice in the summer as usual to have a rest and visit friends. And there another demon hit. He developed a vicious abscess on his tooth, which I can't help thinking was exacerbated by his generally run-down condition. I contacted our friend, Antonio, and he recommended a local dentist. George was in such pain that the dentist put him on an extremely powerful painkiller, something akin to morphine.

Most probably as a result of this, he began to develop fantasies. Two nights later, he called me in my room and I went to see him. But it was not the George that I knew. He rambled on about his fears and insecurities. At one stage, I was terrified that such a noble mind had been overthrown.

In the light of dawn, we decided that he should come off the drug and, by good fortune, his extreme pain had subsided. But there was another worry. The difficulty in walking that he had exhibited at home that summer now became much worse.

There was no way that George was going to conduct his cases with sticks or from a wheelchair. That might have been fine for Perry Mason but not for a man with the pride and dignity of George Carman.

So, having thought about it for a drug-free night, the following day, George told me he had decided to retire. He was only seventy and his mind seemed as good as ever, but his body had betrayed him.

He drafted the briefest of notes for the Press Association, saying that it was his intention to retire because of a 'little local difficulty'. We returned immediately to London. He did not wish to talk to the press but was persuaded to give a brief photo-call in his garden in Wimbledon.

For an ordinary barrister, to retire at seventy was hardly worthy of note. But George was no ordinary barrister, and when George opened *The Guardian* on Wednesday 30 August 2000, he was front-page news. 'Libel legend: George Carman, the master of courtroom cross-examination, retires' ran the headline and beneath it a quarter of the page was filled with a portrait of George.

The *Daily Telegraph*'s front page was dominated by a large photo of George in an open-necked shirt lolling on a sun lounger in his back garden in Wimbledon. 'Carman, king of the libel courts, rests his case' ran the headline of the second lead story.

'Carman quits' tersely topped a paragraph on the front page of *The Times*: 'George Carman QC, the most feared and admired barrister of the age, surprised legal colleagues by announcing that he had made his last appearance in court. He is to undergo treatment for an undisclosed illness.' There was nothing on the front of the *Independent*, but it made up for it by devoting all of page three to him – 'After 47 years "Gorgeous" George Carman QC, the tiny giant of British libel, rests his case.'

The paper went on to quote George:

> 'She danced on the graves of her husband's victims. She is a clever, confident, cold and calculating woman. She has sought to excite sympathy at every possible opportunity in the witness box. The truth and Sonia do not make good bedfellows.'
>
> The words that George Carman QC chose to describe Sonia Sutcliffe, the wife of the Yorkshire Ripper, who was suing for libel, were among the more colourful of his career, though they were in no way atypical.
>
> Such linguistic flourishes – at least in the setting of a law court – may be a thing of the past.

That the papers should mention George's retirement did not come as a surprise. He had acceded to their demands for a photo-call the previous afternoon, but he had declined to elaborate on his 'little local difficulties', merely deflecting their questions with:

> There was an element of choice. I could carry on, but I did not want to expose any client to the prospect that I could not give 100 per cent of myself. It is very sad, really. I have spent forty-seven years at the Bar in a profession I enjoy. It is like losing something irreplaceable in your life, but it happens to us all.

But nothing had prepared him – or me – for this prominent and widespread onslaught of coverage. It was as if a Beatle, a legendary actor or, even, a royal had died, not that a barrister whom few of the papers' readers had ever seen at work had merely announced his retirement.

George was flattered – who wouldn't be? He was secretly pleased, as he had never been one to avoid the limelight. At the same time, he was also somewhat 'choked' by the overwhelming praise.

Michael Mansfield QC, who had only come against George once, wrote:

> He never lets anyone know what is coming next – there is not a flicker of emotion with him. He is not the impassioned speaker that is sometimes suggested. But he never gives anything away – it is like an Exocet missile coming out of the blue. There was a myth about him that during a case he always had something up his sleeve, but I think the thing that is often forgotten is that George obviously did a great deal of preparation.

Joshua Rozenberg, the leading legal commentator, said:

> George Carman was both the best-liked and most feared advocate at the English Bar. He was also the best known. In any

> looming libel battle, the side that was first to pay George a comfortable retainer had an incalculable advantage … His retirement means that the age of the great advocate is over. Many barristers are clever, some are skilful and a few are good-looking. But there are now none left who can fill the public gallery on star quality alone.

My friendship with George was well known in legal circles and beyond, but I had never wanted to share in his prominence. However, the *Telegraph* sneaked a shot of me in one of his photos, enabling it to write, 'Relaxing with his close friend Karen Phillipps at his home in Wimbledon; Mr Carman said that he intended to start writing a book.' We were hardly relaxing together; I happened to be walking past in the background to give the photographers some water.

We discussed this avalanche of coverage over dinner that night and concluded that it would be fruitless to remain silent on the nature of George's illness. The press has a way of finding things out, whether that would be through a casual nurse at one of his radiotherapy sessions or an indiscreet colleague.

George took the bull by the horns. With this unprecedented interest in him and his illness, he knew he would have to speak about it sooner or later, and he wanted to do so in his own words, so he telephoned David Frost.

David had a BBC One Sunday morning show, *Breakfast with Frost*, and George appeared on it the next week, 3 September.

He said that it was his wish to dispel rumours and revealed he had been suffering from prostate cancer for more than three years:

> But much more importantly, I want to send out a message to

> people who do suffer from cancer, to tell them that you can work, you can help the doctors enormously by having a positive attitude, and anybody who has the misfortune to get the disease is not at the end of the road. Having looked at the government figures for cancer research in this country, we are way behind the major European countries and the United States, and I think it is time the problem was addressed by all the political parties.

But then the cancer spread and he had difficulty walking, especially ascending a staircase. So a bedroom was made up in the drawing room on the ground floor of his house. Fortunately, there was a bathroom beside it, but he had increasing difficulty taking baths and getting dressed, so his doctor said he should have 24-hour care.

There was a spare bedroom upstairs which was now given over to his carers who worked a shift pattern. They were usually young women from Australia, New Zealand or South Africa who performed their tasks with a cheerfulness that helped to keep his spirits up. Apart from organising this, I had no part in that aspect of his life. George did ask me to make my base in Wimbledon, so that I could help him.

He had a study lined with legal tomes in the house, but sometimes there was a case or an act that he needed to be referred to, so I could go to the law libraries in the Temple and Gray's Inn, where I was a member, and undertake the necessary research. In truth, although George was supreme in the courtroom, he was not someone who had every precedent or Act at the tip of his fingers, so there was plenty to do.

Of course, he had to hand over any ongoing or pending cases to other members of his chambers, but he wanted to make sure they were thoroughly briefed first. I remember he spent a lot of time on the telephone to Richard Branson, who had sued a journalist personally, rather than the newspaper in which his article appeared, for a story implying he would benefit improperly from his bid for the National Lottery. I think George's advice, in this instance, had been not to sue. Pride, however, was at stake and Branson lost the case. Ever resolute, Branson wanted to appeal but that too, after George had died, failed. Nevertheless, Branson welcomed his counsel on other legal matters.

In fact, George was on the telephone all morning most days. He needed to talk to his clerk, Bill Conner, or Paul, his more junior clerk, about concluded cases and fees but was happy to give his advice freely to any fellow barrister who sought it. He especially loved to speak with Victoria Sharp, who was his junior in a libel case brought by the chef Marco Pierre White. He sued a restaurant owner who had claimed that 'he had served real ink in place of squid ink in a dish of cuttlefish in one of his restaurants'. George handed over the case to his friend James Price QC and would have been pleased to know that just two weeks after he died, Marco was awarded £100,000 in damages and £1.5 million in legal costs. He would have been delighted that Victoria later went on to become a Crown court judge. Also, that his gifted juniors and solicitors – particularly, Susan Aslan, Geraldine Proudler and Jan Tomalin – continued with successful careers. He particularly enjoyed the company of Rosie Boycott, then editor of the *Daily Express*, and her husband, Charles Howard QC; George was their 'matchmaker', reuniting them after years apart. We attended their delightful wedding. Although George worked with several brilliant male juniors regularly, he was an admirer of clever women. He believed they did not have equal opportunities to their male counterparts during his lifetime, in many fields. Silks and judges were predominantly male, as in the world of politics and medicine. Thankfully, there has been an enormous change in this respect, though there is still much more to achieve. There might even be a female president of the USA, and here in the UK, we have our first female Chancellor.

In September, all the members of George's chambers gave him a farewell dinner in the Marie Antoinette room in the Ritz. We came home loaded with cards and presents, many of them books and artefacts relating to his beloved Venice.

George staved off any melancholy or self-pity by investigating his illnesses as he might prepare a case. He read every book on the subject. He went to the Harley Street Clinic for tests and monitoring. He needed a fourth, fifth or sixth opinion. He made an appointment with an oncologist at the St John and Elizabeth Hospital in north London. Bluntly, he asked the man how long he thought he had got. 'Between six months and ten years,' the oncologist replied.

His daily routine was much like it had been at weekends. He pored over every newspaper every day. He was intensely interested in politics, turning on the television to watch the news, *Newsnight* and *Panorama* and following the fall of Yugoslavia's Slobodan Milošević and George Bush's attempt to win the presidency. He had little interest in entertainment programmes and preferred to read biographies and listen to classical music.

Sometimes we ventured out to old haunts in Wimbledon, including our close friend Grace Seymour-Cole's antique shop or a small privately owned tea shop adjacent to the common. We also visited Cannizaro House, an eighteenth-century mansion which had been graced by George III, Pitt the Younger and the Duke of Wellington. It was ornate, but, as George remarked more than once, 'the food does not live up to the furniture'. However, he loved to wander through the gardens with their stunted oaks, camellias, sassafrases and rhododendrons. He also regularly wanted to select flowers for his hallway and dining room from the florist in the village. The days of going into town for dinner at Le Caprice or exotic Indian and Thai meals were over. We enjoyed frequenting a couple of local Italian restaurants in Wimbledon. Lunch and sometimes supper was prepared by George's long-standing housekeeper, Jacki – or me.

His appetite became progressively worse and he was hardly eating at night. But there were good days and not such good ones. If he was in the right mood, I would telephone his son Dominic, who would bring over his children for lunch at the weekend. George had never been very good with little children. Matthew, his eldest grandson, whom he had spent time with as he grew up, would sometimes stay at a weekend if I was there too. We would go on adventures and always had enormous fun, not least my pretending to be a magician. During his retirement George was invited to appear on several television programmes and nearly committed to join the panel of *Have I Got News for You*, but he, correctly, decided against it at the last minute. It would have been a long recording and he didn't know whether his strength would be up to it.

CHAPTER SEVENTEEN

ILLNESS AND DEATH

After the widespread coverage of his retirement, George was inundated with requests by publishers to write his autobiography. Just as he had seen various consultants about his illness, so he diligently checked out the various publishers. He had meetings with three of them. He very much liked Victoria Barnsley, the CEO of HarperCollins, and agreed a contract.

He decided that his autobiography was to include a donation to prostate cancer research. George had held meetings at home in Wimbledon with Professor Gordon McVie, the head of Cancer Research UK, in respect of how he could help others with prostate cancer. Professor McVie, an oncologist, was a vociferous spokesman for patients with cancer and was involved in creating cancer networks linking cancer centres across the country to offer patients who do not respond to conventional treatment the chance to take part in early clinical trials of new treatments.

By December 2000, George was suffering bouts of considerable pain requiring morphine, which made it difficult for him to embark upon the full task of an autobiography, but he listed all his important cases and embarked on his personal chapter.

One night I was awakened by the sound of George calling from his room downstairs. It was 3 a.m. and fearing the worst, I quickly went downstairs. George was sitting up in bed writing in a notebook with a pencil.

'Karen, can you help me draw up a list of guests for my memorial service?' He spoke calmly, as if he were requesting a cup of tea!

We had already agreed that he would like it to be held in St Clement Danes Church, on the Strand. George had telephoned Freddie Forsyth to ask if he would give an introduction welcoming people. I later asked Lord Alexander of Weedon QC to give the main eulogy. George had awakened from a morphine-induced sleep worried that he might insult friends by leaving them out. Together we drew up a large number of names from Cherie Blair to Ken Dodd, from the Lord Chief Justice to Jeremy Thorpe. It was dawn before he slipped back into a restful sleep.

George suggested my mother and Veronica Varney might join us for Christmas. Mercifully, his condition appeared to stabilise in the days after Christmas. George was still good company and had long conversations with us all over the holidays and up till 28 December. After that, he was more tired and declined quickly after 30 December. I telephoned the local doctor to alert him and notified his private nurse Tricia and his son.

By 1 January 2001, he was clearly close to death. He was in a deep sleep, interrupted by moments of sudden waking.

George was very fond of Tricia, who attended to inject him at times with a drug called Zoladex, into his stomach. Tricia always kept in touch and came to be with him in his final hours. She and I sat on either side of George's bed holding his hands. 'We love you and you'll be all right,' she reassured him.

I said, 'I love you, George. Don't worry, we are here.'

At that precise moment, on 2 January 2001, he took his last breath.

It's hard, at this remove, to exactly recall my emotions: numb, certainly; relief to an extent that his suffering was at an end; and deep grief for him and also for me that our irreplaceable friendship of the past fourteen years was over.

Lucretia, my helper from London, in the Philippine tradition, opened the window to let his spirit out. Tricia made contact with his local doctor to ask him to come and certify the death.

When his son Dominic arrived, in the afternoon, he was absolutely devastated. We had spoken at 8 a.m. that day, when I said the local doctor was attending to set up a morphine drip, if he felt it necessary. I had expressed my doubts that George would live more than a few hours. This was the father who had largely brought him up, who helped him get his start in life and to whom Dominic had a very close relationship, the grandfather to his four children.

Father Michael Seed, an adviser to Cardinal Hume, who had often visited George during his retirement returned my call; he had been too busy over Christmas with church services. I said George had asked if he could have his funeral at Westminster Cathedral as he was Catholic, though lapsed. Michael managed after a while to obtain dispensation and arranged for us to use the 'Our Lady Chapel' at Westminster Cathedral for the service. He teased me that in return I would have to help him with some fundraising for his homeless charity The Passage, which I have done so ever since in memory of George. The Orion Orchestra was formed by Toby Purser to raise money in this respect. It continues to raise money for homelessness, a cause close to George's and my hearts.

The following week, a private family funeral was held at Westminster Cathedral. I introduced Dominic to Father Seed. He said Dominic should follow the coffin into the church. Dominic commented, 'I think Karen should walk with me, as she was very close to my father.'

In addition to the family, there were a few friends, including his former clerks Bill, Paul and members of his chambers, such as Gail Carrodus; Jacki, his housekeeper; Tricia, his nurse; Hugh Tomlinson QC; and executors Charles Howard QC and Rosie Boycott, among others. It was a short and simple service, with Dominic as well as George's nephew, Nicholas, giving readings from the Bible.

Afterwards, Matthew, George's eldest grandson, and I, along with Father Michael Seed, accompanied the coffin to St Mary's Roman Catholic Cemetery, Kensal Rise, where a burial plot had been prepared. There was a simple marker by the grave, but later Veronica Varney and I paid for a specially engraved headstone, as George would have wanted this and the executors' budget was limited.

I returned to my flat in Belgravia, feeling drained and down. I was met by a journalist from the *Daily Mail* asking if I would give an interview; needless to say, I refused. A week or so later, a package was delivered from the law firm Farrer's, containing a copy of George's will. Having discussed his ideas for his biography, he surprised me by leaving me all his papers.

I was now busy trying to organise the memorial service which George and I had discussed frequently; it was set for 26 February. Dominic had said he thought it was better for me to arrange it, as I knew what George had requested.

The memorial service was a powerful tribute to George, both in the people who attended and the words that were spoken. Freddie Forsyth set the tone by telling the congregation, 'We have come here not to weep for our friend. George would have found that profoundly silly.' There were, however, tears, not least from me.

Afterwards, we gathered in the Great Hall in Lincoln's Inn for drinks. It was unusual to attend an event there without George, but Jeremy Thorpe and his wife, Marion, and his son, Rupert, sought me out and I spent much of the time with them. Of course, I hadn't known Jeremy at the time of his trial, but George and I had been for dinner at their home in recent years and had spent time with Marion with a dear mutual friend of ours, Lady Katy Salomon. My mother was there and many close friends George had known over the years, including Ken Dodd, Richard Branson, Cherie Blair and Norman Lamont.

Many of George's friends, clients and colleagues wrote afterwards to say how moving the memorial service had been, particularly the beautiful music and the emotional service. It was a heartfelt memorial.

George always hoped that after his death, people would say, 'In spite of all his faults, he was a fairly decent chap and had some talent as a barrister.'

CONCLUSION

The first time we met, George quoted these lines to me from *Julius Caesar*:

> There is a tide in the affairs of men,
> Which, taken at the flood, leads on to fortune;
> Omitted, all the voyage of their life
> Is bound in shallows and in miseries.
> On such a full sea are we now afloat,
> And we must take the current when it serves,
> Or lose our ventures.

This was the inspirational mantra of his life.

George was very conscious of the fickleness of life and the need not to miss any opportunity, however surprising or inconvenient it might be at that time. The reason he worked so hard was that a crucial opportunity, or turning point, if missed could have lifelong consequences. He believed his career at the Bar, when it began, was on 'a full sea' and he 'must take the current' when it came.

That vital turning point arose in George's career when he was observed by the flamboyant, well-known and respected Sir David Napley, president of the Law Society.

George was cross-examining on behalf of the manager of the Battersea Park funfair, who was charged with manslaughter, as a result of a fatal accident. Several children were killed on a roller coaster ride which came off the rails.

George had to take a very important decision as to whether to call his defendant. He was co-defending with a more senior barrister – a QC representing the consulting engineer – and he persuaded him also not to call his client. The defendants were acquitted, as the prosecution had not proved their case. George always said, 'That strategic decision was the principal feature of that case.'

Napley was notably impressed by George and his formidable cross-examining skills and these clever tactics. Napley told George that he would instruct him in his next big criminal case. A short while later, George read press headlines regarding Jeremy Thorpe MP and guessed correctly that he would be Napley's client. George repeated his tactical decision from the Battersea Park case when he represented Thorpe – again, he did not call his client, much to everyone's surprise. Closing speeches had to begin much sooner than anticipated! And so began George's ascent to greatness.

George treated each case as if it were his last, with an extraordinary drive to win and a desire not to be outdone by his opponent or by the occasional 'little obstacles', as he called them, which arose along the way. As Michael Beloff KC stated in interview:

> He had a knack of capturing the jury's attention not just with the well-polished phrases which are legion and legendary but with his intonation. The precise way in which he articulated [Gillian

Taylforth's boyfriend's] alleged words to the arresting office, "I got the urge," sticks in my mind to this day.

Another key moment in George's life was obtaining an invitation for a scholarship place to study at Balliol, Oxford – a chance he nearly missed. As detailed in the Introduction, George kept a constant vigil by the front door, waiting for the post to arrive with news from Oxford about whether he had been accepted. He was there watching when a letter came through the letter box and slipped into a tiny crack in the floorboards. He raced to his father and managed to convince him to pry up the floorboards to retrieve the letter. It was indeed the hoped-for note from Balliol College, offering him a scholarship place. George won the day, the task was fulfilled and so was George's dream! This example demonstrated George's lifelong determination to achieve his goals. He did this by attaining an unvivaed first in law at Oxford, an achievement only parallelled by his colleague Nicolas Browne-Wilkinson, who became a Lord Justice of Appeal. George was also awarded a certificate of honour in the Bar finals in 1953 and came first in the exam. He was delighted to be awarded the King George V Coronation Scholarship. This honour was presented to him by Lord Denning, who became his neighbour in Lincoln's Inn years later.

At a young age, George would be encouraged, a few times a year, to accompany his mother, often late at night, on a reconnoitre by car to her local dress boutique, to approve of her latest 'beaded evening gown design' and placement in the window. George was asked to give a second opinion on the dramatic effect of the display, the lighting and potential appeal to the passer-by – nothing was left to chance!

I am sure this early education enhanced George's constant desire to check and to be meticulous over the facts pertaining to the case in hand. He was always questioning, challenging and rehearsing with juniors and anyone whose opinion he valued. No stone would be unturned before the battle commenced, to eliminate as much of the risk as possible!

This extraordinary fortitude was instilled in him in early life (as we have seen) by his mother, who had a great influence over him and from whom he inherited the qualities of perfectionism and vigorous preparation, often over-preparation… She did not conceal her great ambition for her son, unlike George's father who was not a driving force and suggested George should go to Manchester, if he wanted to attend a university. His Irish mother, Evelyn, always dressed in a black suit with a hat and veil. Her love of music stayed with George all his life; it would provide some solace when his mother died at the early age of forty-nine. George often played on the piano pieces they both loved; he also requested them to be performed at his memorial service, where the eulogy was given by Lord Alexander QC. He was a friend and colleague whom I asked to give this address, at George's suggestion. We had spent hours talking one night, after George called out asking me to come downstairs to his ground-floor makeshift bedroom. We spoke until early in the morning while planning his memorial service. It was very emotional for me, but George treated it as his next project! He dictated a long list of names of colleagues and friends to invite – it was over 700 names long! His relationship with newspaper editors – Alan Rusbridger and others – was close after working on so many cases both for and against newspapers in libel. He also included my mother and friends of mine, such as Jarvis Astaire OBE, whom I met through the Variety Club Children's Charity, of which he had been international president and chief barker. George had been jealous of our closeness, but he had forgiven Jarvis. They spoke several times in the last months of George's life. Jarvis was on the board of the Royal Free Hospital and president of the London Federation of Boys' Clubs – his friend Prince Philip was patron – and he had raised millions for charity in his lifetime. For the memorial service, George was eager for participation by another dear friend, Frederick Forsyth, who had an excellent voice for delivery and chose to lead the bidding-prayer. Professional musicians were engaged for the service, to highlight these important musical memories in George's life. I had suggested the 'Méditation' from *Thaïs*, by Jules Massenet, as it is a particularly beautiful violin solo. George had been moved by the violin concerto played at the memorial service of one of his colleagues, Oscar Beuselinck. George had instructed him in cases over many years. George publicly revealed his love of music when he was invited by Sue Lawley to join her on *Desert Island Discs*. His eclectic taste varied from 'Danny Boy' and 'When Irish Eyes Are Smiling' to Yehudi Menuhin's rendition of Beethoven's violin concerto and the *Warsaw Concerto* – he selected this for me as a surprise.

In addition to music, George loved a good one-liner – and he excelled at making them. Near the end of George's life, Jeremy Paxman interviewed him in December for *Newsnight*, attending his home with a camera crew. George told me his son had telephoned to say he would like to meet Paxman and be present for the interview, so I was happy to have some free time. He told me he enjoyed being interviewed by Paxman and we listened to the fifteen-minute interview just before Christmas. Paxman was regarded as a tough interviewer, rather in the form of Robin Day, George's dear friend who was regarded as the killer interviewer. Day was actually very kind to George; they had a mutual respect, and I have a lovely card he wrote to George thanking him for 'permitting your name to be thundered on my behalf'. The transcript of George's interview with Paxman is presented in Appendix A. George had gone to great lengths with me to rehearse the questions he anticipated and the requisite answers. Paxman was intrigued about his famous one-liners, which often appeared in the press during the opening day or two of a case. Were they planned in advance?

George admitted that, in the Thorpe case, the final address to the jury was conceived and rehearsed two months prior to its airing. Thorpe had previously won millions of votes from people around the country, but it was the twelve jurors' votes that were the 'most precious votes of all'. George felt the case justified high drama and so theatrically moved his eyes and pointed his finger at each member of the jury, saying, 'Your vote, and yours, and yours, and yours.' To the juror or the man on the Clapham omnibus, George's words appeared off the cuff, but they were in fact meticulously planned in advance. The jury – and the public – were under his spell.

Paxman made reference to some of George's other witty quotes, which would stay in the mind of the jurors and press, becoming part of his enduring legacy.

While defending Ken Dodd, George said the unforgettable line, 'Some accountants are comedians, but comedians are never accountants.' He described Sonia Sutcliffe, wife of the Yorkshire Ripper, Peter Sutcliffe, as having 'danced on the graves of her husband's victims'. Neil Hamilton, George said, was 'on the make and on the take', a phrase that was frequently quoted in the press, as George had hoped. As he said in the interview with Paxman, he did not like Hamilton's 'unscrupulous' behaviour.

George also memorably described David Mellor MP QC as 'a man who buried his head in the sand like an ostrich, thereby exposing his thinking parts'. As George told Paxman, this was to settle an old dispute which arose at a Cambridge Union debate, which I attended. I remember the frostiness emanating from Mellor at the conclusion of the debate; he was most annoyed by George's 'put down'. The ostrich quote emanated from the case of *Mona Bauwens v. The People* in 1992. Mellor was the Minister for the Arts under Margaret Thatcher and he and his family joined Mona on holiday in Spain at her friend's large villa at the time of Iraq's invasion of Kuwait. *The People* reported, 'Top Tory and the PLO Paymaster', and Mona sued it for libel.

The People was owned by Robert Maxwell, father of Ian and Kevin, the latter of whom George represented at a parliamentary select committee hearing in 1992, in response to questions about their missing pension funds relating to their father's empire. On George's advice, Kevin refused to say anything during the entire hearing! His father, Robert, sought advice from George regarding a libel case just prior to his disappearance and death in 1991.

There may have been better lawyers, but George was the most effective advocate with a jury. Jurors were transfixed by him, as Lord Alexander commented in the eulogy for George at St Clement Danes Church, he was the correct height for his eyes to peer directly at the jurors for added impact. He would frequently 'pull a rabbit out of a hat'. The crucial video in *Taylforth*, the diary in *Allan*, the BA ticket in *Aitken* and the Mobil Oil note in *Hamilton* resulted from digging where others feared to tread. George was a mixture of vulnerable and a risk taker. He always said that 'he wouldn't be a human being if he didn't expose himself to vulnerability'. And he believed it was important to also be 'passionate about a case'. To make mistakes was 'worthwhile' and 'to not humanise yourself in order to protect' was essential.

He was a great orator and rarely used notes. He admired the great legal orators, including Lord Birkett and F. E. Smith, and he had always been a natural when it came to speaking – he excelled in the Oxford Union when at university. Notably, the first time he spoke there was at the invitation of Jeremy Thorpe, the president, in 1951. Little did either of them imagine how their paths would cross many years later.

George would have enjoyed politics and was considering standing as a candidate for the Conservative Party, however, he was warned by Lord Lawson that being a barrister and politician would result in a serious conflict of interests. As a perfectionist, he would not have been able to operate in both capacities. In later life, he would have enjoyed being appointed to the House of Lords and would have relished debating and listening to all the diverse experts. Alas, it was not to be.

Many of the cases in this book have emanated in the field of libel, something George took up later in his career, in his sixties. In the early years at the Bar, he had advised in criminal cases and represented George Best several times, a client whom I also met. The Georges stayed in touch in later life and Best had a delightfully supportive wife, Alex. (Carman even found himself in the Cromwell Hospital at the same time as Best, both receiving treatment. Alex would pop into Carman's room to see how he was.) George's teething ground at the Bar was spent primarily in Manchester, his negotiating and advocacy skills were developed as a result of his background in civil Factory Act cases. He was regularly instructed by successful solicitors like John Gorna, who became a great friend. George was often claiming damages for individuals against multinational companies or factories where standards had failed. This complex and sensitive advocacy required great tenacity and moulded him into a brilliant cross-examiner possessing a rare rapport with juries.

In libel, as other fields of law, no stone was left unturned, no secret sacred. When asked how he felt about the topics discussed in *Taylforth*, *Allan* and *Sutcliffe* and *Sanderson*, he admitted that he overcame any inhibitions he might have had in order to elicit the truth. This was one of his excellent adversarial skills which other QCs might avoid or elect not to delve into similar depths. He always upheld the principle that 'a barrister was bound by clear rules of conduct from which you could not depart'. However, he firmly believed that 'a member of the Bar could not at any cost avoid your duty of integrity to the court'.

All law students study the case of *Hinz v. Berry*, a sad case in which the Hinz family's stationary car was hit by Mr Berry's vehicle, killing the father. The wife of Mr Hinz witnessed as her husband was killed and her children were injured. She was unharmed but suffered from 'morbid depression'. This was a new area of law, as she sought compensation for her psychological suffering, not physical injury. The Court of Appeal found in her favour and hence the new principle of 'nervous shock'. The case established that a passerby who witnesses an accident and suffers a medically recognised psychiatric illness as a result can claim damages for nervous shock, even without physical injury. The court emphasised the requirement for a close relationship between the bystander and the accident victim to limit potential liability. George succeeded in achieving a high settlement for the family, one of the many high awards he won during his career.

He also held the accolade of winner of the highest personal injury award as a result of a personal injury accident. Similarly, in libel, George was responsible for the largest libel damages award, an achievement that would not be possible in 2024. Damages have been substantially reduced since the excessive awards of the past, due to a more realistic view taken by judges in guiding juries in this respect.

He also enjoyed working on a case for Aidan and Howard Barclay, sons of the owners of the Ritz Hotel in London. They instructed George to obtain a licence for their casino. The application was complex as the Gaming Act of 1968 restricted the number of casinos in London. George enjoyed working on the application, not least because the Ritz Hotel was one of his favourite places for special occasions. It also housed his farewell party – he would have been honoured that the brothers named 'The Carman' room in his memory. Regrettably, the casino is no longer and the hotel was sold.

We worked on a few cases together, where I was instructed as his junior. I have already referred to representing Renate John, Elton's wife, in their divorce case. At my request, George led me in the final stages of financial settlement as Elton had employed a QC.

The 1987 case involving Vivian Price QC, a senior Chancery silk and deputy High Court judge, was very sensitive. Vivian was a colleague from Oxford and had been George's best man. He required a silk and junior, as in Elton's case, of discretion. We did not charge a fee, as was the tradition among the Bar for colleagues.

Vivian kindly gave me a two-volume set of the *Oxford English Dictionary* – was this a hint? It was inscribed with thanks. He was a charming, clever man and was very grateful for our help.

I was very busy with my own legal work at this time, both criminal and civil. George said he would like to introduce me to solicitors as I was relatively new to the Bar. I said I didn't need his help as I had plenty of work from solicitors and from my clerks, so we only worked together on the cases I have referred to here, although he discussed all his cases with me in detail, as discussed previously.

In 1986, George was instructed in a fraud case against Roger Fisher, a leading racehorse trainer based in Ulverston, Cumbria. He was well known for training Ekbalco, one of the best two-mile hurdlers of the early 1980s, winning five important races, including the Imperial Cup.

George asked me to act as his junior and I was instructed to deal with the pre-trial issues with the prosecution junior. The case was to be heard at Preston Crown Court and George was working on another matter at the time of the first court hearing. George presented me with a red bag at the conclusion of this case – an honour to thank a junior for their work. We later both visited the racing stud in Ulverston to meet the client and we both appeared at the trial. The charges related to the fact Fisher had grossly inflated veterinary fees, before submitting them to his client, an Arabian racehorse owner. He was the chairman of the central bank, an important, wealthy businessman called Mr Fakhouri. We all agreed that Fisher would plead guilty to one of the charges. Before a jury, the case provided amusement in cross-examination by George. The main prosecution witness didn't speak good English; he kept prefixing every answer with, 'Mr Fakhouri says…' Fisher was acquitted of the remaining charges and, although hit with a heavy fine, remained a popular trainer for twenty-five years until he died in 2011.

The only other time we were together on a case was in Hong Kong. The 'Carrian' fraud case of Shamsuddin, a Hong Kong banker. The case was listed in the High Court in Hong Kong and was prosecuted by the English Attorney General, Michael Thomas QC. In Hong Kong, solicitors would occasionally instruct QCs from

London in important cases but insisted on having their local juniors. I was asked by George to join him, as he wanted to be sure that he had someone on his team whom he knew and whose instincts he trusted. The facts were complex – I shan't relate, however, the case resulted in the client admitting fraud and bribery. He was sentenced in January 1987 to a very short term for the serious offences of four years in prison. Carman had succeeded again with his persuasive advocacy. Thomas and the prosecution team were not happy. The decision was appealed, and the sentence was increased to ten years.

Michael Thomas and his wife became friends of ours, as we are members of the same tennis club. He returned to London many years ago to undertake a busy practice as a shipping QC. He and I discussed the Hong Kong case with John Mathew QC, another tennis player.

I learned a great deal from working with George, through his professionalism and determination. He had a great ability to analyse every fact with precision – nothing escaped his quick mind and extraordinary memory once he had mastered the facts of the case in hand. He possessed great charm with a jury and held their attention throughout. He was generous, as he sought my opinion throughout the cases we worked on and many we didn't. As I have stated, he would spend hours analysing every detail and particularly his cross-examination and jury speeches. I was considerably junior in call; however, he always said my instincts were good. We rarely disagreed on tactics.

George's life was cut short even while his career was still blossoming. He enjoyed his life as well as working hard, but then illness struck, which he bore with courage and stoicism. At the end of George's life, having distanced himself from religion, it became important once again. His life from the age of seven with the

Christian Brothers, at St Joseph's College, involved strict religious observance. He later moved at the age of fourteen to Upholland Seminary, where he experienced early rising for prayers and meditation. Father Tom Walsh said in his letter to me that 'he felt drawn to the outcasts of the world and there was something of his priestly vocation that lasted through to the end'. It was against this background that he was anxious to have his funeral at Westminster Cathedral, conducted by his friend, Father Michael Seed. His faith had returned and, increasingly, he felt closer to God. It gave him great strength in the last painful days of his cancer. He accepted that he was leaving this world for the next.

When, finally, his life ended after a long struggle, I had the melancholy task of arranging his memorial service, though George was determined it would be a joyful occasion for his friends and colleagues. Everyone was welcomed by eye-catching displays of sunflowers, his favourite flower.

Lord Alexander gave a moving and magisterial address, which is reproduced as an appendix on page 307. I was amazed at the diversity of over 700 people who wanted to attend the service in St Clement Danes Church on the Strand, not far from George's beloved chambers and the Royal Courts of Justice. People crammed into the church, among them Lord Shawcross QC, Jeremy Thorpe, Ken Dodd, Aidan Barclay, Sir Richard Branson, Jonathan Aitken, Lord Norman Lamont, Lord Irvine (the Lord Chancellor), Lord Williams (the Attorney General) and Cherie Blair QC (a former pupil in his chambers). Some were clients, many were dear friends or legal colleagues, others were distinguished figures from the profession and some were there in gratitude for acts of kindness or advice given; it was a remarkable tribute to the man.

George loved the words of Tennyson's poem 'Crossing the Bar'. It is a fitting way to end my tribute to my dear friend:

Sunset and evening star,
And one clear call for me!
And may there be no moaning of the bar,
When I put out to sea.
[…]
For tho' from out our bourne of Time and Place
The flood may bear me far,
I hope to see my Pilot face to face
When I have crost the bar.

APPENDIX A

PAXMAN V. CARMAN

Although George said next to nothing publicly about his illness, he did agree to an interview with Jeremy Paxman for *Newsnight*. Paxman came with a camera crew to the house in Wimbledon and began by asking George jocularly if he enjoyed his celebrity status. George was equally jocular.

CARMAN Mixed feelings, like mixed drinks, are confusion to the soul. I have mixed feelings about it. On the one hand, when you begin to be a so-called celebrity, vanity strikes initially. People recognised you; taxi drivers do, they say things like, 'Are you Jeremy Paxman?' and I say, 'No, I'm George Carman.' Once you have got over the novelty of that recognition, you lose anonymity, you lose privacy and therefore there is a downside as well as an upside to it.

PAXMAN Of course, before you became well known, you had the best part of nearly thirty years in comparative obscurity as a barrister. Did you ever think of giving it up?

CARMAN Oh, yes. Certainly in the early years. I lived in considerable poverty for the first five. I'm publicly quoted, correctly, as saying that in the fifth year at the Bar, I earned as much as a Manchester bus driver without overtime. I washed up in Lyons's. I taught bankers for £2 a night once a week. I taught American soldiers how to read and write, so I didn't do it all with a silver spoon.

PAXMAN The Thorpe case was, I suppose, the first one that brought you to big national attention. Famously, at the end of it, you made a direct appeal to the jury and you said, can you remember what you said?

CARMAN Yes, I do. I said words to the effect that in his time, Jeremy Thorpe had obtained thousands of votes from the people of this country, and now came the twelve most precious votes of all. I went round the jury pointing: 'Your vote, and yours, and yours, and yours,' and went round the whole twelve pointing, saying, 'Those are the twelve most precious votes of all.'

PAXMAN Was that something that just occurred to you on the spur of the moment?

CARMAN No.

PAXMAN So you'd rehearsed it?

CARMAN That took four to six weeks to work out.

PAXMAN Seriously? Four to six weeks?

CARMAN Absolutely, because I was searching around, as I had done in that case and several other major cases, particularly cases which are full of emotions, where emotions were running high – to have an ending that would stay in the jury's mind, inevitably, when they retired to consider their verdict.

PAXMAN Did you know you were going to win?

CARMAN No. Heavens above! If I knew that, life would be easy.

PAXMAN Could you later on read juries?

CARMAN You get instincts. It will vary enormously. The Americans go in for this in a very big way – what they call facial gestures, body movements. They give lectures on it to advocates – as only the Americans would! I think this is instinct and experience. Either you have or you haven't got it. I think it's similar to an actor. He probably gets the feel of what is going on in that audience. The great actor probably knows whether he's getting home or not.

PAXMAN Say you have a particularly sleazy client. Do you have no personal feelings, or are your personal feelings neither here nor there?

CARMAN Certainly all my clients haven't been angels and a few have been far below that. Of course you have personal feelings about your clients – as I think a surgeon would about patients, and no doubt you do about people that you interview. But the real point is to lock your personal feelings securely away in the box until the end of the case and objectively present the case intellectually, making the best points you can.

PAXMAN But when you use some of your famous devastating one-liners about people – for example, of David Mellor, 'a man who buried his head in the sand like an ostrich thereby exposing his thinking parts' – was that something that you personally felt? Was it something that you buffed up beforehand?

CARMAN I had buffed it up a little beforehand. I had heard it before. I did it for two reasons. One, he was a Cambridge man! Two, I debated with him at Cambridge. He was an ex-president of the Cambridge Union and had bullied two of my undergraduate speakers. So I thought, 'You are not going to get away with that,' and I called him in the debate an 'ex-future Prime Minister' and took the occasion of the law case to describe him in those slightly unflattering terms.

PAXMAN That's making it sound slightly like a game, isn't it?

CARMAN No, a skill. An advocacy skill.

PAXMAN Wasn't it settling a score from an old debate?

CARMAN No, it wasn't settling a score. It just came to my mind that he had behaved in a deeply unpleasant way, and I thought, 'Here's just a little bit back, David.'

PAXMAN What about your condemnation of people like Neil Hamilton, whom I think you described as 'slightly unscrupulous'?

CARMAN If I limited it to 'slightly unscrupulous', I am amazed I was so modest! I thought I'd said he was 'a man on the make and on the take' and that to me summarised exactly his modus operandi. You see, the secret, I felt – and I have always felt, as an advocate – is to find a memorable but simple phrase that will stay in a jury's mind, that they won't forget easily and that sums up for them graphically exactly the impression one hopes they're getting about that man from the evidence. The secret is the word 'communication', I suppose.

PAXMAN I don't think many people would care to have been cross-examined by you.

CARMAN I haven't counted. Nothing to fear if they are telling the truth.

PAXMAN I think the anxiety many people would have would be,

in the end, whose private life would stand up to a cross-examination by George Carman? We've all done things we shouldn't have done, that we're ashamed of.

CARMAN Absolutely. So then you make a decision in a libel court whether to claim damages or not. But if you do and you go to a jury and you say, 'Give me loads of money,' you are exposing any weaknesses or deficiencies in your own life for public scrutiny.

PAXMAN But, by and large, a person is well advised to steer clear of suing for libel, aren't they?

CARMAN 'Exercise caution' would be the advice – as I have advised many people and tried to deter many people.

PAXMAN Did your own role, and the fact that you were the most celebrated practitioner in this field, ever trouble you, so that, for example, when Aitken and *The Guardian* got into their spat, *The Guardian*'s editor would – and did – say, 'Let's get Carman quickly before Aitken gets him.' Doesn't that trouble you ever?

CARMAN It didn't trouble me in the least. Jonathan Aitken is (1) one of the cleverest politicians I have ever seen in a witness box, (2) one of the cleverest men I've ever seen in the witness box and (3) one of the most scrupulously prepared men ever in the witness box.

PAXMAN I was thinking more that the outcome of a case could be predicated upon who was appearing for whom.

CARMAN This has been a subject of endless debate of the law. Some of the great advocates of the past have put it as low as 10 per cent differential, some have said as high as 50 per cent. At the end of the day, I wouldn't deny that the role of the advocate plays some significant part.

PAXMAN Does it bother you that you have this image as a horrid man?

CARMAN Oh, I didn't know I had that!

PAXMAN People are frightened of you.

CARMAN People are frightened. I think there is a difference between people being afraid of being cross-examined in a courtroom and people regarding you as a horrid man.

PAXMAN I'm not suggesting personally; they don't know you.

CARMAN Of course not. But the horrid man image would come from the mistaken idea that the barrister is there bullying people all the time, leaning on them unfairly, taking advantage of them in the witness box. That's the way to lose a case. If you have a simple, truthful person, you can never bully them into changing their story if they're telling the truth. The technique to be used in questioning people will vary enormously. If they think they can stand up to it – like an Aitken or like a Neil Hamilton, who had been a government minister, fluent speaker, intelligent man, barrister and so on – those people can well take it on the chin and hit back. But, of course, if you have a more simple soul, you don't lean on them. You ask questions that may probe, but you don't want the jury ever to think that you are being unfair or oppressive.

PAXMAN Now that you have decided to retire on health grounds, do you miss it?

CARMAN Oh, enormously. It's a very addictive profession.

PAXMAN What have you learned from suffering from cancer?

CARMAN I've learned a very great deal, because we all start off in comparative ignorance of it.

PAXMAN And terror, I would imagine.

CARMAN And terror. First of all, it is a disease where the patient can contribute a great deal of help himself, if he or she can retain their morale and their hopes and not lose that. Second, the future of treatment of cancer depends on cancer research. Cancer research depends on money. Money depends on two sources at the moment – government and the charities. I personally believe profoundly that they are the wrong way round. The governments are playing the part of satellite to the charities. It should be the charities being satellite to the government. It is right to say, in fairness to this government, they've woken up late, they're putting more in, but it pales into insignificance to what's really needed. The message is, if I have a moment to say this, government should revisit their contribution to the charities or the cancer areas that require research profoundly, and they could do immense good and save thousands of lives on an annual basis.

PAXMAN Do you think you'll beat it?

CARMAN Oh, I wish I knew! When I was brought up as a Catholic boy, you were supposed to pray to St Jude for hopeless causes, so I've started doing that.

APPENDIX B

JAMES PRICE QC ON GEORGE CARMAN

George knew, better than most, that *everything* that an advocate does or says in court when the jury is present, even the direction in which he looks, matters.

When not on his feet, George sat quiet and still, not slouched, and usually looking straight ahead or at the witness or judge. He listened very intently to everything said. He would permit no distraction from client, solicitor or junior (who have a tendency to want to whisper things to their leader or pass him messages). He rarely made a note. This requires a lot of confidence. Most advocates feel the need to make a note of points to make in answer to arguments their opponent is addressing to the judge, or of points on which to challenge the witness. By concentrating intently, George understood and fixed in his mind what mattered, so that when his turn came, he was able to address the points directly, simply and fluently (and without, of course, burying his head in a note).

When on his feet, he stood quite still and upright, or he leaned *forward* on the lectern for emphasis, hands to his side or resting on the lectern. He never leaned back against the bar, or paced up and down, or made gestures with his arms or hands, or slouched, or put his foot up on a seat or on the rail behind him. In other words, he avoided distracting the jury. When examining a witness, he looked at the witness, not at the jury. He kept an eye on the jury, but never let them realise they were being watched.

His voice was a great asset to him, classless and gravelly (helped, of course, by frequent cigarettes). He did not speak very loudly, sometimes quite quietly. His *manner* of speaking was invariably courteous; I would say sometimes an old-world courtesy. For example, when challenging Mrs Sutcliffe (the wife of the Yorkshire Ripper) on her claimed lack of romantic interest in the Greek travel agent with whom the *News of the World* had linked her, he asked, 'When on holiday, does not the attention of a young man make a lady's heart beat a little faster?' Questions which might be thought intrusive were introduced with an apparently considerate 'Forgive me…' That did not, of course, stop him from asking highly intrusive questions in the most direct way possible, when necessary (as it often was). When not necessary, such a question alienates the jury.

His manner was unhurried. Such a manner inspires confidence in any audience. It also means that things are taken at a pace at which they can be well understood by judge or jury. This is surprisingly rare in advocates, some of whom are so conscious of the amount they have to get through, that parts of what they say or read out are taken too fast to make much impression. George never had that problem, because he never had that much to get through, even in a long and complicated case. He had cut the case down to the points that really matter or, since he quite often worked without a note (or if he had one, did not look at it much), that he remembered. What he remembered, of course, was what mattered. He never ignored what may appear to be obvious. Often the obvious point is the most important one in the case. If so, he kept it at the forefront.

He was quite capable of introducing a little humour into a case to lighten the atmosphere, but he never forgot, and never allowed the jury to forget, that a trial is a serious occasion, especially when serious charges are about. He was invariably respectful to the judge, even when submitting, as always directly and without circumlocution, that the judge had just done something improper.

He was famous as a cross-examiner. But examination-in-chief is as much an art as cross-examination, no easier and no less important in getting your case across to the jury. Two keys to George's technique, in this as in all other aspects of his advocacy, were human understanding and the elimination of everything that does not matter or is on the periphery.

George had an instinctive, as well as developed, understanding of human nature. He knew that, where the witness is going to be attacked as a liar, and it is vital that they should be believed, they must be presented to the jury as a rounded human being. An example is the three witnesses in the *Hamilton v. Fayed* case, who were or had been on Al Fayed's staff and who testified to their involvement in the preparation and delivery of the famous brown envelopes to Hamilton. So, before the witnesses were asked to speak about envelopes, the jury were given a picture of where they came from, their family circumstances, their earlier careers, perhaps their interests, the day-to-day nature of their work and so forth. Thus, the jury could better judge whether they were the sort of people who would lie for their employer or ex-employer.

At every moment, George was conscious of how what was being said would be followed and understood by the jury. The questions were simple and direct. A change of topic would be signalled by some such formula as, 'I move on to ask you about…' If a concept arose that a jury might not be familiar with, he would stop the witness and have them explain in simple language (always identifying himself with the jury as the one who needed to have the matter explained).

When arriving at the nub of the witness's evidence, such as the preparation of the brown envelope, attention would be aroused and focused. There might be a pause, a change in his tone of voice, and often a formula such as, 'Now, Mr B, in your own words, please, would you tell my Lord and the jury how…' He quite often said 'please'.

Half, or sometimes more than half, of what was in the witness's statement would simply be passed over and ignored, so as to get to the points that mattered. George invariably focused attention on the four or five things that really matter in any case, even quite a complicated case, and was ruthless in pruning unnecessary and distracting detail. This was sometimes a rather hair-raising process for those working with him, because on occasion some really quite important points would simply disappear, occasionally because he forgot them. What it showed was that the selection of the points that matter can be bold and that if you deal with every point, you bury the ones that matter.

There is something mythical now about George's cross-examination technique. People ask what was so brilliant about it and what the trick was which so devastated and demolished witnesses. George was not superhuman. Given the material, he would use it to great effect. Without the material, he would make no great impact on the witness. For example, I think that Jonathan Aitken emerged largely unscathed from cross-examination by George, though it certainly exposed improbabilities in his account of the payment of his bill at the Ritz. But a successful cross-examination by George was a thrilling experience for the onlooker, and nobody could do it better. This is partly a question of personality. Though small in stature, he had a commanding presence in court. When he stood up, people paid attention, expecting something to happen. He was never theatrical, often dramatic.

For example, if a witness, such as Jani Allan, when denying an affair alleged by a TV programme, has evinced disapproval of and aversion to adultery, it is not difficult to discomfort the witness, if you are presented (as George was) at the last minute with a diary in which the witness records details of interest in their own handwriting. But few could reproduce the dramatic effect with which George was able to introduce this evidence, having carefully and quietly laid the ground for it by committing the witness to a version of events they would later regret. Then there would be the change of tone which signalled that something was about to happen, and a series of simple and absolutely direct questions, completing the witness's discomfiture.

For the longer or more complicated cross-examinations, George would work from a note – but a fairly short one, which simply identified the points that needed to be made. He always asked simple questions. That sounds easy, but in fact requires great skill and thought, if the ground being covered is at all complicated. One hears a lot of convoluted questions in courtrooms. You are hardly likely to corner the witness if the witness has difficulty following the question. George was always very clear in his own mind exactly where the witness's problem lay on any particular aspect of their account. It is often easy to spot, when reading the witness statements and documents, that the witness has a problem about a particular part of their evidence, or that there is material which discredits them, but more difficult to pinpoint it with absolute clarity. George gave a lot of thought to these points, which enabled him to put them to the witness so simply and clearly that the witness, as well as the jury, were carried along by the logic of it. This was uncomfortable for the witness who can see the logic of your position better than that of their own.

George's cross-examinations were never blunted by the inclusion of too many points or too much detail. He went straight to the point. Nor was there more than the minimum distraction of looking at documents. A witness who is not telling the truth is, of course, often caught out by the contemporary records of the events – correspondence, telephone records and so forth. So, ultimately, a cross-examination may depend on taking the witness to a document which he is going to have difficulty in explaining. But a cross-examination which becomes a paper chase through documents (as many do) is likely to be diffuse. This was not a problem for George, not least because of his almost unbelievable (for a very experienced advocate) inability to find any given document. In a trial of any length, a little heap of paper, in no order, would accumulate along the bench in front of him, and a document handed to him for use in cross-examination would quickly become irretrievably lost, and then he would have to be given it again at the critical moment.

None of this mattered. The helping hand of junior and solicitor was there, and he did not need many documents. If the witness is not very sharp or is ill-prepared or both – and they are lying – they present little difficulty. If they are bright and have thoroughly studied the documents and witness statements (Jonathan Aitken was the model in this respect), they will give the answer you expect, without the necessity of taking them to the document which says it. And so they are led along, until they are confronted with the one document that they cannot explain. It makes for a much more focused, and dramatic, cross-examination. The witness may have spotted their problem in advance. Then they are likely to start demonstrating their difficulty in explaining even before they get there, and that is perhaps even more telling.

Except in cases of complexity, George often made his closing speech to the jury without a note. That makes for wonderful contact with the jury – just leaning forward on the lectern with hands clasped together, looking at the jury. Lesser advocates will be relieved to know that equally, he sometimes read speeches off a typescript. But it was never apparent that he was reading a script.

APPENDIX C

LORD ALEXANDER'S MEMORIAL SPEECH

In every generation of barristers, there are many fine advocates and, indeed, a few who are quite outstanding. Even among such talents, George Carman stood out as the most celebrated jury advocate of the second half of the twentieth century.

He was a great defender in difficult and demanding criminal cases and, in the last decade of his life, this diminutive, dapper man became the dominant, formidable and highly successful giant of the libel Bar.

'Gorgeous George', the nickname thrust on him, was himself a star who battled for a roll call of stars from the worlds of politics, show business and the media. All this, George achieved from a humble home and small beginnings. He was born with no silver spoon in his mouth, nor was his family well connected. He came from Blackpool. His father was an auctioneer. His Irish mother started as a seamstress and went on to be proprietor of several dress shops. She was far and away the most important influence on his life. She imbued him with ambition, drive and a passionate will to win. From a Catholic school, he won a scholarship to Balliol College, Oxford.

There, his initial inclination to become a priest diminished and rather more deliberately he shed his northern accent. He read literature avidly, devouring the rhetoric of great writers such as Cicero, Milton, Macaulay and Churchill. He recognised early, as Lord Denning used so often to stress, that words are the tools of an advocate's trade. His early fascination with language was to serve him well. So, too, was his fine mind. He gained a first-class degree in law, followed by a scholarship from Lincoln's Inn.

He then faced the long struggle to start at the Bar. To get going in practice has always been demanding, but this was never more so than at the time George was called in 1953. Those of us who followed some years later hear stories of many people of notable ability who had failed at the Bar in the 1950s. Work was in short supply and legal aid fees were derisory. So George decided to try his hand on the Northern Circuit, but he had to draw on all his considerable resources of determination to survive at all.

In his first three years in Manchester, he earned, in his own words, 'less than a Manchester bus conductor but without the overtime'. He kept going with the aid of part-time odd jobs: he did libel readings for newspapers, he washed up in a Lyons's Corner House. But a circuit practice was then, as it is now, the best training ground for an all-round advocate.

Life at the Bar has often been compared to life in the theatre: knockabout circuit life is like being a strolling player, sometimes in repertory, sometimes sheer vaudeville with the occasional appearance on the rather grander stages of the greater regional theatres. One man plays many parts, learns in a hurry and acts out before widely differing audiences. Here George Carman added to his intelligence and willpower a down-to-earth, highly effective, sometimes pungent style of advocacy. He learned to be adaptable to different types of work – from crime to divorce to personal injury. He learned, too, to adapt his performances to different tribunals – from lay magistrates to judges sitting alone to shrewd northern juries. It took George almost twenty years to move up through the ranks of juniors, about par for the course for a good circuit practitioner. He developed a large personal injury practice, he advised Manchester United, he appeared successfully for George Best in the last breach of marriage case in this country. In these tough years, his financial rewards were unremarkable. He was to wait a long time for the good fees that clients were willing to pay as they clamoured for his services later on in life.

In 1971, he was rewarded by what all barristers aspire to: he was granted silk. He chose to stay for the time being in the north and he declined a seat in a prominent London chambers. All careers have their defining moments and most of them require a touch of luck. For George, the good fortune was to be noticed by Sir David Napley, a leading solicitor, and chosen by him to defend Jeremy Thorpe on a charge of conspiracy to murder. His opponent was as good as there could be, Peter Taylor QC, later Lord Chief Justice, prosecuting. The case was demanding and knife-edged. George was conscious of the potential prejudice that then existed in that less tolerant age. He had the courage to advise his client not to give evidence. He worked tirelessly on his final speech over four weekends in the solitude of a hotel room. Towards the end, he went for some high drama. He reminded the jury that Thorpe in his time had won millions of votes from people in this country. Now came the most precious and important votes of all. George went from juror to juror, moving his eyes and finger to each member. 'Your vote, and yours, and yours.' It was a *coup de théâtre* few advocates would have dared. But one of George's gifts was a psychological, almost instinctive, affinity with jurors and what they were thinking.

The best advocacy is not just a skill or a craft but an art. Great advocates have antennae which seem to reach out into the minds and emotions of the jury. George had this artistry, these gifts, in abundance. It was 1979; after a quarter of a century at the Bar, he had made his breakthrough. Other notable criminal cases followed fast. George defended Dr Leonard Arthur, charged with the murder of a baby suffering from Down syndrome. Dr Arthur, a noted paediatrician, had prescribed 'nursing care only' for the baby. In his final speech, George said, Dr Arthur 'could, like Pontius Pilate, have washed his hand of the matter. He did not, because good doctors do not turn away. Are we to condemn him as a criminal because he helped two people at the time of their greatest need, condemn him as a doctor because he cared?' No case gave him greater satisfaction.

His list of successes also included the acquittal of Ken Dodd on a charge of tax evasion. Again, he coined a memorable line when he declared to the jury, 'Some accountants are comedians, but comedians are never accountants.' His famous sayings lacked the paradox of Oscar Wilde or the wit of Dorothy Parker. But their clarity and power hit home with juries with deadly effect. These and other one-liners were apparently impromptu but, of course, were the result of hard work and meticulous rehearsal. George now had a different challenge: living up to his own reputation. Every fashionable barrister knows that the spotlight on a trial in open court is a glaring one. You're ultimately only as good as your last case.

Of all of George's successful acquittals, it could be said that a fine barrister might have won each of them. What is remarkable is that George won so many. What is also remarkable is that, close to the age of sixty, he sought out new challenges. His temperament would never allow him to rest on his laurels. He passionately and ceaselessly craved success. He decided that the excitement and the action lay in libel cases. Libel has always been regarded as one of the most important aspects of civil law. It carries, unlike virtually all other civil cases, the right to trial by jury. Many see this right, as Mr Moulder said in Trollope's novel *Orley Farm*, as 'the bulwark of the British constitution'. Libel brings into dramatic conflict the right of an individual to his just reputation, with the freedom of the press to report truthfully and to comment trenchantly. Libel actions, too, have always fascinated the public from the now half-forgotten days before the cinema and television when it was prime entertainment.

George realised that while the details of the libel law were tediously, bizarrely and sometime abstrusely technical, it was good advocacy that swung the results. So he was in his element. His case list over this decade or so was massive. His clients included the *News of the World*, Norman Tebbit, Richard Branson, Elton John, *The Sun*, Marco Pierre White, Christopher Brasher, Imran Khan, *The Guardian* and Mohamed Al Fayed. And so I could go on. Many of them are here tonight and all of them are grateful. In all these cases, for all the unpredictability of jury trials, George was successful.

He did lose from time to time, but he did not do so often. He had a particularly courageous foray to Singapore where he represented J. B. Jeyaretnam, the solitary opposition MP, against the combined assault of the Prime Minister and, even more dauntingly, the senior minister of Singapore. While he lost on liability, damages were limited to 10 per cent of those claimed.

George, like all successful people, had his critics. Some said he appealed to the jury by a conspiratorial nod and a wink disdaining the impassivity which is the conduct of the Bar. He readily acknowledged that he had learned some tricks from the entertainers at the end of Blackpool Pier. It was said that he was sometimes too damned offensive in cross-examination. No barrister should ask a question unnecessary to the presentation of his client's case and George was wholly true to the ethos of his profession and knew this perfectly well. But he also believed that where an unpleasant charge had to be made, it needed to be put fairly and squarely and any advantage rubbed in thoroughly. Few of the clients who depended on his skills at critical moments in their lives complained at the vigour of his presentation.

Sometimes, too, he seemed to pull rabbits out of a hat. In several of his cases, evidence arrived at the last minute and created the advantage of surprise. But no one could properly suggest that George kept this material up his sleeve. Its late arrival reflected the fact that, together with his solicitors, he was conscientiously and tirelessly searching right up to the final stages of the case for any material that would help to establish the truth. His solicitors, with many of them here tonight, knew just how hard he drove them, just how hard he worked with them so tirelessly. The roll call of cases had no pattern; this list of clients no common thread. George did not just appear for newspapers or just against them. He represented, as a barrister should, all comers. He gladly accepted the difficult cases and the uphill task brought out the best in his fighting spirit. He made the claimants for whom he appeared feel that their reputation would be properly protected. But he also made the media feel in his last decade that they could, after all, win libel cases if they took a vigorous line of attack. No wonder he was first choice. Individual cases, in their time, are of great importance to the protagonists and of great interest to the public. But as the autobiographies of past barristers show, their interest tends to fall and stale with the perspective of time.

So what are the lasting achievements by which George Carman will be remembered? I hope aspiring barristers will remember him for his sheer skills. To appear against him was to know that you were engaged in a titanic contest, with his straining every sinew, preparation, concentration and thoroughness of advocacy to sway the jury. His opening might seem like total hyperbole, but it did not strike the jury that way. He was a devastating cross-examiner. 'To be Carmanised', as one of his victims put it, 'was a dire experience.' He was a terrier who first snapped at the heels of a witness, then dug his teeth in and did not let go. He bonded with juries and studied tirelessly. In this, his small physical stature helped: standing in counsel's robes with the jury at a higher level, he could look each juror in the eye and build his bond with them. He could look at the same time at the judge, jurors, witnesses and yet have one eye on reporters as he delivered a telling phrase.

When once asked his own formula for success, he responded, 'Hard work, dedication, passionate commitment, a belief that a greater responsibility rests upon you in terms of the client. And a constant vigilance of self-criticism to see how you can improve.' He was immensely thorough and believed you could never be over prepared. And he had that essential quality without which no advocate is complete: courage.

George did not become a judge. In 1982, he nearly went to Hong Kong to take up a judicial appointment. Fortunately for the Bar, and his clients, he changed his mind. I know that at one time, he had strong ambitions to become a High Court judge, but, in truth, he was a born advocate and had no lasting regrets. The last time I talked to him, he suddenly said, 'I'm getting worse. I don't have time to get to restrooms and will not have time to get my autobiography done. But I have no self-pity and have had immense good fortune in my life.' It was the law that shaped George's life and was his principal passion. His marriages were not a success. He blamed that on himself, although it did not stop him liking the company of women. He had a constant thread of deep affection linking him to his son, Dominic, himself a wordsmith. Father and son were close and would discuss George's cases. He was glad, too, to have grandchildren, Matthew, Kristin, Charlie and Isabel. In the last fifteen years of his life, he enjoyed a regular companionship with Karen, herself a barrister on whom George practised his speeches and to whom he turned for criticism of his performance in court. Together they enjoyed theatre and holidays and restaurants. Karen helped him through his final demanding months and eased his loneliness.

For I sense George was lonely. He was not easy to read. One part of him enjoyed the company of the stars for whom he appeared and dining at the Ritz and Le Caprice. In private life, he was warm, wry and engaged in sometimes quizzical conversations. He was never stuffy and mixed easily with the young. He liked young people and those who wanted to give Bar a go.

But he did seem to withhold some of the depths of his personality. Why was he so private? Was it because of the failures in his personal life, or were those failures because he found it difficult to reach the depths of intimacy? Or was it because all else in his life was dominated by the law and his care for his clients and this passion left little room for anything else? It's idle to speculate because we shall never know. But nor, in the long run, does it matter to us. It matters to us that what he achieved was of prime importance to his clients and a fine advertisement for our profession. The Bar is an independent, individual and sometimes maverick trade. It relies on skill, courage and the fearless pursuit of truth. It is there to protect the individual against the juggernaut of the state. Great advocacy before juries has, since the time of Thomas Erskine and, indeed, long before, been seen as essential in a free country. George Carman, because of the fame he won, demonstrated these values to a wider public. His fame and the interest he aroused helped the readers of broadsheets and tabloids alike to understand the Bar and so to understand why the advocate is important to society.

George professed only the most modest aspirations for his own obituary. 'What I would like them to say is, in spite of all his faults, he was a fairly decent chap and had some talent as a barrister.'

That is far too slight an assessment. What George strove for and achieved was a reputation as a winner, a tireless *batailleur*. He said:

> What matters in life is a passionate commitment to something which you profoundly believe in. In my case, this was the professional work of a barrister and, above all else, that the decision that this is perhaps to be the most important thing in your life. Not the achievement of the successes you have, but the achievement of deploying what talent you have in the interests of others.

By these highly demanding standards, George Carman's life served his clients well. He brought great lustre to our profession. One of his finest predecessors as a jury advocate Norman Birkett once wrote, 'Many opinions have, in the view of those best qualified to judge, that simplicity of speech linked with the expression of the deepest feelings of mankind, which always has power to stir the blood.'

George Carman had these rare skills and he used them to the very full.

APPENDIX D

VERONICA VARNEY'S MEMORIES OF GEORGE CARMAN

When George Carman QC died peacefully at home on 2 January 2001, the world lost a famous and highly respected advocate, who loved his work and was sought after by clients and solicitors. Sadly, he was forced to retire several months before, due to progression of his prostate cancer affecting his mobility, which would have implications for his courtroom work. One of his greatest concerns was over the many pending cases and the clients that he would let down. This came second to his deeply personal sadness at giving up the Bar, which had given meaning to his life. For the illness itself, he showed no fear and didn't complain, viewing the cancer in a detached way since the diagnosis.

On 2 January, I also lost his close friendship and remember with affection all the times that we spent together and the endless evening discussions, meals out and shows we had shared since our first meeting with my friend Karen Phillipps.

A few days before George died, he told me that he had never expected death so early in his life. I replied that few people had achieved in their lifetime what he had! Since he had been a chain-smoker, his statement did surprise me for a moment, as it suggested that he never saw smoking as linked to a shorter lifetime.

His complete calm and acceptance of his death showed courage.

I believe that George always knew he had the gift and ability to become a very distinguished lawyer, and until he proved it to himself, he was a restless man earlier in his life. But this changed with success.

George was determined he would make something of his life. As a child, his mother presented a great role model of a driven and successful businesswoman who worked hard with her dress shops and clearly stood out as ahead of her time combining the roles of a housewife, mother and career woman. He spoke of her to me often. He described her as successful and they shared the closest bond. His father was a more relaxed and content man, who was not dynamic and had the attitude of going with the flow of life. This was very different from George and his mother. As a result, George did not identify very much with his father during his lifetime and spoke only a little about him to me.

His mother's financial success did benefit George's education. George frequently discussed his early Catholic upbringing and life as an altar boy, along with his mother's aspirations for him to be a priest. He described his memories of time in the seminary and his visit to Rome, which he viewed as a prelude to progression of a career 'of the cloth'.

George was strong enough to not follow his mother's career choice and the excuse was his 'discovery of girls'! I believe this represented to him a belief that he may not conform to the priesthood with uncertainty about faith, lifestyle and lack of academic challenge, for one of such solid intellect.

George had excellent teachers who recognised his academic talents. He never criticised the Roman Catholic faith but never spoke in detail about any belief in God to me. He did, however, welcome meetings with Father Michael Seed and had long discussions of great interest to him in the months after he retired.

George was always certain that he made the correct decision not to pursue the priesthood but often expressed interest in what may have happened had he done so. His university, Balliol College, had produced many famous lawyers, judges and politicians and was well suited to George's ability. The reputation and expectation, as George said, was to work hard and succeed.

George told me that for much of his time at Oxford, he was preoccupied with thoughts of girls and what the sexual experience might be like, wasting hours or days at a time. This was set against a background of Catholicism, which generated conflict. His studies were affected and he was warned he'd need to work hard especially in his final year. This he did, and he passed out with a first-class degree in law. He was eager to get engaged during college, but this did not occur, although he did marry his first wife shortly after leaving college.

The degree did open doors but did not secure a large income, leaving George on the bottom rung of a very long ladder. He said work of variable intellectual challenge frustrated him and was unsettling. In addition, he was extremely sad over his mother's death when he was in his early twenties. She had been a close confidante and adviser and expected high standards from George. This may have led to some of the unchecked heavy drinking that followed. He always spoke of his mother's ovarian cancer and watching their GP draw off pleural fluid from his mother's chest while she was leaning over the kitchen table to improve her breathlessness. He said he visualised all these images for very many years and it took a long time to recover.

George said income in his early Manchester years was less than a bus driver and the next work assignment was always uncertain. He considered leaving the Bar at one stage, due to the poor income and scarcity of work. He had endless gratitude for his then mentor, who told him not to give up and assured him that 'his time would come'. George listened and heeded his words of encouragement, which prevented the loss of a yet undiscovered and brilliant future barrister.

George had great respect for the average man in the street, surviving by hard work and, in his day, with often little education. He knew them and how they thought and reacted to life. He had a fascination with the human condition which he always spoke of in every aspect of life, be it in the courts with the jury or life in general. He felt that the pressures of life and the complexity of survival in our world had interesting effects on human reactions.

The George that I first met was a man in his fifties, having relocated to London in the mid-1980s from Manchester. He appeared fundamentally a man's man but enjoyed the company of women socially.

In contrast to most lawyers, George was a clear and concise communicator with a very attractive speaking voice that was very easy to listen to. His stories of past cases were animated and interesting without any chance of being boring. He enjoyed the challenge of current court cases and described past court successes and equally analysed the failures, but to me he never bragged.

George always had sympathy with the losers in court even when found guilty, as he felt for the effect on their life and their family. This was expressed privately once the courtroom battle was settled.

He never harboured any vendetta, no matter how hard the courtroom battle had been. He liked those who lived life on the edge and risked it all; they appealed to him.

In George's company, you were aware of his intellect and ability to rapidly assimilate and understand information including that well outside his field, such as medicine or science, along with stimulating and enquiring questions. He would grasp facts rapidly and always say 'understood' or 'indeed', which meant no further explanation was required.

George's intellect and broad education, including an extensive knowledge of literature, allowed him to see relevant parallels with his clients and his legal cases. He would sometimes use quotes from Shakespeare during his summing up to the jury with great effect that was both humorous and memorable and later quoted by reporting journalists.

George described his defence of Dr Leonard Arthur from the charge of manslaughter in 1981 as an important case to him personally. He was also impressed by the level of knowledge in the medical expert witnesses and felt that he too may have enjoyed an academic medical career.

He was not a great lover of small talk and told me he did not truly enjoy celebrity parties and would limit how many he attended, despite many invitations. This may explain why he always spoke of the law or world affairs to all who would listen, rather than mundane small talk about the weather.

When out socially with George, I noticed that he could and would converse with everyone – including taxi drivers, waiters, cleaners and security people – without any pomposity and would generate an interesting conversation of relevance to them, whether he knew them or not. I could see how this gift allowed George to relate so well to people of the jury, leading to journalists reporting his 'mesmerising effect' upon them.

George had a good constitution and was seldom ill nor tired in mind or body; he disliked neuroticism and never spoke nor worried about symptoms or illness, both before and after his diagnosis of prostate cancer. He studied and understood all the reports and scans in respect of his prostate cancer and any progression of his condition just like a 'brief' in law. He would show his reports to me and others to update us and get our opinion. He went to court daily, despite early morning radiotherapy, and thought nothing of this and made no fuss whatsoever.

He enjoyed a peaceful home and appreciated outdoor space following his move from central London to Wimbledon in the 1990s. His gardens in Wimbledon were peaceful and a delight to sit in. I felt it represented his escape from the pressures of court life. His hobbies were walks around Wimbledon Park and Cannizaro House, seeing West End London shows and eating out at restaurants, especially for Thai food. He was generous and would insist on paying for everyone present, and it would be very difficult to convince him otherwise.

He was happy to entertain at home or at restaurants – Karen's mother Audrey and my mother Jean were frequently invited. They liked him and found his conversation and company of great interest. My mother had especially followed many past criminal cases including Jeremy Thorpe long before we knew George. Hearing first-hand the full stories of cases gave added interest and was captivating.

Invitations would be extended for festive celebrations to them to come to his Wimbledon home. The central London life of drinks after court reduced after he moved to Wimbledon, as he tended to work more from home.

George was more focused on other people's lives as a source of conversation than himself. He seldom spoke about his own personal issues, although his childhood, Roman Catholic upbringing and time at Balliol were discussed. He did discuss his ex-wives, describing their work and how they met and married but clearly his career interests trumped his interest in marriage. He talked about his son Dominic and his grandchildren frequently. All three grandsons went on to study law and became solicitors.

George had beautiful Venetian artwork at home and often holidayed in Venice. Another destination he enjoyed was Dubai, which he first visited for the case of Sheikh Maktoum and then returned to a few times, before it became fashionable and overcrowded.

When I visited George at home, he would offer wine and food. He was happy to be visited and particularly enjoyed one-to-one conversations. He was a true 'wise owl' people would go to for advice. He gave his house and driveway entry code to friends and the location of the key to his front door without fear. George would sit and talk for hours. He had humour, charm and charisma and in conversation, he gave you 100 per cent of his attention. Time would fly by due to the interest of the subject. George would largely chain-smoke, drink coffee and have a glass of wine. Discussions with George made you realise his advanced understanding of all manner of emotions that could drive jealously, violence, deceit or drug and alcohol misuse.

He detailed accounts of court cases from the past, which were delivered concisely with the human element emphasised. They were all fascinating and included many that never reached the newspapers from his time in Manchester. The more famous cases that changed George's career would reveal the enormous amount of thought and time that was required for the winning formula. Active court cases took over his thoughts and he gave all his intellectual capacity to them to get to the winning formula. He never indicated insecurity over his work to me. His focus was on the client. His sense of duty to his clients and the effects of his advocacy on the outcome of a trial drove him to do his very best in the courtroom.

When his sister died, he was sad that they had not had a close relationship. He recalls the differences in their lives, as his sister was a housewife. He found this hard to relate to and felt she had no idea about more important issues in life and the 'bigger picture'.

George showed little interest in material things. Although he dressed smartly and looked after his possessions, luxuries were seldom a topic for discussion. I never knew him to brag about anything.

Between 1991 and 1996, I was working 100 miles from London and saw less of George as a result. When my mother died in 1993, he phoned to see how I was. I remember and appreciate his thoughtful phone call and comforting words and kindness, which have not been forgotten.

After I moved to Surrey in 1996, we were less than ten miles apart and we met more frequently, as I worked in Wimbledon two afternoons each week. I remember George's phone call at my new house when the hall was full of unpacked boxes and the ringing phone was difficult to find. He told me a CT scan had shown a single bony metastasis in the pelvis, with no clear primary tumour. George was calm and explained that he would be having a biopsy from the area. The biopsy gave no definite primary site. I was convinced it was prostate cancer from the outset. Extensive tests were performed but nothing was confirmed. Due to the uncertainty in the first three years, radiotherapy was given to the pelvic bony tumour and a wait-and-watch policy with regular scans was adopted. George remained well and unperturbed by it all, including a great number of invasive tests. Eventually, further prostate biopsies proved positive. I remember George telling me in Wimbledon high street, about eighteen months before he died, that he accepted that the prostate cancer would at some point kill him. He had never spoken like that before!

After that announcement, his scans gradually showed new bony tumours in the pelvis, until there were effects on his standing and walking which forced him to retire.

It was a very sad time discussing with George the awful dilemma of whether he could continue to work for a few more months or not. He was objective and calm about situations that had suddenly arose, but he was hugely disappointed and concerned about making the best decision for his clients, so as not to withdraw partway through their court case.

George was a close and confiding friend whom I greatly admired and loved. We had a similar outlook on life, including the importance of a sense of purpose in life. I greatly respected his intellect and his non-neurotic approach to life and illness. We both enjoyed genuine conversation and we could discuss any topic, including my research, for which he left money in his will.

It was so sad to see his life end while he had such interest in everything and was more in demand than ever workwise. Due to his problems with walking, I would sometimes pop round to check he could get up the stairs safely at night. His glance towards me conveyed his frustration without complaint – nor were words required.

When George died, I was working locally in Wimbledon and arrived at 4 p.m. I went into George's room alone and sat quietly there for thirty minutes. I had a feeling of great sadness and loss that extended to his advocacy and the law. I also had that feeling of disbelief which occurs when someone dies, even when the death is expected.

I drove home later after George's death, still numb. The evening TV news was already announcing George's passing and the papers had full stories for days and weeks. I was unable to attend the funeral due to work commitments. I did attend his wonderful memorial service, which included so many people that George had worked with, including clients, judges, politicians, clerks, clergy, family and friends.

I enjoyed the tributes to George and was thankful and proud to have known him and for the close genuine friendship and respect that we shared. George was unique and I thank him for his great friendship. He touched very many lives and took with him his amazing gift of advocacy. He will never be forgotten.

ACKNOWLEDGEMENTS

I have been greatly helped by many friends, colleagues and former clients of George Carman in the completion of this book. I very much appreciate all the friendship, time, support and patience they have exhibited. Writing a book can be a lonely occupation, but they have lessened this state and kept me very busy.

Thank you to those many people who originally encouraged me to write this book in George's honour, Jarvis Astaire, Norman Lamont for his constant guidance, Iain Johnstone, Tim Hartnoll, Ted Fort, Chris and Ali Griffiths, John Matthew QC, Simon Heffer, Audrey Phillipps, Veronica Varney, Paula, Henry Crawford, Dani, Penny and Dennis Marks, Jeannette Owide, Steve Richards, Keith Richards, Michael Beloff KC, Tom Grant KC, James Price QC, Jonathan Sumption KC, Graham Boal QC, Rosamund Horwood-Smart KC, Julian Bevan QC, Stanley Brodie QC, Philip King QC, Gerrard Tyrrell, Susan Aslan, Michael Cole, Jeffrey Archer, Nigel West, Sasha Swire, Judge Rob Rinder, Jonathan Caplan KC, Heather Rogers KC, Tony Clover KC, Rosie Boycott, Charles Howard KC, Hugh Tomlinson KC, Sir David Napley, Alastair Hutchinson, Raine Spencer, Aidan and Howard Barclay, Michael Seal, Danny

Unger, Lady Colin Campbell, Simon Astaire, Lady Katy Salomon, William Dartmouth, Christina, Leo and Elena Drollas, Ludka, Robin Syret, John and Jenny Brinkley, Simon and Chris Weber, Joe Thai, Philippa Juul, Viv Levan, Anna Watts, Sue, Michelle and Steve, Carol Gilbert, James Aukland, Peter Begg, Eleanor and Alex Jensen, Simon and Tricia Mansfield, Bernard Anscombe and many tennis friends, also supportive neighbours, Urszula, Olivia, Simon, Kim, Ed, Gerry and Ping and Miranda and Khaled, Joanna Birch Jones, Mathew Steeples, Melinda Kilkenny, Victoria Davies Jones and Deborah Moore.

To the hard-working, delightful teams at Lucio, Mosimann's, Jones Family Kitchen, Chucs Belgravia and Olivomare and ULI in Notting Hill, for giving me respite when cooking at home is too time-consuming.

Thank you to all who have contributed in any way with information about the cases or about George as a colleague with interesting, often humorous facts of which I was unaware.

I am dearly grateful to my pupil master, Patrick Talbot KC, Charles Sparrow QC, my first head of chambers, Margaret Puxon KC, Michael Latham, Lord Campbell of Alloway, my second head of chambers and the amazing clerks. Also George's ex-clerks Bill Conor and Paul and the many members of chambers who gave friendly advice, like Elizabeth Appleby KC and other tenants in my pupillage years.

During part of lockdown I was given respite in Hampshire by my dear neighbour Kata and her son Arthur and her wonderful team. As a consequence of a fractured left wrist and foot at my tennis club, due to a slippery surface, I was unable to write, except awkwardly, with my right hand, to drive, or to be very independent. It resulted in an enormous protective splint and a further operation headed by Max Horowitz at Chelsea and Westminster Hospital.

Also, an amazing team of physiotherapists and Sue Donnolly, a private physiotherapist who ensured treatment continued via Zoom for months from her family home in Ireland.

Thank you to Toby Foxcroft for his amazing therapy bed, provided for sports recovery, Patrick for his therapeutic sports massage, James Dabbs for a return to training, The Light Centre, Frederica for Pilates and Trinny and Natalie for their online classes, Fabio for his professional hair treatments, Anna and all at Chloe for respite in a busy month.

To Lady Winnie Forsyth, JJ and Cora for breaks in Surrey to escape to peaceful countryside and to Count and Countess Flamburiari and their kind staff for annual breaks with my dear friend to write in the magical 'garden isle' of Corfu on their sun-kissed terrace and translucent sea.

To Gillian and her family for a tranquil break in Arran, to Kari Teiderman, who allowed me to relax with her and her husband Carl in Windermere on a deserted beach with peace for inspiration.

Thank you for recent help by Niki Cole and her team for assistance regarding a book launch and Liz Brewer for her encouragement and ideas about promotion.

To Jenny Rowcliffe, Guy and Digby for undertaking regular proofreading of chapters, scanning photographs and keeping me sane. To Graham Ogilvie and Morris Leslie for encouragement over the years with practical matters.

To Jan, Dennis and Meghan Cassidy, Nick Daniel, Toby Purser, Peter and Keith Shepherd and Father Michael Seed for their support as a result of the formation of the exceptional Orion Orchestra, where I enjoy great relaxation listening to beautiful music.

Lastly, thank you to my publisher Biteback, particularly Olivia, my editor, Ella, my sub-editor, and their team. Also, my editor Tom

Henry and agent Jaime Marshall, who has been at the helm on a few occasions with excellent advice. I would also like to thank Nigel Newton of Bloomsbury for being the first publisher to place confidence in me.

I apologise for anyone I have failed to mention: please do forgive me, and I hope you will come to my book launch, where I can thank you personally.

INDEX

INDEX